THE EXCLUDED THIRD

Studies in Critical Social Sciences Book Series

Haymarket Books is proud to be working with Brill Academic Publishers (www.brill.nl) to republish the *Studies in Critical Social Sciences* book series in paperback editions. This peer-reviewed book series offers insights into our current reality by exploring the content and consequences of power relationships under capitalism, and by considering the spaces of opposition and resistance to these changes that have been defining our new age. Our full catalog of *SCSS* volumes can be viewed at https://www.haymarketbooks.org/series_collections/4-studies-in-critical-social-sciences.

Series Editor
David Fasenfest (York University, Canada)

Editorial Board
Eduardo Bonilla-Silva (Duke University)
Chris Chase-Dunn (University of California–Riverside)
William Carroll (University of Victoria)
Raewyn Connell (University of Sydney)
Kimberlé W. Crenshaw (University of California–LA and Columbia University)
Heidi Gottfried (Wayne State University)
Alfredo Saad-Filho (Queen's University, Belfast)
Chizuko Ueno (University of Tokyo)
Sylvia Walby (Lancaster University)
Raju Das (York University)

THE EXCLUDED THIRD

Contribution to a Dialectical Anthropology

FERNANDO HADDAD

TRANSLATED BY
DANIEL HAHN

Haymarket Books
Chicago, IL

First published in 2024 by Brill Academic Publishers, The Netherlands
© 2024 Koninklijke Brill NV, Leiden, The Netherlands

Published in paperback in 2025 by
Haymarket Books
P.O. Box 180165
Chicago, IL 60618
773-583-7884
www.haymarketbooks.org

ISBN: 979-8-88890-518-0

Distributed to the trade in the US through Consortium Book Sales and Distribution (www.cbsd.com) and internationally through Ingram Publisher Services International (www.ingramcontent.com).

This book was published with the generous support of Lannan Foundation, Wallace Action Fund, and the Marguerite Casey Foundation.

Special discounts are available for bulk purchases by organizations and institutions. Please call 773-583-7884 or email info@haymarketbooks.org for more information.

Cover design by Jamie Kerry and Ragina Johnson.

Printed in the United States.

Library of Congress Cataloging-in-Publication data is available.

To Roberto Schwarz

Contents

Acknowledgements IX
About *The Excluded Third* X

1 Introduction: toward a New Utopian Horizon 1

2 New Forays from Biology into the Humanities 7
   1 The Role of Sexuality 11
   2 Evolving and R-evolving 17
   3 The Life of Culture 24
   4 Culture, Language and Evolution 32
   5 Sociobiology and Super-Organisms 34
   6 Psychology of Culture 40

3 Toward a Dialectical Anthropology 46
   1 Cultural Niches and Frontiers 53
   2 The Primitive Exchange Economy 71
   3 Alienization and Materialism 76
   4 Marxism and Anthropology 84

4 Symbolic Language and the Time of Culture 95
   1 Philosophies of Language and of Culture 110

References 149
Index 157

Acknowledgements

In the process of developing this book, I immersed myself in a bibliography that had previously not been well known to me, as recommended, principally, by the biologist Carlos Navas and the anthropologists Rui Murrieta and Lilia Schwarcz. From there, I exchanged a few valuable phone calls with Eduardo Viveiros de Castro, Lucia Santaella, Carlos Fausto, Miguel Nicolelis, Sebastião Milano, Sandro Cabral, Carlos Melo, Victor Marques and Stelio Marras, who set me off onto new lines of enquiry. Finally, the first draft was read by Lilia Schwarcz, Sidarta Ribeiro, Vladimir Safatle, João Paulo Bachur, Gabriel Chalita, Gabriel Galípolo, Ricardo Musse and Frederico Haddad, who shared significant and beneficial notes. Ricardo Teperman and the team at publishers Zahar/ Companhia das Letras (Ivan Marsiglia, Érico Melo, Baby Siqueira Abrão, Fábio Bonillo, Camila Saraiva and Ana Maria Barbosa), of course, read the text and made some pertinent final observations on content and form. Roberto Schwarz and Luiz Felipe de Alencastro are interlocutors of a lifetime. Ana Estela, Frederico and Ana Carolina are life itself. To all of them, my thanks.

About *The Excluded Third*

This wide-ranging study probes deeply into questions of great intellectual significance and import for human life. Challenging and thought-provoking.
– *Noam Chomsky*

The Excluded Third is a piercing appraisal of the cultural dynamics that animate our politics. Drawing on an impressive range of philosophical and anthropological sources, Haddad makes a case for rehabilitating the concept of dialectical change, as a first step to rescuing the study of humanity from the spectre of pseudo-science.
– *David Wengrow, co-author of* The Dawn of Everything: a New History of Humanity, *and Professor of Comparative Archaeology at University College London.*

An impressive tour de force, an update on the debate between disciplines as diverse as biology, linguistics and anthropology. Weaving a complex dialogue between so many different perspectives has never been more necessary and *The Excluded Third* does this masterfully and boldly.
– *Sidarta Ribeiro, neuroscientist, author of* The Oracle of Night: the History and Science of Dreaming.

CHAPTER 1

Introduction: toward a New Utopian Horizon

When the world's most important linguist came to my house, Brazil was going through its most dramatic political period since redemocratization. In an outbreak of political incommunicability, a significant part of the country seemed oblivious to the crossroads we had reached between barbarism and civilization. Noam Chomsky had come to pay a visit of solidarity to former president Lula, then being detained at the headquarters of the Federal Police in Curitiba, and Perseu Abramo Foundation staff connected us.

On 30 September 2018, a Sunday, the Massachusetts Institute of Technology (MIT) professor and his wife, the Brazilian translator Valéria Chomsky, sat down at the table of the home where I grew up, in São Paulo's Planalto Paulista neighborhood, for breakfast with me, my partner Ana Estela, and two other guests, literary critic Roberto Schwarz and his wife Grecia de la Sobera.

Chomsky, a distinguished human rights activist, was worried at the rise of the far-right candidate Jair Bolsonaro, against whom I would be competing, the following Sunday, in the second round of the presidential elections. And so, I found myself, in the space of a week, in conversation with one of the great living humanists and going to the polls to face off against a psychopath. I could feel the clash of irreconcilable perspectives.

The MIT professor was asking us about the condition of the left in Brazil and the difficulties in building a broad front against Bolsonaro. I replied, and took advantage of the situation to question him about linguistics. At one point, I asked Chomsky a question that, I can now see, was directly related to what I was going through at that time—and which would later trigger the spark that produced this book. Would it be possible to explain Einstein's theory of relativity to an isolated community? And could we understand their world view? The reply was unequivocal:

> There's nothing in the psychic structure of any human being that would impede them from perfectly understanding, in their own terms, the theory of relativity or the cosmology of an isolated people.

Chomsky then explained, in the light of his theory of generative grammar—which conceives of language through the relationship between the properties of the human mind and the biological organization of the species—that we humans came into the world equipped with the linguistic capacity to allow us to move between different universes. What matters is an underlying grammar that organizes the world and is common to the human species in general. For somebody concerned with questions about the incommensurability of cultures and world views, untranslatability and irrationality, it was encouraging to hear this idea repeated at that historic moment, just as we were experiencing the troubling feeling of living with a section of the country with whom no common denominator seemed possible.

Actually, it was not the attacks, the lies and the accusations I endured from the Bolsonarista groups that I found most striking. It was the brazenness with which my rival candidate—who from the first months of the campaign had tellingly refused to debate—talked of unimaginable things: praise for the dictatorship, for torture and killings, just to give a couple of illustrative examples. Faced with barbarism, it is amazing how people of judgment opted to ignore it—or just to live with it.

On the eve of that fateful election, I thought only of avoiding the tragedy that would prove inevitable, given the political circumstances. Following the defeat, I decided to write a book. At the start of 2021, the Covid pandemic gave me the opportunity and the time to prepare it. It was also a way of protecting my mental health amid all the outrages perpetrated by Bolsonaro and the virus.

This book seeks to offer an immanent criticism of the mainstream of biology, anthropology and linguistics. It seeks to restore the humanities to their proper place with their critical eye on the dilemmas being faced by humanity, while also paving the way for a more generous reception for the historical materialism of new approaches, especially anthropological ones, which have been gaining ground in the last decades.

Some seminal works of Marilyn Strathern, Viveiros de Castro, Philippe Descola, the later Ingold, etc. call the subject/object binary into question. The main objective of this study is to complement theirs: to demonstrate how this relationship was formed and why it moves us away from any evolutionist perspective of the social sciences.

Just as biology, when faced with physics and chemistry, invokes properties that are transcendent or emerging from a more complex dimension like life—which in no way denies the properties of inorganic matter—the humanities should invoke what is particular to culture in relation to life in order to secure their specificity, without any need to deny any of the properties of biology. To put it another way, just as physicists and chemists can contribute to the elucidating of the mysteries of life without, nonetheless, trying to reduce them to molecules, biologists can find support for their research in the cultural dynamic without reducing it to genes or other replicators.

I argue that the variation/selection formula, which is appropriate for describing the dynamics of biological evolution, does not apply to culture. The cultural dynamic requires that we find some other concept than *evolution* to describe it.

The critique of the mainstream begins with the following assumption: that contradiction is a specific aspect of humans, and, without considering it, you lapse into a pseudoscience, which often only serves to justify ideological conceptions that are positivist in nature. Without dialectics, I wish to show, the humanities fall prey easily to approaches that try to bring the human cultural dynamics close to a process of differentiation that is still prisoner to the variation-selection binomial.

The hypothesis I mean to defend is that culture does not proceed by evolution, rather it *r-evolves*, a neologism that seeks to clarify that cultural 'evolution' does not occur in the same terms as biological evolution. The verb 'r-evolve' is intended precisely to convey more appropriately the idea that cultural changes occur in a process that is contradictory, dialectic.

Just as the shift from physics and chemistry to biology is transcendent, when through physical-chemical processes life is established, the shift from biology to culture is likewise a transcendent movement, in which one dimension does not deny its predecessor, notwithstanding the disruptive nature of both: the origin of life and the appearance of human language. If symbolic language is actually a result of evolution, it produces some 'other' nature that goes beyond the biological.

As the biologist François Jacob suggests, the 'three natures'—physical, biological and cultural—are distinguished from each other by their relationship to the arrow of time. We live in one world with three temporalities: the fundamental laws of physics are symmetrical across time; in the case of biology, the past and the future represent entirely different, asymmetrical directions; and symbolic language, a precondition of culture, typical of humans, gave us the capacity to travel in time and to invent a future.

It is precisely in the temporal dimension that we find the key that allows us to understand why cultures r-evolve: symbolic activity does not only produce identity and difference; it also produces *contradiction*. The symbol liberates human beings from the immediacy that is typical of non-human beings and allows them to *project themselves forward*. The appearance of symbolic language propelled the human being into a third dimension of temporality that makes us capable of imagining, jointly, objectives and perspectives that might be common, different or contradictory.

So, the future projects of different human groups can be in harmony with each other, or they can antagonize. If, biologically speaking, the chances of human beings speciating are remote, cultural speciation is a frequent occurrence, a radical schismogenesis. When cultural speciation occurs, however, what is produced is not difference, but contradiction. This process, which I call *alienization*, does not create a biologically different species, but a 'species' that can be *culturally antagonistic*.

The title of this book is a play on words. The famous principle of the excluded third is one of the laws of thought that seek to banish contradiction from the domain of formal logic. I decided, provocatively, to name an existing contradictory character after this law. In this way I do not only seek to re-enthrone dialectics within the humanities, but to do so by positioning contradiction in the right place: in cultures' relations with each other. The *excluded third*, in the eyes of ego and alter, both is and is not a human being. We could characterize it as *radically other (autrui)*, like Levinas (1991). I prefer, however, the Freudian *Unheimlich*, which moves into the idea of ambivalence and can extend psychoanalysis even beyond psychism. It is this figure, a kind of dialectical haunting, that will allow us to conceive of contradiction as a triadic relationship between ego, alter and alien, without which the cultural dynamic cannot be understood.

At a certain point, societies incorporate the excluded third by subjugation, a process by which slave-owning conquerors tame the dominated, reducing them, via a process of depersonalization, to inorganic elements of their own reproduction. In this context, not before, the subject-object relation is established. Historically speaking, the very first object of a human being was another human being. The objectification of nature is not originary but derived. Only then does the separation of culture and nature occur. The meaning of slavery, a product of alienization, seems, thus, much more profound than the fathers of historical materialism could have supposed, due to anthropology being at such an incipient stage in their day, for which, to their credit, they demonstrated a growing interest. Recent anthropological approaches to the nature/nurture binary, if correctly interpreted, can play a role for historical materialism that is equivalent to those which genetics fulfilled for the theory of evolution, that is, to enable a modern synthesis of the humanities. In this journey, we will find linguistics especially useful, particularly the debate between Chomsky and Tomasello, mediated by Humboldt's still important pronominal linguistics, as we shall see.

When one human group subjugates another, spiritual and material needs are formed that go beyond physiological necessities. The very concept of scarcity gains a new meaning in the passage from ecological societies to economic ones. And, as soon as these dyadic relations between the dominators and the dominated are established, an external alienized group is reconfigured to structure a triadic relationship, from outside. The r-evolution of culture occurs, then, through dialectical triadic relationships that dissolve and are permanently replaced.

By situating contradiction in human cultures' relationships with each other, we come to understand religion and economics as two of its forms of expression, mediated through language. The phenomena analysed by Feuerbach and Marx, whose backdrops are religious and economic alienation respectively, seen from this perspective, are derived from a more fundamental process, in which symbolic language recovers its precedence, without falling into Hegelian idealism or dispensing with dialectics, as in the case of Feuerbachian contemplative materialism.

What this is, then, is an interpretation that remains within the field of historical materialism while at the same time incorporating the anthropological perspective. What I propose, therefore, is a potential beneficial synthesis in which materialism is anthropologized and anthropology is made dialectic, moving away from the reductionist conceptions of culture that take some potency away from the contribution that the humanities can bring to science.

From this perspective, the history of societies has been the history of the struggle around alienation, on the one hand, and depersonalization, on the other. History does not have one motor, but two, an external one and an internal one, that propel it; and the attempts to explain the major historical transitions using exclusively internal causes or exclusively external ones can be considered, by that reasoning, to be mere simplifications.

Of the theoretical theses I defend in this book, a whole line of political action can be drawn. Especially since one of the conclusions reached is that, from a biological or cultural point of view, there is absolutely nothing to prevent the human species from conceiving of itself as a single group, once it is opened to radical otherness. Undoubtedly, we have to keep in mind the idea that the problems we are facing today are pervaded by many questions—there are ecological, national, ethno-racial problems, problems of gender and class and of specific groups—that ought to be considered in all their specificity, without however losing sight of the idea of recovering a broad, global view of human emancipation.

If human language frees us from the immediacy of the present and launches us into historic time, we are fated to weave the web of our social lives from the symbolic threads of identity, of difference and of contradiction. There is, however, no space for something that can might the name 'reconciliation.' What we call 'emancipation' should, therefore, be considered in the light of a rereading of the dialectic (keeping at some distance from the Hegelian framework), in which contradictions are no longer resolved in a process of returning to identity—since identity and contradiction only serve to reinforced one another—but in a process of continual extending of the spectrum of difference.

Dealienizing practices, in every aspect of social life, economic life, political life, racial life, sexual life, etc. are easy to imagine, along with the historic consequences of their success: a growing sense of satisfaction in the face of fewer material and spiritual needs. That is not, however, this book's immediate aim. Its aim is simply to bring to the discussion some new theoretical bases for human emancipation, without which what we think of as a utopian horizon will never occupy the progressive imagination.

CHAPTER 2

New Forays from Biology into the Humanities

> The precondition of treating 'nations' as generic beings is that the development of each nation can be seen as a typical, closed cycle of the same kind as the development of individual living creatures.
> MAX WEBER

∴

The relationship between biology and the humanities has always been controversial, since the dawn of time. The demarcation of the fields is, to this day, the subject of heated debate. However, ever since the modern synthetic theory of evolution, which got an extraordinary push from the 1930s, the profusion of scientific publications proposing new approaches has been remarkable. This movement gained even more traction with the advent of the biolinguistic revolution proposed by Noam Chomsky. This book sets out to challenge that argument, following three paths that, ultimately, will meet. While the disciplines of biology, anthropology and linguistics intermingle throughout the work, the emphasis of each chapter is different. This first chapter lays out some contemporary 'schools' of the biological thinking that ventures to think about human societies based on its own premises. There has often been partnership between biologists and anthropologists, but within this closeness there do remain mutual accusations of undue biologisms and anthropomorphisms. It is a subject that inspires much attention, and which is not unrelated to that argument about the worn-out old question of reductionism that also played out among biologists, on the one side, and physicists and chemists, on the other, as we shall see below.

In the opening chapter of *Animal Species and Evolution*, Ernst Mayr outlines the modern synthetic theory of evolution and refers to the threats to its development. The weakness of non-Darwinian pre-synthesis theories, according to him, rested in the fact that all their versions explained evolution based on one single factor: the principle of internal self-improvement (Lamarck); the induction of genetic change by the environment (Étienne Geoffroy); catastrophism (Georges Cuvier); evolution through isolation (Moritz Wagner); or mutationism (Hugo de Vries). Evolutionary synthesis, meanwhile, innovated in its introduction of a theory of evolution based on two factors: mutation and also the selective effects of the environment, or, in other words, the constant production of *variation* and natural *selection*.

The modern theory not only surpassed the others in explanatory power but also moved away from old mistaken philosophical conceptions. On the one hand, *preformationism*, according to which evolution did not produce actual change, but merely the maturing of inherent potentials; on the other, *typological thought*, for which the variability observed was only the shadow cast by immutable underlying ideas that corresponded to what truly was real and permanent. These ideas were definitively pushed away by the modern synthesis.

Mayr now suggests a new threat, *reductionism*, or the expression of the laws of evolution in terms of the laws of physics. Going against this trend, Mayr offers an argument that is a practical corollary of the modern synthesis: "since every individual is unique, strict evolutionary reversibility is a logical impossibility" (Mayr 1966: 6). It is not hard to see that reductionism is a kind of preformationism in the opposite direction. The impracticability of reductionism is, according to him, particularly remarkable in one significant event in evolution, the emergence of new species, which sees the appearance of "essentially irreversible discontinuities with entirely new potentialities" (Mayr 1966: 11).

The argument about reductionism becomes even more complex when the question moves into another dimension. There is debate about the extent to which the supposed laws of cultural evolution can be reduced to or expressed in terms of the laws of biology. In spite of considerable efforts by zoologists, and primatologists in particular, to identify 'culture' in the non-human animal kingdom (use of tools, control of fire, sign languages, technical learning, moral sense, individual recognition, etc.) the uniqueness of the human species has almost always been reaffirmed, though almost never adequately.

According to Mayr,

> the 'closed' program of genetic information is increasingly replaced in the course of this evolution by an 'open' program, a program which is so set up that it can incorporate new information. In other words, the behavior phenotype is no longer absolutely determined genetically, but to a greater or lesser extent is the result of learning and education.
> MAYR 1966: 636–47

The capacity to transmit non-genetic components of culture, including all kinds of scientific and technological information, has made mankind, according to Mayr, the master of his environment, a being emancipated from his natural conditions of existence. This has even raised the question of whether or not mankind would remain subject to natural selection. Mayr, for example, states that there is actually no evidence of any significant biological improvement in the human species in the last 30 thousand years, and, rather the contrary, he warns of the signs of likely genetic degradation as a result of modern life.

Mayr then invites those who are persuaded that a kind of adverse natural selection is working on modern man, reducing the frequency in the human species' gene pool of the most desirable genes and combinations of genes, to think of incentivizing countermeasures, given the unfeasibility of authoritarian proposals that are scientifically viable but not very socially palatable.

> In our present society, the superior person is punished by the government in numerous ways, by taxes and otherwise, which make it more difficult for him to raise a large family. Why, for instance, should tax exemption for children be a fixed sum rather than a percentage of earned income? Why should tuition in school be based, in large part, on the ability of the father to pay rather than inversely on the achievement of the student?
> MAYR 1966: 661

The blunt reasoning, as you can see, shows up difficulties in passing from one dimension to the other, from biology to culture, and vice versa, from the cultural dimension to the biological, on a subject as commonplace as population theory, a subject that is at the root of the development of the theory of evolution. In fact, Mayr's suggestion, ludicrous to anyone of his intellectual scope, cannot even be characterized as Malthusian; it is Galton-style eugenics, pure and simple.

The relationship between Malthus and Darwin was for a long time poorly understood. Darwin's brief reference to the Malthusian doctrine of the power of geometric growth of organic beings led him to conclude that more individuals of each species are born than can survive, favoring by natural selection those with just the slightest adaptive advantage over the rest, given their complex and changing living conditions.

Darwin realizes, as a result, that competition did not only occur between species, but between individuals within a species, without which natural selection would be impossible. But Malthus shows his clear opposition toward the improvement of the human species by eugenic methods, a trivial fact observed among breeders of animals who practiced and still do practice artificial selection and crucially important for shaping the theory of evolution.

The Anglican priest cast doubt on whether "since the world began, any organic improvement whatever in the human frame can be clearly ascertained" (Malthus, 1985: 129), though he did not rule out the possibility of a small improvement, not as regards intelligence, according to him, which is of dubious hereditary transmission, but perhaps as regards physical strength and beauty. Nevertheless, the nonsense of condemning to celibacy those individuals who are ill-adapted left human beings with two possibilities.

Faced with the hypothesis that population grows by a geometric progression, and the means of subsistence by an arithmetic one, Malthus says that, in the absence of preventative controls (late marriages and less numerous offspring) all the way along the social scale, 'obstacles' to population growth would be imposed—war, plague and hunger—that affect the less well-favored classes of society more directly.

Malthus, a reader of Condorcet, opts to disregard that writer's observations of the effects of the progress of the human spirit on social dynamics, including population. The evolution of culture—science, art, agriculture, industry, politics—progressively alters the technical and moral conditions that open up entirely new perspectives to the human species and make the premises of Malthusian population theory contingent. In any case, the idea of offering fiscal stimuli for a superior person—whatever that might mean—to choose to raise a larger family seems to fall victim to an even shallower reasoning than that which leads to the idea that physics and chemistry can do without the advances of biology for explaining life.

Behaviors that might go against the natural biological impulses—rich families that are small, celibacy, etc.—prompted biologists to turn to a number of causes to explain them. In a curious passage in *The Selfish Gene* (Dawkins, 2006), for example, Richard Dawkins turns—to explain voluntary celibacy—to the laws governing cultural evolution, placing a new character onto the stage, the selfish meme (a unit of cultural evolution that can self-propagate). A selfish gene (a unit of biological evolution) associated with celibacy, says Dawkins, would, for obvious reasons, be doomed to failure; but a meme of celibacy, the writer points out, would have a good chance of surviving in the meme pool as a "minor partner in a large complex of mutually assisting religious memes" (Dawkins, 2006: 119). Thus, the individual, the vehicle for the propagation of genes and memes, is transformed into a battlefield (and the site of self-interested cooperation) in which the selfish meme of celibacy can hypothetically defeat all that same organism's selfish genes. Obviously, a possible meme of true altruism would have theoretical repercussions that Dawkins acknowledged but chose not to explore: "We, alone on earth, can rebel against the tyranny of the selfish replicators" (Dawkins, 2006: 201). The statement is manifestly illogical. According to Dawkins's model, the altruism meme is, hypothetically, as selfish as all of an organism's genes and memes. Serving as the vehicle for any one of them would not make us rebels. The statement, however, is revealing about the questions and contradictions to be faced.

In time, the idea became established that cultural evolution is not to be confused with biological evolution. Just as physicists and chemists can contribute to the elucidation of the mysteries of life, without seeking to reduce it to molecules, biologists can find support for their research in the evolution of man without reducing it to genetics. Nevertheless, although the argument about reductionism has been left behind, the recourse to analogies and homologies has not always been adequate for mapping and framing the problems arising from this three-dimensional approach (physical, biological and cultural).

There are many questions that spring from this perspective: 1) is it possible to speak about cultural evolution? and to what extent?; 2) can cultural evolution be explained by the same two factors—variation and selection—that determine biological evolution?; 3) on which unit does selection, whether natural or cultural, act: gene (meme), individual or group?; 4) is it possible to draw a parallel between biological evolution and cultural evolution?; if we take Dawkins's arguments further, would it be possible to think about new analogies, like those of the cultural genome, cultural species, the flow of memes between different cultural species, etc.?; 5) how are biological evolution and cultural evolution related?; coevolution, interdependence, a dialectic relationship, a sequential one (in the same or some other dimension)?[1]

1   The Role of Sexuality

At this point it would seem appropriate to ask, as a preliminary, whether culture is so distant from biology as biology is from physics. Anthropology and biology quite often resort to linguistics and philosophy to answer this question, as well as the other questions raised above, which flow from it, given the implications of one or other answer.

Let us take the evolution of sex as an example. One way of approaching the subject is to examine the advantages of the variety resulting from sexual reproduction. Some specialists have emphasized that sex constitutes a defence against pathogenic agents. Since germs reproduce much faster than complex organisms, they are likely to evolve during the lifetime of the host, dodging their immune system, effective though it might be. Since sex entails

---

[1] There are other less ambitious perspectives, applying the theory of evolution (variation/selection) only partially: the evolutionary of knowledge, the evolutionary theory of economic change, etc.

the exchange of half an individual's genes for the genes of another individual of the same species, the recombination gives the offspring an initial advantage in the race against the germs.[2]

It is worth pointing out that not all sexual reproduction is beneficial. Every organism lives with harmful mutations that, when they become dominant within a population, are eliminated by natural selection. Most harmful mutations, nevertheless, are recessive and only cause harm when they accumulate within a population, increasing the likelihood of two carriers mating. This likelihood increases significantly when close relatives procreate, since they share genes, including recessive genes that are highly dangerous and potentially lethal.

According to Maynard Smith, there are two ways for animals to reduce the probability of crossing with close relatives: by recognition and refusal; and by the dispersal of offspring before they reach sexual maturity. There are mechanisms of the former type that work in plants with seeds, but in multicellular animals, endogamy has been avoided when the second mechanism is considered.

Moreover, more than going by phenotypical similarities, animals tend to treat those that raise them as parents and those with whom they're raised as siblings. There is a striking account of children raised communally in a kibbutz where, despite the lack of a social pressure against marriage within members of the group, there was not one single case of this type in more than 2700 marriages between adults from the second generation of that community. The human being's search for a partner seems to be directed toward someone who was not familiar to them in childhood.

It is reasonable, therefore, to suppose that, just like other primates, humans similarly develop barriers against incest. Maynard Smith finds it strange to consider it a taboo, when it seems no more than a biological adaptation reinforced by various different cultures. Thus, according to Maynard Smith,

> When Lévi-Strauss (1968) asserts that the incest taboo is the characteristic feature which originated human culture, it is in one sense tautologous and in another manifestly false. If the emphasis is on the cultural connotations of the word 'taboo,' the statement is tautologous since there can be no culture without culture. If the statement implies that animals do not have practices which avoid incest, then the statement is false.
> SMITH, 1978: 143

---

2 See Smith (1978).

It is worth noting that the cultural manifestation of this biological orientation varies from society to society, not always consistently with the degree of genetic kinship, and that the various patterns of behavior do not evolve genetically as adaptations to each one of these societies, which, however, does not allow us to underestimate the evidence that our ancestors avoided marrying close relatives even before they had acquired the ability to speak. In this way, sexual reproduction would be, according to Fisher, the only adaptation that evolves through *group selection, being a characteristic that is disadvantageous to the individual but advantageous to the survival of the species.* The mechanisms for preventing endogamy would actually strengthen the argument.

Maynard Smith returned to the subject twenty years later (Smith and Szathmáry, 1999), reasserting that group selection can be important in the maintaining of sex in superior organisms. Yet he made two observations that would justify some reservations: 1) the existence of superior taxonomic groups that are totally parthenogenetic (females that procreate without needing males to fertilize them); 2) the existence of species in which the same individual produces descendants that can be sexual as well as asexual.

These considerations provided the supporters of sociobiology with some encouragement (Wilson and Wilson, 2007). Seeking to study social behavior from a purely biological perspective, they returned to the debate based on the latest research and turned to Darwin himself to rethink and update their theoretical bases. In a very famous passage from *The Descent of Man* (1871), Darwin observed:

> It must not be forgotten that although a high standard of morality gives but a slight or no advantage to each individual man and his children over the other men of the same tribe, yet that an increase in the number of well-endowed men and an advancement in the standard of morality will certainly give an immense advantage to one tribe over another. A tribe including many members who, from possessing in a high degree the spirit of patriotism, fidelity, obedience, courage, and sympathy, were always ready to aid one another, and to sacrifice themselves for the common good, would be victorious over most other tribes; and this would be natural selection.
>
> DARWIN, 1871: 166

It is clear from the quotation that the underlying reasoning is flirting with the principle of group selection. Though Darwin is not referring in the first sentence to an individual's harm to the benefit of the group, but to the 'slight or no advantage' of the adoption of altruistic behavior, in the second he does talk explicitly of individual sacrifice for the common good. It is worth noting that the 'common good,' in this case, is the defeating of other groups, that is, altruistic behavior is not explained by natural selection within a single group, but requires natural selection between groups. According to Edward O. Wilson and David S. Wilson, the maxim of the latest version of sociobiology could be expressed thus: the selfish individual defeats the altruistic individual within the group, but a group of altruistic individuals defeats a group of selfish individuals:

> For this to happen, an advantage at a larger scale (between groups) must exist to counteract the disadvantage at a smaller scale (within groups). Second, a higher-level unit (such as a social insect colony) can become endowed with the same adaptive properties that we associate with single organisms. There can be such a thing as a superorganism.
> WILSON and WILSON, 2007: 330

This movement causes sociobiology a certain awkwardness. We should recall that its aim is to explain social behavior from a purely biological perspective. It would be very hard to demonstrate that the behavioral difference between two tribes could be explained from a strictly genetic point of view. One of the most frequently raised issues in the broader debate over evolution is that the rhythms of biological and cultural evolution are altogether different.

It would be very hard for a behavioral divergence such as that described by Darwin to be the product of a genetic alteration. A genetic determinism like that would sound implausible and over-the-top. The new version of sociobiology must therefore appeal to more complex genotypical-phenotypical relationships, in which modest genetic alterations between groups can result in substantial hereditary phenotypical variations between them. Only in this way can it remain faithful to its theoretical bases, but at the rather high cost of almost equating cultural features with phenotypical ones.

Biological thinking attempted to put forward other ways of dealing with altruistic behavior, getting around the hypothesis of group selection. One of them, associated with the name of William D. Hamilton, was named kin selection. The so-called 'Hamilton's Rule' postulates that:

$$r \times B > C$$

where C is the reproductive cost to the individual who performs the altruistic act, B is the additional reproductive benefit obtained by the recipient of the altruistic act and r is the genetic relationship of the receiver to the performer.

Haldane simplified the argument with a humorous phrase: "I'd lay down my life for two brothers or eight cousins."[3] Since a sibling has half the other's genes, and a cousin has an eighth, Hamilton's Rule suggests that the exchange imagined by Haldane could be fair or even beneficial, seen exclusively from a genetic point of view. By this reasoning, organisms would be altruistic only in relation to their own genes, and not in relation to the group to which they belong.

Another alternative to group selection was proposed by Robert Trivers: reciprocal altruism, or evolutionary game theory. This involves considering the combined strategic behavior of the participants in a game that can favor cooperation. In that environment, the cost and benefit of each choice is not fixed but depends on the choice made by at least one other player. In the original 'prisoner's dilemma' game, two prisoners (number of players $N=2$) are offered two possibilities: remain silent or confess to their joint crime.

If one of the prisoners, in confessing, bears witness against the other and that other remains silent, the one who confessed walks free while his silent accomplice serves a ten-year sentence. If both stay quiet, the police can only condemn them to six months' imprisonment each. If they both betray their partners, each one does five years in prison. Since the behavior of the players cannot be determined *a priori*, there is nothing to recommend an attitude of cooperation. A prisoner would only stay quiet if he was certain the other would do the same, but in that case, it would be worth confessing (betraying) and vice versa.

Dilemmas such as these can be resolved through the practice of iterative games, repeated indefinitely, with the widest range of strategies, which comes close to simulating real-life situations. Some models suggest that cooperative behavior can emerge and remain stable even in quite competitive scenarios. This would give rise to what Maynard Smith (1993) calls an 'evolutionarily stable strategy,' defined as one which, when adopted by the majority of members of a population, cannot be overcome by an alternative strategy, making itself immune to betrayal.

Both formulations assume that the total population is divided into groups, segmented by r (degree of kinship) or N (number of players). Let us go back to Darwin's example. In a tribe, the degree of kinship between its members is presumably greater than the degree of kinship of one of its members in relation to the members of the neighboring tribe.

---

3 Haldane quoted by Lewin (1974: 325).

If we do not limit the range of r, we can bring the kin selection close to the group selection. The same reasoning can be applied to evolutionary game theory when N is expanded to reach the scale of a group. This theoretical approach, however, does not favor the theory of group selection, since there is no space in these models for genuine, disinterested altruism. Altruism, according to the biological approaches, always ends up being the product of some selfish calculation.

We will now return to the subject of the evolution of sex, unquestionably the best argument in favor of group selection. Let us analyze it in the light of the selfish gene theory. Dawkins recognizes the paradox: why did females capable of producing daughters that were identical replicas of themselves evolve and start producing eggs that contain only 50% of their genes and depending on males for their reproduction? Dawkins suggests that the paradox is resolved if, instead of going up a level—from the individual level to the group—we were to move down one, to the gene, in order to identify where, according to him, natural selection actually operates.

For Dawkins, the gene is ideally the 'indivisible' chromosome fragment that reproduces 'exact' copies of itself for 'eternity.' Ideally, because the words in quotation-marks need relativizing. They are justified if we compare the gene to the group, to the individual or to the chromosome. The gene's distinction as regards longevity, fertility and faithfulness of copy qualifies it as a candidate for the 'fundamental unit of natural selection.'

Overdoing it with the anthropomorphisms, Dawkins states that, at a gene level, altruism is necessarily a bad deal. Genes compete directly with their alleles to conquer the same locus in the chromosome of future generations. The gene for blue eyes is a rival to the gene for brown eyes. Relative to the other genes, however—those that do not occupy the same locus in the chromosome—the gene adopts a cooperative attitude to ensure the survival of the individual in whose organism it is to be found, at least until that individual reaches reproductive age.

It follows that even deadly genes, so long as they are late acting (post-reproduction), can survive in the gene pool, this being one possible explanation for the natural aging of these ephemeral beings that are organisms. The gene is thus competing with its alleles and cooperating with the others solely and exclusively to guarantee its own survival and not that of the other genes, of the individual or of the species.

Dawkins believes he has found, through this perspective, the key to explaining sexual reproduction. In treating the individual as a survival machine constructed by a confederation of genes, 'efficiency' from an individual's point of view becomes irrelevant. Sexuality starts to be considered the attribute of a single gene, just like eye color. "A gene 'for' sexuality manipulates all the other genes for its own selfish ends" (Dawkins, 2006: 44). In this way, if sexual reproduction benefits the gene responsible for the characteristic of this reproduction, then this, according to Dawkins, is explanation enough for the existence of sexual reproduction.

This explanation is manifestly tautological, since, if natural selection operates at gene level, its manifestation is at individual level. It is the individual who lives or dies. Sexual reproduction brings unquestionable benefits to the individual in an environment that is fast-changing, especially when the challenge comes from pathogenic agents in rapid evolution, as we have seen above. Not being the same, there is more chance that one of the two descendants produced sexually will be able, even in the short term, to survive in the event of intense competition. Besides, individuals produced sexually can have a smaller load of harmful mutations. If we imagine a finite population subject to continuous mutations that are slightly harmful, in the absence of any individuals without harmful mutations, it would be impossible to produce any of the latter without sexual reproduction.

Everything contributes, therefore, toward a sexual population evolving more quickly to adapt to a changing environment. And if we consider that the environment of a species also consists of other species of competitors, predators and parasites, then "when any one species changes, this is experienced by other species as a change in their environment, inducing them to change, and so on" (Dawkins, 2006: 44).

Sex, then, totally alters the dynamics of evolution. Anthropomorphic analogies in biology, as we can see in the use of the selfishness/ altruism binary, involve risks as great as—as we will discover—biologizing anthropology.

2 Evolving and R-evolving

Similar complex questions led some biologists to invoke Hegelian dialectic, as received by Engels, to overcome certain difficulties (Haldane, 1937). That does not refer only to what Maynard Smith calls 'major transitions in evolution,' such as the origins of life, sex or human language, but to the most banal evolutionary mechanisms, such as those presented by the modern synthesis.

The first clash occurred, back in the thirties, between one of the fathers of the modern synthesis, the Marxist biologist J.B.S. Haldane and the eminent economist Abba P. Lerner. Haldane's argument was, in fact, rather schematic. For him, the dynamics of evolution allow for revolutionary changes that the Hegelian system of thesis, antithesis and synthesis are able to clarify. However, he was warned by Lerner that this idea was inappropriate (Lerner, 1938), as there would not be in nature the *contradiction* in the Hegelian sense that that triad requires. Taking Haldane's formulations as an example, Lerner states that, in the 'heredity> mutation> variation' triad, for example, the antithesis (mutation) is merely an expression of the synthesis (variation) in other terms, while in the 'variation> selection> evolution' triad, the thesis (variation) and the antithesis (selection) are not in contradiction, rather they combine to produce the synthesis (evolution). Note also that the theory of punctuated equilibrium, from Gould and Eldredge, which moves away from the idea of evolution as gradual and continuous and considers evolution in leaps, does not escape the same criticism that was made of Haldane.

Later, oblivious to Lerner's warnings, other biologists, such as Richard Lewontin and Richard Levins, for example, tried to recover the idea of a dialectics of nature, this time in reference to the metabolic interaction of the organism with its environment, which, as we shall see, has nothing dialectic about it. Before them, C.H. Waddington and Ivan Schmalhausen, more appropriately, broached similar topics from the perspective of cybernetics, developed in the 1940s. The metabolic interaction with the environment gains significance here too, but if Lewontin and Levins (2007) highlight the organism's relationship with its environment, Waddington (1942, 2015, 2016) and Schmalhausen (1960) emphasize the metabolic interaction within the organism itself, understood as the locus of the interaction between the genes and their environment.

The works of Lewontin (2002) and Lewontin and Levins were crucial for the development of the theory of niche construction. Meanwhile, the works of Waddington and Schmalhausen were precursors to the effort to combine evolution and development. Beginning from common perspectives, researchers from these two fronts are seeking to build bridges with a view to an extended modern synthesis. Without getting into the controversial question of how much this movement away from a genocentric vision is promising for biology (it is undoubtedly promising for the humanities, as we intend to explain), the fact is that these contributions, when they try to enter the field of culture, do not keep a prominent place for symbolic language. They treat it as a product of evolution like other important arrivals, like the appearance of the eye or the opposable thumb, but not as something that launched us into a dimension beyond biology.

Among the important biologists who did not make this mistake, one name stands out: Ludwig von Bertalanffy, who, beginning with cybernetics, developed a general systems theory that, when it is dealing with culture, finds itself in dialogue with linguistics, specifically the linguistics of Benjamin Lee Whorf, the limitations of which we will deal with in due course.

Another important biologist who sought to differentiate the biological dimension from the cultural one was Dawkins himself, as mentioned above. But that does not mean that the simplifications proposed by Dawkins and his followers (Blackmore, 1999; Dennett, 2017) are acceptable—on the contrary. And it is in the cultural dimension that they are found to be even more problematic. Dawkins claims to be such an enthusiastic fan of Darwinism that he does not want to see it limited to the biological dimension, and he asks whether the principles of biology might, like the laws of physics, have a similar universal validity. It is culture that makes the human species unique, and language, the basis for culture, seems to 'evolve' via non-genetic means. Dawkins appears convinced that cultural transmission is analogous to genetic transmission. The chief property of genes is that they are replicators. And the culture broth gave rise to a new type of replicator: the meme.

Just as the gene propagates within the gene pool from one body to another through reproduction, whether sexual or not, memes propagate from one brain to another through communication. Biological selection produced the human brain, which supplies the culture broth from which memes emerge. This would have given rise to a new kind of evolution which, according to Dawkins, is much speedier and is not necessarily subject to biological evolution, though respecting the same dynamics of replication.

Dawkins recognizes the difficulties in the analogy, which do cause him some reservations. In the first place, memes are not high-fidelity replicators like genes. Cultural transmission is not a physical-chemical operation, and it is subject to countless distortions of understanding, interpretation, translation, etc. Secondly, for memes, there is not necessarily any equivalent to rival alleles. So, some doubt arises about whether we can assign them the bad habit of being selfish. Dawkins replies in the affirmative, arguing that a meme, in occupying a brain's finite memory, must do so at the expense of rival memes.

Curiously, however, Dawkins does not carry the analogy all the way through. In dealing with multicellular bodies, for example, he recognizes that, although they are colonies of selfish genes, they behave like a coherent whole, like a unit with centralized coordination, to the detriment of anarchy, to such an extent that the communal nature of the genes cooperating reciprocally becomes recognizable. However, Dawkins does not ask what the analogs would be of the organism and the species in the memetic universe.

Wouldn't it be a good idea to speculate about the concepts of *personality* and *culture* in the light of this exercise? Just like their body, shouldn't a person's mind be seen as a coherent unit from a memetic point of view? Just like a species, shouldn't the meme pool be regarded as a specific culture? Would it be possible to think of a 'genome' for each culture? Is a culture a superorganism?

Dawkins only explores these questions superficially, and memetics concludes at a dead end, which doesn't come close to enabling it to handle the logical problems posed some time ago by analytic philosophy, some of which will be discussed below.

Nevertheless, memetics does have one advantage over sociobiology. It recognizes that cultural evolution is not reducible to biological evolution. Making use of the concept of the extended phenotype, Dawkins could have fallen into a trap and followed another path. Conventionally speaking, a gene's phenotypical effects were those produced exclusively in the organism where they are found. Dawkins broadened this concept. Phenotypical effects come to be seen as those prompted by genes not only in the organism where they are found, but also in the world the organism inhabits. Following sociobiology, culture could be seen as something developing out of from that vision. Fortunately, this is not what Dawkins does. He even suggests that,

> we do not have to look for conventional biological survival values of traits like religion, music, and ritual dancing, though these may also be present. Once the genes have provided their survival machines with brains that are capable of rapid imitation, the memes will automatically take over.
> DAWKINS, 2006: 200

This contradicts head-on what is argued by, for example, the sociobiologist Edward O. Wilson in his book *On Human Nature*, where we read:

> Can the cultural evolution of higher ethical values gain a direction and momentum of its own and completely replace genetic evolution? I think not. The genes hold cultures on a leash.
> WILSON, 1978: 167

Schematically, then, if, for sociobiology, genes never lose command, for Dawkins, it is the biological principles, and not genes themselves, that rule in other dimensions—in the case of culture, through new replicators: memes. Nevertheless, two observations are worth making: in the case of memes, *acquired* characteristics can be transmitted from one generation to the next—which doesn't happen with biological transmission—giving cultural inheritance a Lamarckian shape; and it is possible to rebel against genetic inheritance in the name, for example, of religion or nationalism. Although Dawkins doesn't explain, from memetics, what he understands by religion and nation (the concept of memeplex, understood as being a 'coadapted meme complex,' adds little clarity), the simple concession made to the relative autonomy of culture will be fundamental to the development of the premises I am arguing for in this study.

Contrary to what Dawkins maintains, however, for reasons that we will elucidate below, the variation/ selection formula, so appropriate for describing the dynamics of biological evolution, does not apply to culture. Strictly speaking, we will have to find another concept that is not *evolution* to refer to the cultural dynamic. The hypothesis that I will attempt to demonstrate is that culture does not evolve, it *r-evolves*. I am making use of a neologism to make it clear, in advance, that cultural 'evolution' does not respect the same logic as biological evolution.

It is not possible to biologize the cultural dynamic. The variation/ selection factors, so apt for describing biological evolution as expressed in the modern synthesis, are inappropriate for explaining the cultural dynamic. The verb 'r-evolve' is intended to convey the idea that cultural change involves a dialectical, contradictory triadic process, which will be described below, and which is not found in the biological dimension.

Let us return to the argument about reductionism: when we say that the laws of biology cannot be reduced to the laws of physics, or that culture cannot be deduced from genetics, what do we actually mean? We note that Dawkins defines the organism as a colony of selfish genes. In spite of this, he recognized that, through the interested cooperation between genes themselves, the organism behaves like a unit that is so coherent and integrated that his own definition of an altruistic vehicle for selfish genes eventually sounds implausible.

In no process is this cooperation so evident as in homeostasis, in which the internal equilibrium of the organism's various chemical compositions and functions is maintained. In the words of Norbert Wiener, "our inner economy must contain an assembly of thermostats, automatic hydrogen-ion-concentration controls, governors, and the like, which would be adequate for a great chemical plant" (Wiener, 1985: 115). Small variations in body temperature, in the toxic concentration arising from a part of those ingested products that are not used, in osmotic blood pressure, in the level of leukocytes, etc. can mean death to the organism. These physiological controls are biocybernetic, that is, they operate though feedback chains.

Jacques Monod showed that these biocybernetic controls operate in the organism on a microscopic level. It was known that the nervous system and the endocrine system assured the coordination between organs or between tissues, that is to say, between cells. It was discovered, then, that "within each cell a cybernetic network hardly less (if not still more) complex, guarantees the functional coherence of the intracellular chemical machinery" (Monod, 1972: 77).

Among the regulatory proteins, it is the allosteric enzymes that stand out, distinguished from the rest because, in addition to the classic catalyzing function, they have the property of electively recognizing, by stereospecific association, compounds that increase or reduce their activity in relation to the substrate, without maintaining any chemically necessary relationship with it, neither structural nor reactive, conserving the homeostatic state of the intracellular metabolism in a way that is effective and coherent. Monod writes:

> Physiologically useful or 'rational,' this relationship is chemically arbitrary—'gratuitous,' one may say ... The way in which allosteric interactions work hence permits a complete freedom in the 'choice' of controls, having no chemical requirements to answer to, will be the more responsive to physiological requirements, requirements, and will accordingly be selected for the extent to which they confer heightened coherence and efficiency upon the cell or organism. In a word, the very gratuitousness of these systems, giving molecular evolution a practically limitless field for exploration and experiment, enabled it to elaborate the huge network of cybernetic interconnections which makes each organism an autonomous functional unit, whose performances appear to transcend the laws of chemistry if not to ignore them altogether.
> MONOD, 1972: 77–78

It is as if the organism, though observing the laws of physics and chemistry, found a way of transcending them to the benefit of its preservation. The functioning of the organism—and thus its physiology—'commands' the process of chemical reactions that will in fact occur to the benefit of its stability.

If every organism, without exception, is merely the result of the combination of no more than twenty amino acids and four types of nucleotides, it is the gratuitousness of their cybernetic systems that ensures them transcendence in relation to inert matter and allows them to attain their own life and internal coherence, like a machine that constructs and reproduces itself, or even like a *teleonomic* system endowed with a plan recorded in it from the beginning.

Monod extrapolates the reasoning to the universe of culture and, in a way, prefigures the outlines of meme theory. He talks about the temptation for a biologist to compare biological evolution with cultural evolution. If the organism transcends the laws of physics, while observing the properties of atoms and molecules, then ideas, to Monod, would transcend the biosphere, retaining some of the organism's properties. Just like organisms, ideas also evolve, via various mechanisms of recombination, fusion, transmission, etc. and selection—here, too—does play a major role in the process.

As we shall see, biologists become prisoners to this type of analogy, and having been more convincing when explaining biology's transcendence in relation to physics, they are less successful in clarifying what changed in the shift from biology to culture. The truth is, anthropologists and sociologists, even those who recognize the cultural dimension's specificity, adopt positions very close to what Monod is suggesting.

In fact, there is a related difficulty for physicists in relation to biology and vice versa. Monod owes much of his approach not only to cybernetics but also to quantum mechanics, and the discussion that he struck up with the physicist Walter Elsasser was crucial in the maturing of his formulations (Elsasser, 1966). However, it is in biology itself that he finds the organism's specific properties and tries to extrapolate them to culture.

The neurophysiologist John Eccles also resorted to quantum physics to try to lay out a bold hypothesis about the mind-brain interaction. Ever since Herbert Feigl, the mind-brain dualism had been passed over in favor of the thesis that, in some way, mental events are identical to some special class of neural events. Nevertheless, in a 1986 essay (Eccles, 1986), Eccles invokes the work of Henry Margenau to improve upon the approach that he himself and Karl Popper had suggested to clarify the matter (Margenau, 1984).

For Margenau,

> the mind may be regarded as a field in the accepted physical sense of the term. But it is a nonmaterial field, its closest analogue is perhaps a probability field.
>
> MARGENAU, 1984: 97

It is upon this field that, according to Eccles, mental events act, modifying probabilities in a way that is analogous to quantum mechanics, as if the mind were playing the role of the observer in Schrödinger's experiment.

At the tips of nerves, where electrical signals are transmitted between one nerve cell and another, there is a collection of vesicles arranged on the inner side of the axon, each of them containing different groups of neurotransmitters, since, when a signal is transmitted, only some of the subgroups of vesicles release their particular content. Margenau asserts that

> in very complicated physical systems such as the brain, the neurons and sense organs, whose constituents are small enough to be governed by probabilistic quantum laws, the physical organ is always poised for a multitude of possible changes, each with a definite probability.
>
> MARGENAU, 1984: 96

It is in this context that the mind would operate like the observer in a quantum experiment that affects, by the mere alteration of the probabilities of the vesicular emission, the state of these emissions within the brain and, through it, the physical machinery of the body, offering responses that are not pre-codified in the genes.

It is clear that, though much has been written since Eccles and Monod, the more recent theories of consciousness and life, for some time, do not imply dualism, or vitalism—on the contrary. The transition from physics to biology and from biology to culture are transcendent or emergent movements in which a more complex dimension does not deny the preceding one, despite the disruptive nature of the origin of life as well as that of the appearance of human language. And these *shifts from one dimension to another* are not to be confused with the *transitions within the same dimension*, in the sense that Maynard Smith gave to the expression in the field of biology—another recurring source of misunderstandings.

The transition of solitary individuals to colonies (bees, ants, termites), to cite another example (like the origin of sex) pointed out by Maynard Smith, occurs within the biological dimension and should not be confused with the shift from biology to culture—which, in this author's terms, is observed as a mere transition from primate societies to human societies characterized by language. Despite the specificities pointed out by the author himself, rather than as a transition, this move should be characterized as a true change of dimension. Language is the result of evolution, but it produces a new nature that, paraphrasing Monod, *appears to transcend, if not to escape, the laws of biology*. My assessment, which will be clear at the end of this book, is that the *three natures*—physical, biological and cultural—(or two, if we want to combine under the concept of the first both the inorganic and the non-human organic, and, like many sociologists, call the cultural universe the 'second nature') can be distinguished from one another, as François Jacob suggests, by each dimension's relationship to temporality. In the relationship between culture and *the arrow of time*, as I hope to show, we find the key to understanding why cultures r-evolve in a projective dynamic that is wrapped in contradiction. But I won't get ahead of myself.

3 The Life of Culture

It is worth our returning to some recent contributions made by biology to the understanding of culture because, while they are not very promising, they do approach certain aspects of the problem beyond sociobiology and memetics that will merit consideration later. I will start with Peter J. Richerson and Robert Boyd's approach, in *Not by Genes Alone*. To these authors, culture, which is essential for understanding human behavior, is *part of biology*, although "culture and cultural change cannot be understood solely in terms of innate psychology" (Richerson and Boyd, 2005: 4).

As culture affects the success and survival of individuals and groups, cultural variants spread the same way as genetic variants, with the advantage that cultural evolution produces exotic adaptations to changing environments much more quickly than biological evolution does. The environment, which is, in turn, shaped by cultural evolution, ends up affecting which genes will be favored by natural selection. "Culture has shaped our innate psychology as much as the other way round" (Richerson and Boyd, 2005: 4). Thus, culture should be seen as a cause of human behavior, so long as we do not lose sight of its connection to biology.

In defining culture as information that can affect human behavior, acquired by some kind of social transmission, Richerson and Boyd adopt the popular thinking to explain the dynamics of cultural evolution. In this way, they dispense with the hypothesis that cultural information needs to take the form of a meme that is discrete and faithfully replicable like genes. That does not imply, for them, that cultural evolution cannot be thought of in Darwinian terms, nor that culture is a phenomenon disconnected from biology, as some anthropologists claim. These authors reject the view that "first we got human nature by genetic evolution; *then* culture arose as an evolutionary by-product," (Richerson and Boyd, 2005: 12) as if human nature merely supplied a blank slate on which the culture would be written.

The ideas that humans adopt, according to Richerson and Boyd, beyond the process of selection to which they are subjected, typical of cultural evolution, also depend on innate predispositions and organic restrictions that make them more or less attractive. "Individuals with different psychologies will acquire different beliefs and values that will lead to different fitness outcomes." We interact with the environment and with each other all the time. "Thus, culture is neither nature nor nurture, but some of both" (Richerson and Boyd, 2005: 8, 11). In a coevolutionary dynamic, the genetic elements of our psychology shape the culture, just as cultural variation shapes the environment in which our psychology evolves.

The interest sparked by this perspective comes from the fact that the populational approach to culture makes it possible to reposition the subject of group selection within new molds. It is no longer a matter, in sociobiological terms, of thinking about the group as a big family, in which the 'average' kinship is greater than that between groups. Even the very scale of modern societies would not recommend that perspective. It is a matter of recognizing the specificity of the culture and its own dynamics. Unlike Dawkins, who allows greater autonomy for cultural evolution, Richerson and Boyd adopt a position of gene-culture interdependence, in which culture is impacted by *superimposed instincts* of kin (biological) and group (tribal) and affects them directly.

The authors criticize the evolutionary psychology and cognitive anthropology that emphasize the process of cultural differentiation as resulting from genetically transmitted information, conjured up by environmental suggestion. To these schools of thought, culture is not learned: natural evolution would have favored the selection of cognitive modules that, having mapped out particular environments, offer a menu of adaptive cultural behaviors, just the same way as a child is suited to speaking any language, independent of their origin. Richerson and Boyd think differently: cumulative cultural adaptation cannot be based on genetically codified information, and, although one can conceive of an innate 'universal grammar,' corresponding to the capacity for language, those languages used by human groups are taught—that is, they are transmitted culturally.

Faced with this argument, two questions emerge: how does a group maintain its cultural coherence? And how do groups remain culturally differentiated from each other? Beginning from a simplistic model of cultural transmission, Richerson and Boyd believe that a society's individuals have a conformist bias. The authors understand there to be two decision-making forces when it comes to cultural evolution: guided variation and biased transmission.

In the case of the first, a generation's beliefs are linked to the next generation, in such a way as to allow learning to lead to a cumulative change, in a process geared toward the increase of adaptation. In the second, closer to natural selection, the biased transmission results from the comparison of two cultural variants already present in the population, in a process of selection in which the individuals tend to choose the social model that is most common or most prestigious. In both cases, without there being a more marked change to the environment requiring new adaptive responses, the conformist tendency will be the one that is more emphasized, and in this way, it will be favored by natural selection. Culture can thus be seen as a *superorganic* phenomenon, as some anthropologists believe (Kroeber, 1952), but without disregarding its interconnections with the biological aspects of our behavior and our anatomy.

Since, to these authors, culture does not presuppose human language, but only some capacity for learning—the rather debatable choice of one group of biologists and anthropologists, as we shall see—they suggest the hypothesis that the drastic climactic variations of the Pleistocene could have favored cumulative cultural adaptation. The period of climate deterioration is contemporary with the increase in the brain size of various lineages of mammals, a change that would be related to a greater behavioral flexibility, including a longer juvenile period for learning.

With this conception of culture, it might seem paradoxical that drastic changes took place in the Holocene, a more recent period that saw a dramatic fall in climate variation. However, if we consider the conscious construction of a second nature by means of symbolic language, found in human beings, as an event that alters the environment more dramatically than a climactic change, we would have strong arguments for explaining the even more accelerated cultural evolution in that period. As Richerson and Boyd maintain:

> However wild cultural evolution has subsequently run, it arose by natural selection operating to build a complex adaptation in response to specific adaptive challenges. *Culture is an unusual system of phenotypic flexibility only because it has population-level properties.* But even in this it has numerous analogs in the history of evolution; for example, coevolution mutualisms ... We leave it for readers to decide for themselves the extent to which human gene-culture coevolution achieves a status in the history of the evolution of life akin to the rise of the eukaryotic cell.
> RICHERSON and BOYD, 2005: 147; italics by the author

In this attempt to mediate with sociobiology, the authors move away from Dawkins's conception that memes have the ability to rebel against genes and adopt the approach that disadaptations are not consistent with the theory of evolution since Darwin, rather they are explicable through a coevolutionary competitive process in which slow genetic evolution cannot defeat rapid cultural evolution. Culture, itself a product of evolution, allows a faster and less costly form of adaptation than genes. It becomes even more effective if the transmission of information doesn't just happen from parent to children, like genetic transmission, but involves all the information that is available in the social environment—which on the one hand expands the sample from which useful information is extracted, but also increases the odds of disadaptation. Cultural variants (or memes) are not rebels; in truth, the evolutionary speed makes room for cheating.

Group selection is, according to the authors, one of these cheats of culture toward biology. Human culture allows rapid and complex adaptations to variable environments. This makes the inheritable cultural variation between human groups grow, as well as the persistence of the difference between them, which is favored by the cultural conformism within each group. Cultural evolution, in turn, favors the innate psychology suited to each environment, which also reinforces the distinction between human groups, to the point where certain ethnicities make use of the same kind of taxonomy to classify other ethnic groups and animals and plants, as if other ethnic groups were of a different 'species' (Gil-White, 2001).

As a result, along with the selection of genetically determined kin, there arise, as a result of the gene-culture coevolution, 'tribal instincts' that impel us to collaborate with a much larger group of people who are culturally distinguishable, but not genetically related. And the greater the benefit of cooperation, the more the symbolic bonds will be reinforced by other means, such as punitive moralities and coercive institutions, toward even greater and more complex aggregates that, because of the social effects they bring about (hierarchy and inequality), demand sophisticated sources of legitimation.

The process ends up favoring the innate psychology that 'has the expectation' that, on the one hand, social life will be structured by norms and that, on the other, the social world will be divided into culturally different groups. As a result, moral and institutional innovations that make large-scale societies possible, but which maintain the 'social grammar' of a tribal community, tend to spread.

Note that, although the results of this approach come close to those of sociobiology, group selection in this case is a disadaptation that is justified from an evolutionary perspective by the greater speed of responses to changing environments. Selfish cultural variants, poor analogs of genes, tend to spread as replicators, even at the cost of genetic aptitude. Dobzhansky stated in a famous article that "nothing in biology makes sense except in the light of evolution" (Dobzhansky, 1973). To these authors, the same would apply to culture: "Nothing about culture makes sense except in the light of evolution" (Richerson and Boyd, 2005: 237).

As for the 'status' of culture, from Richerson and Boyd's perspective, it gains and loses power: it gains (when compared with sociobiology) because culture, in transforming the environment, alters the conditions in which psychology evolves; it loses (in comparison to memetics) because culture remains on the leash of genes.

> *Culture is on a leash, all right,* but the dog on the end is big, smart, and independent. On any given walk, it is hard to tell who is leading who.
> RICHERSON and BOYD, 2005: 194; italics by the author

Like Dawkins, Richerson and Boyd believe that culture evolves, a premise that this study seeks to refute. But unlike him, these authors suggest, to the approval of evolutionary psychology, that human beings acquire, over the course of their biological evolution, some instincts particular to the species, such as tribal instincts, which are absent from the memetic perspective. Religion and nation are, to Dawkins, the cultural work of memes, not of genes, which is very interesting to highlight, as we shall see.

Nevertheless, I do not believe that Dawkins carried his reasoning all the way through. From a memetic perspective, if a group adopts the same cultural variants, its members could be seen as 'cultural relatives' whose brains operate as vehicles for the culture, through which cultural variants or memes are replicated. Going even further down this same path, different cultures could be seen as the equivalent of different cultural species made up of individuals (people) with their own memeplex (personality).

This line of reasoning could serve as inspiration for recovering some analogies with aspects of anthropological and sociological thought. However, if Dawkins followed this line of reasoning, he would see that his replicator/vehicle model could not be easily applied to the case of memes. Genes of the same organism cooperate with one another because they share the same exit route to the future: the gamete. There is no equivalent to the gamete where the brain is concerned. Besides, the brain is not born with a memeplex (the complex of memes of the same individual) all ready. The process of selection of cultural variants that make up an individual's personality happens over a lifetime, in a process of socialization and individuation about which Darwinism has little to say.

It is worth mentioning, in passing, one theory that seeks to complement the coevolutionary approach from the idea of niche construction and its impact on biological evolution and cultural change. This perspective, according to its proponents, flows from Dawkins's above-mentioned concept of the extended phenotype, an inspiration that Dawkins himself refuted. To Dawkins, as we have seen, genes can be expressed phenotypically outside of the vehicle carrying them, that is, they can extend out into the world.

Laland et al. piggyback on this idea and expand it: "Niche construction refers to the activities, choices, and metabolic processes of organisms, through which they define, choose, modify, and partially create their own niches" (Laland, Odling-Smee, and Feldman, 2000: 132–3). If an organism is continuously altering its environment in the same direction and this change is reinforced by subsequent generations, this can give rise to a new source of selection, such that new generations inherit not only their ancestors' genes but also an ecological legacy, in a process of feedback in which the adaptation is not a mere response to environmentally imposed problems but a two-way street.

Besides, since an organism alters not only its own environment but that of other species, too, niche construction can unleash evolutionary events that realign a number of ecosystems over time. The gene-culture coevolutionary view, according to the authors, is insufficient precisely because it does not grasp that the model is only complete if, in more complex situations, niche construction is added.

Reciprocal altruism, from this perspective, could even have a broader reach, between species and intergenerationally, gaining an ecological dimension. It is interesting to note that, in adopting an ecological perspective, the selfishness/altruism binary, in practice, simply dissolves and loses any empirical reference, as I had indeed already suggested.

To this school of thought, even if humans are not the only living things capable of transforming the environment around them, with impact on evolution, they do it preferentially via culture: "Culture now becomes merely the principal way in which we humans do the same thing that most other species do" (Laland, Odling-Smee, and Feldman, 2000: 137).

In *Evolution in Four Dimensions*, Eva Jablonka and Marion J. Lamb (2014) argue that this approach is especially relevant to animals that inherit a niche from their ancestors in the form of cultural features and artefacts, as human beings do. If in that context, for example, a cultural change were to take place that was persistent and stable, it could feed back to the evolutionary process with consistent genetic alterations; otherwise, if the cultural change is not continuous or is unstable, there is clearly no way for genetic evolution to go along with it. The authors recognize that there are not many examples of coevolution[4] but believe that this is due to the fact that not a lot of researchers are committed to this sort of study, which is hardly a very convincing argument to justify the total lack of any robust evidence.

The advantage of the theory of niche construction, according to Jablonka and Lamb, is that it offers concepts of environment and of variation that are much richer than those used by Darwinian theory:

> The environment has a role in the generation and development of cultural traits and entities, as well as in their selection, and the new cultural variants are usually both constructed and targeted.
>
> JABLONKA and LAMB, 2014: 218

---

4 The work of anthropologist William Durham (1991) is still the most widely cited.

Variation is not always random in its origin and functionally blind, but it can arise as a Lamarckian-style response to conditions of life. Cultural Darwinism, in these authors' view, does not incorporate the fact that the creation, preservation, transformation and suppression of cultural variants "are all linked to the network of interactions that forms the wider cultural system" (Jablonka and Lamb, 2014: 218).

However, as Steven Pinker points out, both the thesis that humans are evolving biologically and the thesis that culture evolves in the manner of biology are questionable. Brains, he says, evolve according to the laws of natural selection and genetics, but they interact with one another according to the laws of cognitive and social psychology and of human ecology (Pinker, 1997: 208).

The cultural dynamic, therefore, respects another logic, which is neither Darwinian nor Lamarckian, since cultural products arise from mental computations which 'invent and direct the mutations' and 'understand the characteristics acquired.' Passive minds, which simply accept the environment's cultural variants uncritically, would be eliminated by natural selection, giving way to those that assess, discuss and perfect ideas in order to simulate and plan their actions. From these considerations, Pinker introduces another paraphrase: "Nothing about culture makes sense except in the light of psychology" (Pinker, 1997: 201).

Note that, from the perspective of evolutionary psychology, the concept of cultural evolution does not make much sense. The statement that "nothing about culture makes sense except in the light of psychology" obliges one to situate the nature/ nurture dichotomy elsewhere: after all, what is innate to the human brain? Evolutionary psychology tries to answer this question, approaching only its assumptions (from hypotheses about the evolution of the human brain up to its current form, reached during the Pleistocene), but without dealing with the question about the subsequent cultural dynamics, about which it has little to say. As John Tooby and Leda Cosmides stress:

> Adaptive tracking must, of course, have characterized the psychological mechanisms governing culture during the Pleistocene, or such mechanisms would never have evolved; however, once human cultures were propelled beyond those Pleistocene conditions to which they were adapted at high enough rates, the formerly necessary connection between adaptive tracking and cultural dynamics was broken.
> TOOBY and COSMIDES, 1989: 35

Genetics only established the parameters that define the boundaries of culture, and the Darwinian theory of natural selection can only enlighten our understanding about the dynamics of human culture if it settles for promoting an understanding of its points of support, without seeking to explain its development.

4 Culture, Language and Evolution

At the root of those problems faced thus far, as becomes ever clearer, is the very definition of culture and its relation to symbolic language. In my view, there is no culture without symbolic language. Culture is the product of symbolic language; or alternatively, culture is the second nature that symbolic language produces. The brain producing symbols is such a disruptive event that it set the fathers of the theory of evolution, Charles Darwin and Alfred Russel Wallace, who agreed about all the rest, against one another. To call anything produced before symbolic language 'culture' is a misconception. For the purposes of this book, symbolic language is that which makes it possible to 'travel in time,' a precondition for what I understand by culture. We shall come back to this.

We know that aperiodic crystals (DNA), being a strand of different units, are able to transmit information and to originate life if they are associated with a metabolic-homeostatic system. Symbols can, likewise, transmit information, but it is worth investigating how the symbol and the gene differ, and what is the particularity of the social mechanisms that originate culture and determine its dynamics.

Returning to Jablonka and Lamb's book, these authors argue that evolution happens in four dimensions—genetic, epigenetic, behavioral and symbolic—with their respective inheritance systems, which interact with one another. This view does still owe a great debt to the sociobiological perspective. Sociobiology in the 1970s sought to present a new synthesis (Wilson, 1975). Edward O. Wilson wanted to go beyond the results obtained by the successful modern evolutionary synthesis since the 1930s. The initiative produced more confusion than certainties.

The theorists of coevolution and of niche construction are currently trying to remedy sociobiology's inadequacies with a move toward an Extended Evolutionary Synthesis (Laland et al., 2008, 2015). Nevertheless, the treatment given to the symbolic dimension is insufficient and impoverishing. In aspiring to situate the symbolic inheritance system among the between three others, these aspects do not comprehend its transcendent nature, in the non-metaphysical sense that Monod gave the word.

The appeal to Ernst Cassirer's authority to support this choice proves curious. In *An Essay on Man*, which Jablonka and Lamb cite, Cassirer (1944) begins from the thinking of Estonian biologist Jakob von Uexküll who, in his celebrated works, adopts a vitalist view that is critical of Darwinism. Cassirer does not seek to make a critical evaluation of Uexküll's biological principles, to which we shall return later, but to borrow his schema and terminology to posit a more general question. To Uexküll, the simplest organism is not merely adapted to the environment, but totally re-adjusted. There are no inferior and superior organisms, but perfection everywhere.

Every organism, in accordance with its anatomy, has its own receptor system, via which it receives external stimuli, and its own effector system, via which it reacts to them, forming a single intertwined chain or a functional circle. Knowing its anatomy, we can reconstruct its unique way of experiencing reality. There are, therefore, as many different realities as there are different organisms. Every organism has a world just of its own because it has an experience just of its own, such that the realities of two different organisms are incommensurable with each other.

Cassirer asks, then, what would be different about man. Is a human merely a living being who, given its own particular anatomy, experiences a unique reality incommensurable with the other realities of other species? Or is there something more than this? "The functional circle of man," answers Cassirer,

> is not only quantitatively enlarged; it has also undergone a qualitative change. Man has, as it were, discovered a new method of adapting himself to his environment. Between the receptor system and the effector system, which are to be found in all animal species, we find in man a third link which we may describe as the *symbolic system*. This new acquisition transforms the whole of human life. As compared with the other animals, man lives not merely in a broader reality; he lives, so to speak, in a new *dimension* of reality.
>
> CASSIRER, 1944: 24

Cassirer uses the concept of *dimension* in a quite different sense to that used by Jablonka and Lamb.[5] The symbolic dimension projects man beyond biology. Humans do not lose the condition of biological beings for this reason, just as life doesn't stop being a handful of 'matter.' When aperiodic crystals combine with chemically arbitrary cybernetic systems, which are more useful from a physiological point of view, the conditions are created for what we call life.

---

5 Dobzhansky (1962) produced a more acceptable reading of this writer.

The arbitrariness or gratuitousness of regulatory systems are common to every form of communication that is complex, genetic or symbolic.

There is also a tradition in sociology (Parsons and Luhmann, for example) that will take inspiration from biocybernetics (referenced in the work of Uexküll himself and of Bertalanffy), to try to elucidate the social mechanisms that regulate the cultural dynamic. Nevertheless, it is important to note, with Cassirer, that man is not simply a social animal:

> Man, like the animals, submits to the rules of society but, in addition, he has an active share in bringing about, and an active power to change, the forms of social life.
> CASSIRER, 1944: 223

Emphasizing the crucial difference between *social* and *cultural*, increasingly important in the debate between biologists and social scientists, the philosopher goes on:

> Human culture taken as a whole may be described as the process of man's progressive self-liberation. Language, art, religion, science are various phases in this process. In all of them man discovers and proves a new power—the power to build up a world of his own, an 'ideal' world.
> CASSIRER, 1944: 228

5   Sociobiology and Super-Organisms

The difference between the social and the cultural is a good starting-point for setting out the series of problems faced by the social sciences in defense of the specificity of their object. Sociology's interest in biology precedes the establishment of biology itself as a discipline. The founder of sociology, Auguste Comte, devotes one class (42ème *leçon*) of his *Course of Positive Philosophy* to a debate between Lamarck and Cuvier that anticipates, albeit in a nascent form, many of the subjects that would be systematically dealt with by the theory of evolution in the decades that followed. Herbert Spencer's sociology, meanwhile, gave rise to countless controversies that, frankly, were no good for Darwinism nor for the humanities, social Darwinism being the product of a major misunderstanding by him and his followers.

In *First Principles*, Spencer defines evolution in purely mechanical terms:

> Evolution is an integration of matter and concomitant dissipation of motion; during which the matter passes from an indefinite, incoherent homogeneity to a definite, coherent heterogeneity; and during which the retained motion undergoes a parallel transformation.
>
> SPENCER, 1867: 281

It is not hard to see how far Spencer's definition takes him from Darwin. The basis of Darwin's theory is not the progression of incoherent homogeneity and coherent heterogeneity, but the variability of lifeforms. The two-stage process of variation by natural selection makes these lifeforms into single entities that in no way represent moments of evolution of a total system. The variation/selection mechanism produces sequences of irreversible forms, but without determined directionality.

As a cumulative sequence of appearances of these entities, evolution can only be understood in retrospect. The theory of evolution has nothing to say about the future of evolution. Thus, natural selection does not necessarily involve progress; it just takes advantage of the beneficial variations that best adapt the organism to its conditions of existence. There is no evidence for a law of necessary development, as is indeed suggested by the coexistence of more complex and less complex lifeforms.

Spencer's definition not only doesn't limit the concept of evolution to the organic, but it attributes a progressive unidirectionality to it. Although he describes the process as merely teleomatic, in which a certain result is reached exclusively as a result of physical laws, Spencer comes close to an early sociobiological view in suggesting that organic development and social development are subject to the same principles.

Human societies are treated as superorganisms, analogously to colonies of insects and certain other groups of vertebrates, an approach that is much to the taste of contemporary sociobiology. If we consider the suggestive substitution of the principle of natural selection by the slogan 'survival of the fittest,' we can glimpse the possible Spencerian ways of approaching the relationship between human societies, to the point where Walter Bagehot (1872), a contemporary of Darwin's and Spencer's, stated that fighting between tribes and nations is no more than the Darwinian struggle for existence and evolution by natural selection. We recall that *The Descent of Man*, published by Darwin not long before this, includes passages, already quoted above, that allow for this controversial perspective, which sociobiology would embrace in defense of the theory of group selection, in contrast with that found in *The Origin of Species*.

The first chapter of *The Principles of Sociology* is entitled "Super-organic Evolution." After having dealt in previous works with the inorganic evolution of inanimate objects and the evolution of discrete organic aggregates, Spencer (1876) will devote himself to the evolution that begins beyond the combined efforts of parents in relation to their offspring, still within the context of organic evolution. Social insects are the best-known example. In some of the most advanced insect societies, the division of labor reaches the point where it relies on different classes of individuals who are structurally adapted to different functions, as is the case with soldier, worker and slave insects. Spencer also mentions the existence, in certain situations, of a rudimentary system of sign language and of complex activities of mining, construction and transportation.

In spite of this, he recognizes that social insects are no more than one big family, the uniting of the children of one single mother, even if they belong to various classes of individual, and finds in the coordinated action of birds and in the associating of mammals for activities of hunting, defense and protection, rudimentary forms of superorganic evolution. Going further, Spencer observes among some groups of primates the nascent presence of subordination, property, the exchange of services, the adoption of orphans, etc.

The evolution of human societies, the highest order of superorganic evolution, while it emerges from these less-high orders of the animal world, also surpasses them in extent and significance in terms of growth, structure, and function, with it falling to an actual discipline, sociology, to study them. But sociology ought to do this by adopting the same procedure that other sciences devote to the analysis of inorganic evolution and organic evolution, that is, via the observation of the particular forces of the object under consideration, its nature or intrinsic factors, and of the forces to which it is exposed, its environment or extrinsic factors. In the case of human societies, on the one hand, the physical and emotional features of its members, their intelligence and way of thinking, and on the other, the climate, the terrain, the flora and the fauna.

Spencer's theory then begins to express what he calls 'derived factors.' Human action radically alters the organic and inorganic environment around it, allowing the development of new and complex forms of cooperation in agricultural and industrial activities. Human societies grow and become the superorganic environment for others, determining new forms of political organization and governmental action.

As they gain in prominence, these industrial and governmental activities come to exercise a greater influence over the actions, feelings and ideas of the individuals that constitute it, adapting them to social demands, while at the same time these requirements are themselves reformulated to suit them to the demands of the individuals. The dynamic is completed with the emergence of a secondary environment, more important than the first, made up of superorganic products commonly characterized as artificial but which in Spencerian philosophy should be considered to be as natural as any other product of evolution: artefacts, writing, science, religion, art, etc.

For Spencer, therefore, the second nature is not artificial. Everything is natural: superorganic products are treated on the same level as sub-organic elements. As a result, it is also not possible so speak of coevolution; there is only evolution: the same teleomatic process operating in the inorganic, organic and superorganic worlds. In that sense, Spencer's philosophy is even more comprehensive than sociobiology.

The Spencerian theory of evolution reaches its tentacles backward, toward the inorganic world, and forward, toward the superorganic world. It does not, therefore, fit into any of the major contemporary aspects of biological thought about culture: sociobiology, memetics or coevolution. Rather it comes across as a kind of positivist 'phenomenology of nature.' The proximity to sociobiology, however, is worthy of note. As Alfred L. Kroeber pointed out in *The Nature of Culture*, while Spencer recognizes that insect societies merely simulate social aggregates, he was not especially impressed by what separates them from human societies.

The issue still merits some consideration. Unbelievably, this subject, under the name of *eusociality*, has occupied some biologists, thanks to Edward O. Wilson's extraordinary obsession with returning to a subject that had already seemed properly clarified. Wilson recently joined up with two colleagues, Martin Nowak and Corina Tarnita, to return to the argument made in earlier works that "relatedness is better explained as the consequence rather than the cause of eusociality" and to reassert group selection, once again:

> Eusociality, in which some individuals reduce their own lifetime reproductive potential to raise the offspring of others, underlies the most advanced forms of social organization and the ecologically dominant role of social insects and human.
> NOWAK, TARNITA, and WILSON, 2010: 1057

The article paved the way for the publication, two years later, of *The Social Conquest of Earth*, which was harshly criticized by Dawkins (2012), the book in which Wilson puts human societies into the field of eusociality, seeking to demonstrate the fundamentally biological basis for what Spencer understood as derivative factors or second nature.

The article also prompted an uncommon reaction from more than a hundred evolutionary biologists in defense of Hamilton's original hypothesis about kin selection (Dawkins, 2012), according to which the 'altruism' between two organisms is 'proportional' to their genetic closeness. The authors counter-attack sociobiology, turning to the striking example of sex allocation, that is, the ratio of investment in males vs females. This is well-known material in which the results of kin selection are very robust, since Trivers and Hare, among others, tested out hypotheses raised by Hamilton himself.

In simplified terms, a colony of hymenoptera (ants, wasps and bees) has a queen that stores for life the sperm received on her nuptial flight, which, in turn, fertilize a portion of the eggs as they mature. It is an intriguing situation because the non-fertilized eggs develop into males, and the fertilized ones, into females, a phenomenon known as haplodiploidy. The male, therefore, has no father, and all the cells in its body contain just one group of chromosomes coming from the mother (haploids). As a result, a male's sperm are necessarily all the same.

This means that the children without fathers, the males, carry 50% of their mother's genes, just like the females. Nevertheless, their sisters (diploids), unlike their brothers, not only have 50% of their mother's genes but also 100% of their father's, given that the father's sperm are all alike. The degree of kinship between full sisters, therefore, is 75%, not the 50% that you find in normal sexed animals, while the degree of kinship between them and their brothers is only 25%.

Counterintuitively, from the brothers' perspective, the chance of their sisters carrying one of their genes is 50%. In this framework, the queen and her male children are indifferent as to the sexual ratio between males and females, while full sisters have a bias toward females, that is, toward more sisters. The balance of the colony, from an inclusive fitness perspective, therefore favors investment in females, which has been established empirically.

According to Wilson's critics,

> the quantitative success of this research is demonstrated by the percentage of the variance explained in the data. Inclusive fitness theory has explained up to 96% of the sex ratio variance in across-species studies and 66% in within-species studies.
> DAWKINS, 2012: E1

Kroeber emphasizes that social scientists, having few accomplishments they can lay claim to on the cultural plane, will not infrequently resort to whatever is to hand to produce results by force, with materials and models that come from physics or biology. These hard sciences, meanwhile, faced with the 'fragility' of the humanities, often attempt to find a solution to cultural phenomena in causes that are physical or organic. These movements reinforce each other.

With sociobiology, something different happens; it takes one characteristic of human societies, the cooperation between individuals who are not genetically related, and seeks to transpose it onto the non-human organic world as a strategy for arguing that everything can be explained by genes. Kroeber published his essay entitled *The Superorganic* in 1917,[6] in which he sets out his understanding that human progress and culture are

> so unmistakably similar to the evolution of plants and animals, that it has been inevitable that there should have been sweeping applications of the principles of organic development to the facts of cultural growth.
> KROEBER, 1917: 164

Reasoning by analogy, in this case, would be entirely justified. However, this sort of behavior does often create a predisposition to adopting a less rigorous scientific attitude to support that analogy, even when the results from the research contradict one's assumptions.

According to Kroeber, this is the case with the analogy between insect societies and human societies. Some insects are sociable beings because they associate, but they do not have culture. The sociability of the insect is determined by its genetic inheritance. The process of developing culture occurs by accumulation, not necessarily related to hereditary agents. The distinction between insects and human beings is not based on a difference of degree, but a difference of type. We will not find in the superiority of any one characteristic feature, such as intelligence, an explanation that will distinguish the two processes.

Instinctive activities of non-human animals are even capable of extraordinary feats, of causing astonishment. What distinguishes us is that we are organic beings that produce culture.

> The attempt today to treat the social as organic, to understand civilization as heredity, is as essentially narrow minded as the alleged medieval inclination to withdraw man from the realm of nature and from the ken of the scientist because he was believed to possess an immaterial soul.
> KROEBER, 1952: 32–33

---

6 In biology, the eusocial colony was considered a superorganism by Wheeler (1911).

For Kroeber, the confusion between the organic and the cultural is due, deep down, to the incapacity to distinguish between the mental and the cultural. As biology tends to correlate, and sometimes co-identify, the human brain and the mind, and does so in a way that is grounded scientifically, it is then led, by an extrapolation that is not justified, to identify mind and culture. It is one thing to admit that everything cultural only exists through the mental, the basis of which is organic; it is something else entirely, something quite different, to imagine that one can explain culture in physiological and mechanical terms.

> That heredity operates in the domain of mind as well as that of the body, is one thing; that therefore heredity is the mainspring of civilization, is an entirely different proposition, without necessary connection and without established connection with the former conclusion.
> KROEBER, 1952: 40

As a flow of the products of mental exercise, culture is, essentially, not individual. Imagining that a culture can be understood through the organic make-up of its members is to take it as the mere aggregate of psychic activities or as a product of minds that are shaped organically, not as an entity beyond these minds. Culture, for Kroeber, is a leap into a new dimension, like the first occurrence of life in the universe. And though it is still ingrained in it, it transcends it. What does this transcendence mean?

If we have referred earlier to the same problem in neurophysiological terms—the mind/brain binary dealt with at the physical level of neurons, hormones and neurotransmitters—we should now, taking Kroeber's explanation, examine the discussion around the psyche/culture binary, as it was organized by evolutionary psychology, which studies the brain as a system for information processing, without reference to neurophysiological processes, in its challenge to Kroeber's own anthropology, as well as that of Durkheim and Geertz.

6 Psychology of Culture

In a classic text entitled "The Psychological Foundations of Culture," John Tooby and Leda Cosmides set the terms of the clash: "Human minds, human behavior, human artifacts, and human culture are all biological phenomena—aspects of the phenotypes of humans and their relationships with one another" (Tooby and Cosmides, 1992: 20–21). To other authors, taking the human being apart into biological and non-biological aspects is to fall back into the old pre-modern dualism of the western tradition which has disappeared from the horizon of modern science. We have already seen, through Monod and Eccles, the existence of an alternative path between monism and dualism that the authors do not explore. Still, it is worth setting out the argument, for reasons that will soon become clear.

Tooby and Cosmides want to replace what they call the Standard Social Science Model (SSSM) with the alternative Integrated Causal Model (ICM) which, they argue, breaks with the dualist view. To do so, they present, step by step, the considerations that motivate the former model. In the first place, the SSSM begins from the supposition that genetics cannot explain why culture is something shared by members of a group but not necessarily between different groups, which can differ from one another dramatically.

This gap is reinforced by the fact that children are born the same as one another and become adults who are different from one another to the same extent that they grow up in varied cultural environments. Human nature, which is common to all those of the species, does not seem to be the cause of cultural variation, which can, in turn, only be explained by what children learn from other members of their local group according to a paradigm that is pre-established and external to the individual which shapes their mind, taken to be a tabula rasa.

Culture, therefore, is something extrasomatic or extragenetic, a group of non-biological variables that organizes and gives substantial form to human life based on the group's own historical-cultural dynamics. In Kroeber's words: "The only antecedents of historical phenomena are historical phenomena" (Kroeber, 1915: 287). According to the SSSM, from this perspective, psychology should study the process of socialization with a focus on the process of *learning*, through which children assimilate culture that is transmitted more or less accurately by the group from generation to generation.

Natural evolution simply replaced the systems of genetically determined behavior with general-purpose mechanisms of learning and cognitive processes that are independent of content, and the explanation for the existence of similarities between members of the same group is due merely to the existence of separate flows of transmission of the informational substance that constitutes culture. Culture, therefore, according to the SSSM, has little to do with biology or human nature or any genetically inherited psychological design, whose innate aspects have only negligible ability to explain it.

The model put forward by Tooby and Cosmides (ICM) starts from different assumptions. It should be presented with some care because its central argument places evolutionary psychology in a curious position both in relation to the standard model of the social sciences and also in relation to certain aspects of sociobiology. Evolutionary psychology, on the one hand, does not look into which differences between individuals and groups of individuals are caused by distinctions in their genes and, on the other hand, it doesn't rule out the existence of a psychological architecture that is typical for the species, which is *universal and genetically inherited*, that contains mechanisms resulting from natural evolution, specialized in resolving long-lasting adaptive problems.

We should note, above all, that evolutionary psychology denies the existence of any scientific evidence to support any racist explanation for the differences between human beings. In addition, it embraces the theory that, just like the human body, the human mind also evolved phylogenetically; just as teeth and breasts are absent at a child's birth, certain psychic mechanisms manifest ontogenetically only during the process of the individual's development.

In this way, the standard social sciences, according to Tooby and Cosmides,

> [fail] to appreciate the role that the evolutionary process plays in organizing the relationship between our species-universal genetic endowment, our evolved developmental processes, and the recurring features of developmental environments.
> TOOBY and COSMIDES, 1992: 33

The SSSM are reluctant to give up on the theory of the almost infinite malleability and plasticity of the human mind; even if they do understand it as an operational system, they consider it to be like a general-purpose computer in order to escape from a determinist vision that naturalizes unwanted behavioral and social results and, in this way, they seek to weaken the significance of the biological forces that act upon human behavior.

For Tooby and Cosmides, however, this is a mistake. The idea that an infinitely malleable and generic psychic architecture is more responsive to the environment fails to recognise that, without specific mechanisms resulting from evolution, we would not have the abilities needed to survive.

> Our ability to perform most of the environmentally engaged, richly contingent activities that we do depends on the guiding presence of a large number of highly specialized psychological mechanisms.
> TOOBY and COSMIDES, 1992: 39

Faced with infinite possibilities of behavior, there is only a small group of desirable solutions to every set of circumstances. In that context, the extreme flexibility of an operational system is not a virtue, quite the contrary; adaptive flexibility prevents us from getting lost in a series of mistaken possibilities and thus requires a guidance system. An organism would not have time and information available to allow it to solve problems of great complexity without specific rules of domain of relevance, specialized processes and prior hypotheses to guide them.

This only seems limiting to us if we consider just two alternatives, the brain as a generic system or the brain as one single specialized system. Nevertheless, as soon as we consider the likeliest hypothesis that the brain is made up of a well-articulated group of specialized mental organs, this impression vanishes. The human brain is not more flexible because it has freed itself from 'instincts;' rather it is more flexible precisely because during the process of evolution it incorporated more 'instincts.' The modern debate about the psyche-culture relationship should therefore be centered, according to the ICM, on the nature of the dedicated evolutionary psychological mechanisms, which, far from causing constraints and imposing limits on us, expand our field of activities, which are impossible in their absence.

According to evolutionary psychology, human nature is the same everywhere. Natural selection, associated with sexual recombination in species with an open population structure, such as humans, tends to produce uniformity in adaptations, especially those that form interdependent structures that limit the variations able to happen without compromising the integrity of the adaptations as a whole. This means that the inherited group of specialized mechanisms is common to all human beings, with small variations from individual to individual, albeit operating in different circumstances. And just as phenotypes differ from genotypes, that is, the observable expression of a feature differs from its inherited basis, the distinction ought also to be drawn between manifest behavior and evolved psychology, breaking up the cultural differences into variable environmental raw-materials and a uniform underlying design. In this way,

> all humans share a universal, highly organized architecture that is richly endowed with contentful mechanisms, and these mechanisms are designed to respond to thousands of inputs from local situations. As a result, humans in groups can be expected to express, in response to local conditions, a variety of organized within-group similarities that are not caused by social learning or transmission. Of course, these generated within-group similarities will simultaneously lead to systematic differences between groups facing different conditions.
> TOOBY and COSMIDES, 1992: 116

Another consequence of the argument underlying ICM is that there is no distinction between what is biologically determined and what is not biologically determined, but there is between psychological mechanisms open to various environmental factors that produce variable manifest behavior and psychological mechanisms closed to external influence that produce uniform behavior.

Meanwhile, the environment, understood in a limited way as the relevant part of the universe that interacts with the developing organism, is also a product of evolution, including the physical and biological worlds and, in the case of humans, culture. The universal architecture of our minds, both physiological and psychological, the interaction both between them and between them and the natural and cultural environment relevant to their development, make up a metaculture that is ultimately what allows so many children to understand what is culturally variable and anthropologists to conduct their ethnographic work.

> It is probably more accurate to think of humanity as a single interacting population tied together by sequences of reconstructive inference than as a collection of discrete groups with separate bounded 'cultures'.
> TOOBY and COSMIDES, 1992: 121

As we will later get the chance to clarify, from this book's perspective, both these alternatives are false, unless the word 'interaction' is assigned a very particular meaning.

For evolutionary psychology, what we call culture, in the classic sense, is, therefore, merely a residue, a subgroup of contingent cultural phenomena that exist in a mind and which, through interaction and observation, are recreated in other minds by low-fidelity inference mechanisms in an epidemiological kind of process, which is insufficient to produce a discontinuity in the evolution of culture that transports humans to an autonomous realm that transcends biology. Evolutionary biology, in this way, rehabilitates the old 'nature not nurture' formula, without conceding to any racialist perspective but remaining equidistant from the anthropological approaches that argue for culture's transcendence over genetics.

From that perspective, there is no such thing as a culture 'out there,' external to the individual; it is the design of the human psychological architecture that structures the nature of social interactions and the transmission of representations between individuals. The social system is like an ecosystem structured by a process of feedback directed by the dynamic properties of the human mind, and it is through their common psychological architecture that the secondary anti-entropic effects of the social dynamic should be analysed, not through some supposed functionally integrated mechanisms belonging to the social system as though that itself were an organism.

But what do these specialized psychological mechanisms consist of, after all? First, we would like to lay out the following examples: the mechanism for partner preference (Buss et al., 1992), the mechanism for sexual jealousy (Wilson and Daly, 1992), specific mechanisms of sexual creativity (Miller, 2001), signals communication emotion between mother and baby (Fernald, 1992), the mechanism for detecting social cheating (Cosmides and Tooby, 1997), etc. These mechanisms are certainly not exclusive to the human species; we have already seen that many biologists talk naturally about animal consciousness, animal culture and animal psychology.

Nevertheless, if what distinguishes human beings, according to evolutionary psychology, is precisely the fact of possessing more instincts, not fewer, it is interesting for us to ask about those specific instincts of humans to which the researchers pay attention. Three of these, being most significant, deserve mention: the language instinct (Pinker, 2007), the tribal instinct (Richerson and Boyd, 2005), and the religious instinct (Boyer, 2001).

These 'instincts' are associated with human culture, and it seems obvious that the two latter ones are clearly dependent on the first, since tribe (nation) and religion presuppose symbolic language. This means that to clarify the question of whether human culture is a mere phenotypical expression of evolved human psychology or whether biological evolution hurled the human being into a dimension that transcends biology itself, it seems clear that the debate over the status of language is unavoidable.

It is here, in my opinion, that evolutionary psychology's major vulnerability is to be found.

I will seek to show, over the course of this book, that language, though a product of biological evolution, cannot easily be considered an instinct. Going further, I will defend the hypothesis that the tribe (or nation) and religion not only have symbolic language as a pre-condition, but that they are also a result of how cultures r-evolve.

So just as important as characterizing human language is understanding whether the so-called tribal and religious 'instincts' assumed by evolutionary psychology are innate or whether they are a product of the historical development that unfolds according to laws that are analogous to evolutionary biological laws or according to actual r-evolutionary laws that this study seeks to reveal.

CHAPTER 3

Toward a Dialectical Anthropology

> What we need is to reconstitute an ontology or, at least, an anthropology that is dialectical.
> JEAN-PAUL SARTRE

∴

> Here I and my culture are primordial, over against every alien culture.
> EDMUND HUSSERL

∴

Martin Harris (1968) points out that Franz Boas never rejected the Darwinian theory of evolution, an opinion that Tim Ingold (1986) would later take on. Boas, in fact, rejects evolutionary parallelism and the universal patterns of progress. On this, his position is entirely in agreement with Darwin's as expressed in *The Origin of Species*. The Boasian rejection of biological reductionism should not obscure the analogies that the father of American anthropology drew between biological evolution and cultural evolution, as Ingold made a point of stressing.

Boas defines culture as

> [the] totality of the mental and physical reactions and activities that characterize the behavior of the individuals composing a social group collectively and individually in relation to their natural environment, to other groups, to members of the group itself, and of each individual to himself. It also includes the products of these activities and their role in the life of the groups. The mere enumerations of these various aspects of life, however, does not constitute culture. It is more, for its elements are not independent, they have a structure.
> BOAS, 1938: 159

Note that the definition does not immediately exclude the existence of a non-human animal culture. Phenomena of material culture, such as the use of artefacts, and even social habits, like those cases of gregarious animals and social insects, can be observed in the non-human animal world. However, Boas prefers to call them animal habits or lifestyles, reserving the word *culture* for the species whose non-stereotypical behavior cannot be characterized as instinct, but which depends instead on a transmitted tradition that presupposes the use of symbolic language, that is, the human species. I should say, once again, that this study takes that same position.

There are certain features that are common to all cultures: the cooking of foods, the use of tools, a belief in the supernatural and in a multiplicity of worlds, the idea of a human soul, the grammatical structure of languages, etc. Boas admits, to the approval of evolutionary psychology, that, just as analogous forms in plants and animals can arise independently, these common cultural features could also have arisen independently as a function of the identity of the human being's mental structure. But it could also be the case, according to him, that these similarities are due to two kinds of historical relations. Those features common to all humanity could represent cultural conquests from a period preceding the dispersal of humans, suggesting the possibility of a common cultural antiquity; or the common features are due to the process of diffusion of culture whose elements sometimes travel at great speed.

Specifically with relation to languages, Boas, in the light of the available historical evidence, did not believe that the number of languages could have been smaller in the past than currently. Rather, everything suggests that the number was greater, it being impossible to assert whether, in times even further back, all languages were related to a single mother-language. The likeliest thing is that, in primitive conditions, groups were much more isolated from one another than they are now, each with its own language and its own culture.

Boas attributes the course of Tylor, Morgan and Spencer's research to the influence of Darwin's work, as they had focused their analyses on the theory of biological evolution applied to cultural phenomena, relating these phenomena to the development and advance of civilization. As we have seen, *The Descent of Man* allows for this interpretation. The constant increase in empirical knowledge and its technical application in new inventions, as well as the illusion of a moral progress of civilization strengthened the idea of a single line of development of culture, a view prominent in the anthropological works of the late 19th century.

As for the perspective in *The Origin of Species*, however, nothing could be more misleading. Boas and Darwin, as Ingold pointed out, seem to be pretty well in agreement as regards some of the properties of biological evolution and cultural evolution. In both cases, it is hard to talk about progress or unilineal evolutionary sequence. In relation to industrial development, obviously, everything suggests a movement toward growing complexity; but in relation to everything else, something quite different happens.

Many primitive languages are more complex than modern ones. We can also find, in primitive cultures, more complex forms of religion and sophisticated systems of social obligations. Even with the economy as a whole, there is no parallel development that is comparable. You need only think about the independent development of agriculture and cattle-raising, even in chronological terms.

Would a pastoral group be more evolved than an agricultural tribe? Impossible to say. Besides, people whose material culture is very poor often have a high level of social organization. On the other hand, materially rich cultures can deprive considerable sections of their members from the enjoying of these spoils, relegating the subordinate layers of society to the satisfying of only their bare necessities.

We must also consider the relationship between one culture and another. The ethics that can today justify improving the well-being of one culture at the expense of the other, according to Boas, are the same that previously might have encouraged primitive man to consider every outsider an enemy to be killed.

To Boas, "cultural phenomena are of such complexity that it seems to me doubtful whether valid cultural laws can be found" (Boas, 1940: 257). With culture being an integrated whole whose elements have an effect on each other, the attempt to deduce cultural forms from one single cause are doomed to failure.

We are not denying the importance of certain factors for the shaping of cultural forms, such as geography and economics. But even these crucial factors must be relativized. Very different cultures can cohabit in the same environment, and societies with comparable levels of economic development can differ greatly in terms of art, religion and the other elements of culture. "Cultures differ like so many species, perhaps genera, of animals, and their common basis is lost forever" (Boas, 1940: 254).

That last analogy, which associates cultures with species, undoubtedly brings Boas close to Darwin, as Ingold points out. Dobzhansky, years later, would consider it acceptable to "distinguish evolutionary changes in cultures as analogous to anagenesis and cladogenesis in biological evolution" (Dobzhansky, 1962: 10). One interpretation that I suppose is acceptable of Boas's formulations would consider the possibility that, at the time of human dispersal, a process of cultural differentiation analogous to allopatric cladogenesis took place, through which a geographical isolation (allopatry) between populations of the same species interrupts the gene flow between them and, as a result reproductive isolation between them can occur, allowing for the possible formation of a new species.

Nevertheless, Boas himself recognizes a fundamental difference between cultures and species, which makes the analogy a questionable one:

> Animal forms develop in divergent directions, and an intermingling of species that have once become distinct is negligible in the whole developmental history. It is otherwise in the domain of culture. Human thoughts, institutions, activities may spread from one social unit to another. As soon as two groups come into close contact their cultural traits will be disseminated from the one to the other.
> BOAS, 1940: 251

I believe that we can find in biology an analogy that is more consistent with Boas's considerations. It allows us better to explore the author's limitations and potential, while simultaneously giving us the opportunity to bring in a new character who is crucial to the development of our argument. The suggestion comes from Ernst Mayr, who introduces us to the concepts of the superspecies and semispecies. For Mayr, "a superspecies consists of a monophyletic group of entirely or essentially allopatric species that are morphologically too different to be included in a single species" (Mayr, 1966: 499).

Now, the allopatric populations of which the superspecies is composed are designated as semispecies when they have not completed the process of speciation, though the geographical barriers are notable: "Gene exchange is still possible among semispecies ... but not freely as among conspecific populations" (Mayr, 1966: 502).

Biologically speaking, the chances of human beings speciating are remote, at least for as long as planet Earth is our only home. Culturally speaking, however, human beings can be seen, from Boas's perspective, as a large cultural superspecies made up of semispecies separated by cultural barriers, which are generally surmountable, *but not always*. This last hypothesis, of a possible 'unsurmountability' between cultures, in the specific sense of contradictory perspectives or conflicting projections in time, which obstruct the process of reciprocal exchange, will be of the greatest importance in our explanation of how cultures r-evolve.

The possibility of a total cultural speciation is, in a sense, considered by Boas and, when it occurs, the consequence of the interruption to the genetic exchange by cultural causes can be tragic. Primitive man's inclination toward treating an outsider as an enemy to be exterminated is mentioned by the author more than once. But Boas does not draw all the conclusions from this fact. Complete cultural speciation, which we shall call *alienization* (to keep us away from the theories of *alienation* of Hegel, Feuerbach and Marx), would suggest very powerful forms of de-eroticization of the species.

If incest marks the boundaries of mating according to degree of kinship (a relatively small group of individuals), alienization marks the boundaries of mating with an outsider, an almost unlimited circle of non-relatives. Note that alienization does not create a biologically different species, but a *culturally antagonistic species* in which the gene flow is obstructed not by natural barriers but by cultural coercion. In other words, complete alienization gives rise to a new figure, the excluded third, generating a dialectical triadic relationship between ego, alter and alien.

In the literature that I consulted, the only place I found a correlated term, applicable to anthropology, was in Freudian psychoanalysis: *das Unheimliche* (the uncanny).[1] *Heimlich* (homely):

> *Heimlich* thus becomes increasingly ambivalent, until it finally merges with its antonym *unheimlich*. The uncanny (*das Unheimliche*, 'the unhomely') is in some way a species of the familiar (*das Heimliche*, 'the homely').
>
> FREUD, 2003: 134

The excluded third is an inherently contradictory character, who simultaneously is and is not of the human species. They adhere perfectly to two observations from Freud on the subject:

> In the first place, if psychoanalytic theory is right in asserting that every affect arising from an emotional impulse—of whatever kind—is converted into fear by being repressed, it follows that among those things that are felt to be frightening there must be one group in which it can be shown that the frightening element is something that has been repressed and now returns. This species of the frightening would then constitute the uncanny, and it would be immaterial whether it was itself originally frightening or arose from another affect. In the second place, if this really is the secret nature of the uncanny, we can understand why German usage allows the familiar (*das Heimliche*, the 'homely') to switch to its opposite, the uncanny (das *Unheimliche*, the 'unhomely'), for this *uncanny element*

---

1 The translator Paulo César de Souza highlights the inadequacy of the translation of the term, and draws attention to the solutions adopted in some foreign editions: *lo siniestro, lo ominoso, il perturbante, l'inquiétante étrangeté, the uncanny* (Freud, 2010).

is actually nothing new or strange, but something that was long familiar to the psyche.
    FREUD, 2003: 148; final italics by the author

Maynard Smith rightly criticized Lévi-Strauss's statement that the incest taboo started culture. As we have seen, the statement sounded false to him, or tautological: false because there are many non-human species that avoid incest; tautological because taboo *is* culture. In fact, what happens is something different. Culture creates a new sexual barrier which pushes preferences in the opposite direction to the natural inclination to get some distance from close relatives. So, it is now a matter of getting some distance from strangers. This means that it was not the incest taboo that started culture, as Maynard Smith rightly noted; rather it was culture that, in creating a force acting the opposite way to that biological predisposition, denaturalizing the search for a partner and redefining the field of sexual choice, created the need for a barrier that placed a limit on this new force, pursuing the same motivation as the biological force (avoiding the biological complications of incest). The incest taboo is, therefore, from the cultural point of view, a consequence of alienization that, in directing the sexual impulse towards those who are more familiar or acquainted, forces the construction of a second cultural barrier that is not identical but harmonized with the biological one. A process of dealienization would, of course, have another consequence, namely, to re-eroticize civilization in relation to cultural barriers—but not to biological ones. This is the correct way of approaching the incest taboo from an anthropological point of view.

Lévi-Strauss (1952), like Boas, does not ignore the matter of alienization. In *Race and History*, he recognizes that the notion of humanity, encompassing the whole species, independent of the few ethnicities and many cultures that exist, arose recently in one particular region.

There prevailed, over the course of history, an ethnocentric view according to which a people will look at others as barbarians or savages, now stripping them of the smallest degree of reality, transforming them into ghosts or hauntings, now attributing vices or inhuman natures to them. But when Lévi-Strauss talks about 'a certain optimum of diversity,' he is more concerned with the process of homogenization of cultures, with some persistent superstructural differences maintained, than with its extreme opposite, antagonistic heterogeneity.

Diversity, for him, is a natural phenomenon. It results both from the isolation of groups and also, more regularly, from the desire of nearby groups to distinguish themselves from each other. It would not even be possible to conceive of one single process of development of culture, whatever it might be. That would imply, in practice, denying true diversity.

The difference between cultures would be determined exclusively by the different stages at which they find themselves, resulting from progressing at different paces, not from a divergence between the actual developments of each one. Nevertheless, nothing in the history of peoples suggests such a hypothesis, quite the opposite. Lévi-Strauss is not thereby seeking to deny the reality of some kind of human 'progress', if we can call it that, but prefers to present it from a different perspective.

What characterizes those cultures that manage to realize the most cumulative forms in history? For Lévi-Strauss, the so-called great civilizations, which so impress us, were never made up of isolated cultures, but of coalitions between cultures that combined their conquests and inventions, whether voluntarily or involuntarily.

That is the main reason why Paleolithic cultures did not come together very much. While humanity was dispersing geographically, these human groups were differentiated from a cultural point of view, but they combined little.

> A culture's chance of uniting the complex body of inventions of all sorts which we describe as a civilization depends on the number and diversity of the other cultures with which it is working out, generally involuntarily, a common strategy.
>
> LÉVI-STRAUSS, 1952: 42

The combining of cultures is, therefore, a precondition of big civilizations, which makes it even more of a nonsense to talk about civilizations that are superior or inferior. The most cumulative cultures do not exist in themselves; their size is not a product of their nature. They are the characteristic form of 'social superorganisms' made up of distinctive cultures and their specific way of coming together.

Even dramatic historical events like the colonizing of Latin America by the Europeans are laid out by Lévi-Strauss in this interpretative key. The collapse of the civilizations of the New World when faced with the arrival of a handful of conquistadors from the Old World was due, according to Lévi-Strauss, less to the fact that the Americas had less cultural diversity than to the fact that, being a region more recently settled, the Amerindian peoples would have had less time to diversify, thus presenting a more homogenous panorama.

The cultural coalition of the American peoples brought together fewer partners that were different from one another than the coalition from Europe, the locus of the fusion of Greek, Roman, Germanic and Anglo-Saxon traditions, and Arab and Chinese influences, these traditions themselves being the results of other, even older coalitions.

The contribution of one single culture, therefore, has less to do with its individual realizations than with a certain *differential distancing* of itself in relation to the other cultures, the civilizing process being, to some extent, a paradoxical phenomenon in which the fruitfulness of coalitions increases as a function of the diversity between cultures; a diversity that continuous progress tends, in turn, over time, to homogenize. And precisely by weakening what causes it, progress gradually loses traction and cumulative momentum.

According to Lévi-Strauss, this fate can only be compensated for by two kinds of events: the first consists of *internal* differential distancings, in which the division of a society into distinct groups and classes is deepened and, perhaps, social inequalities increase; the second, to a great extent conditioned by the first, consists of incorporating, for good or ill, new cultures into the social superorganisms, a means amply used by the European powers through colonialist and imperialist practices.

Whatever the path taken, the civilizing process depends on the continuous replacement of diversification: global civilization can only be the planetary coalition of cultures each of which maintains its originality; equalized into one single way of life, humanity will remain ossified.

1 Cultural Niches and Frontiers

Lévi-Strauss's reading of the arrival of the European conquistadors and the resulting colonialism is instructive. The genocide of the Amerindian peoples and the importing of African slave labor, in the terms that he proposed, are treated by the same name as coalitions that create social superorganisms, as if the historical processes of social formations differed in manner and degree, but not in nature.

Genocide and enslavement are played down by a 'technical narrative', operating under the mantle of science. With this, *structural anthropology*, in not considering the triadic relationship in which the process of alienization transforms difference into contradiction, and differential distancing into antagonism, loses in realism and critical power. The same thing happens when it is called upon to comment on internal differentiation, which Lévi-Strauss, to his credit, recognizes as being conditioned by external differentiation. In his interpretative key, internal differentiation (castes, classes, etc.) is seen merely as a positive compensation for the loss of dynamism resulting from the homogenization between cultures that progress itself encourages, putting itself at risk.

Internal differentiation is, therefore, incorporated in the manner of Durkheim, who dealt with the process of constitution of social structures based on a combinatory logic. If Boas, as we have seen, calls more attention to the phenomenon of dispersal and cultural speciation, Durkheim attempts a more detailed description of the phenomenon of binding the species together and the consequent *organization* of society.

If, from the external point of view, Durkheim, along the same lines as Boas, considers societies as 'individualities' belonging to social species, from an internal perspective he sees them as an organism. What Lévi-Strauss would later call a superorganism would be a special case of a coalition of organisms. Also, according to him, just as a physiologist studies an organism's functions, it falls to the sociologist to assess the health of each social species, according to its particular characteristics, without falling into the temptation of judging an institution, a moral maxim or a practice in themselves, indiscriminately for any social type, disregarding each one's particular stage of development.

The main weak point of Comte's philosophy, according to Durkheim, is precisely his having underestimated the existence of social species. Beginning with the idea that there is a continuous evolution of the human genus, Comte thought it possible to represent the progress of human societies as identical to that of a single people, it being down to philosophy to find the order to this evolution.

For Durkheim, however, what exist are particular societies that are born (like a social species), develop (in accordance with their own historical phases) and die (incorporated into other societies or not):

> A people which takes the place of another is not merely a prolongation of the latter with some new features added. It is different, gaining some extra properties, but having lost others. It constitutes a new individuality, and all such distinct individualities, being heterogeneous, cannot be absorbed into the same continuous series, and above all not into one single, series. The succession of societies cannot be represented by a geometrical line; on the contrary, it resembles a tree whose branches grow in divergent directions.
>
> DURKHEIM, 1982: 64

Social morphology should establish and classify social species. Societies are made up of parts that are added to each other by the gathering of the peoples who precede them. The simplest society is the horde. The gathering of hordes makes up the clan. The juxtaposing of clans gives rise to poly-segmental societies that, in a permanent combinatory process with other societies, become ever more complex.

In this process, however, the combining of populations from different species can also happen, located on different branches of the genealogical tree of social types, prompting the formation of new species. And in this, for Durkheim, the social world diverges sharply from the biological one: in the social world, societies, like the individualities of different species, are crossed, originating new species, hybrid social types; the rare 'biological-style reproduction' occurs in an 'asexual' way, through a process of colonization, and, even then, only while the new colony remains isolated, not mixing with other social types.

One extreme example of radial hybridism is offered by the Roman Empire, which brought together peoples of the most diverse natures. Yet Durkheim observes, in a simple footnote, something highly significant:

> However, it is likely that in general the distance that separated societies composing it could not be too great; otherwise, no social communality could exist between them.
> DURKHEIM, 1982: 117

For Durkheim, although everything that exists breaks down into elements of the same nature, the differences of association give rise to the most varied forms of organization. It is these differences of association that explain the distinctions between living beings and inorganic molecules, between multi- and uni-cellular organisms, between man and animal, and, ultimately, between human societies and the individuals that constitute them. Even if cells contain more than molecules of raw material, that form of molecular association is the cause of something new, life, the germ of which cannot be found in any of the elements that constitute it. And just as biological phenomena cannot be explained, analytically, by physical-chemical phenomena, so sociological phenomena cannot be reduced simply to psychological ones.

> By aggregating together, by interpenetrating, by fusing together, individuals give birth to a being, psychical if you will, but one which constitutes a psychical individuality of a new kind.
> DURKHEIM, 1982: 129

Hence Durkheim's reference to the moral community.

This is why, in agreement with Durkheim, sociology should not allow itself to be fooled by certain human features that are apparently innate, such as feelings of religiosity, sexual jealousy, maternal love, etc. since the manifestations of these inclinations differ so widely from one society to the next that, stripping away all the difference, the psychological residue left in all human beings is limited to something that's situated at some distance from the facts it seeks to explain.

And just as contemporary psychologists see the advantage of psychology over neurology, Durkheim sees the advantage of sociology over psychology: the object, in the two pairs suggested, is easier to reach.

Human society is, therefore, an organism that cannot be reduced to its constituent parts. It has its own existence, external to the individual, and it imposes itself upon him, exercising a kind of coercion that is the *spontaneous* product of reality. This is also, therefore, including for Durkheim, a second nature or *sui generis* nature in which "the determining cause of a social fact must be sought among antecedent social facts and not among the states of the individual consciousness" (Durkheim, 1982: 134). This does not imply that individual originality has no role in social evolution; however, it cannot do much if the conditions on which the evolution itself depends have not already been realized in some way.

Pursuing this line of reasoning, when societies are hybridized, forming new types, the role of the individual experiences a change. Initially, the combination occurs between societies of the same nature. The first polysegmental societies are made up of similar and homogenous segments, juxtaposed 'like the rings of an annelid'. New-order combinations, however, give rise to completely different organisms, in which the constituent parts are not of the same nature, nor are they arranged in the same way; rather they comprise a system of different organs, each with a special function, coordinated and subordinated to a central organ that exercises moderation over the organism.

And just as cells in multicellular organisms are specialized, the individuals who make up a complex society take on different and complementary functions by means of the division of labor. Unlike cells, however, individuals do not inherit the characteristics from their parents, and the distribution of social functions can stop responding to the distribution of natural aptitudes and talents.

As the progress of division of labor implies ever-increasing differentiation, it is down to society to ensure equality in the external conditions of struggle, in such a way as to allow each individual to find happiness in the realizing of their nature, according to their ability, carrying out those functions to which they are suited.

Durkheim believes that the differences in birth between the rich and the poor would lessen, leading to greater harmony between individual natures and the social functions carried out by individuals, but he did consider the hypothesis of a caste system producing solidarity, so long as it is rooted in a given society's nature.

Durkheim also doesn't highlight the difference in nature between the process by which a tribe is formed from clans and the process by which a 'Rome' is formed from the subjugation of one tribe by another, a situation in which the dominated are transformed into a part of the inorganic conditions of reproduction in the life of the dominators.

Now, the so-called 'Neolithic Revolution' reaches its peak with two extreme events of great impact: writing and slavery. The effect is comparable only to the taming of fire, a decisive event in the process of anthropogenesis. What the mastering of fire represented for the body, the Neolithic Revolution represented for the mind. Writing frees the mind, externalizing a series of processes that it fell to it to perform (memory, algorithms, routines, etc.).

The 'agglutination' of societies, in this case, produced a new phenomenon, a counterpart to alienization. Societies that incorporate the excluded third through subjugation end up with individuals who are depersonalized: neither people nor animals—a *domesticated alien*, to be precise. Parenthetically, the so-called process of self-domestication of the human species, to which many scientists have given their attention, from Johann Friedrich Blumenbach to Richard Wrangham, can only be understood if based on contradictory human relations of this nature. It is worth noting that Émile Benveniste had already observed that the term *pasu*, in the ancient Vedic texts, referred to movable property, the ownership both of domesticated animals and also of subordinated domestic serfs and slaves (Benveniste, 2016: 28–30). And he added that, while the word 'slave' is associated with the concept of strangeness, foreignness, the word 'free' is associated with the idea of a friend, belonging to a group, well-born. More recently, it has also been pointed out that in the ancient Sumerian world, the term *amarKUD* was applied equally to castrated animals and castrated slaves. Like the incest taboo, the castration complex should also, as you can see, go through an anthropological examination.

It is important to clarify, from the outset, that what we are calling a 'process of depersonalization' is not restricted to phenomena from the world of work; it is therefore not limited to the concept of class or caste, but it does allow us to consider, under the same name, outlandish processes of domination involving situations that are very different but equally oppressive, in relation to gender, race, sexuality, etc. which form a real matrix of subjugation that is idiosyncratic in nature, in which human beings are subjected to conditions analogous to those described above.

Wherever you look, without considering a dialectical triadic relationship, you will lose sight of the critical and specific dimension of the cultural dynamics of human societies. A society's conflicts and discords are not, as Durkheim believes, the product of pathological forms of division of labor that stop producing solidarity. Rather, they are an expression of the internalizing of contradictory relations that structure essentially divided societies.

In this way, the division of labor into which the social process of subjugation culminates actually serves the self-preservation of the subjugated whole. The history of societies has been the history of the struggle over alienation and depersonalization. It has two motors, one external and the other internal, that propel it; and the attempt to explain the great historical transitions by exclusively internal or exclusively external causes have generally been impoverishing, a risk that the German Historical School, the Annales School and World-Systems Theory have sought to avoid.

We recently used an analogy inspired by Ernst Mayr to present this dynamic. We thought of the human species as a biological superspecies made up of cultural semispecies capable of speciating. We can go a little further and state that, depending on historical events, cultural subspecies can merge (identity), or remain distinct in relative equilibrium (difference), or be alienized toward mutual annihilation or subjugation. Complete cultural speciation, alienization, does not produce difference, as in biology, but *contradiction*, which makes it impossible to deal with intercultural phenomena from a biological perspective. And so culture does not evolve, rather it r-evolves. The concept of r-evolution is aimed precisely at considering a process that is itself inherently contradictory.

This approach also brings great advantage as concerns the traditional opposing views of continuity and discontinuity of cultures, getting around a crucial problem in anthropology, like the definition of the borders that bound cultures. Kroeber, for example, rejects the comparison between cultures and organisms; for him, cultures are

> obvious composites: more or less fused aggregates of elements of various origins, ancient and recent, native and foreign. They are therefore more truly similar to faunas and floras, which are also composites or aggregates of constituent animal or plant species which often are of quite diverse origin in space and time.
>
> KROEBER, 1952: 57

Robert Lowie refers to culture as a "planless hodgepodge, that thing of shreds and patches called civilization" (Lowie, 1920: 441). Ruth Benedict is even more direct:

> It is, so far as we can see, an ultimate fact of human nature that man builds up his culture out of disparate elements, combining and recombining them; and until we have abandoned the superstition that the result is an organism functionally interrelated, we shall be unable to see our cultural life objectively, or to control its manifestations.
> BENEDICT, 1923: 84–85

In an article published in 1935, Radcliffe-Brown criticizes this perspective: "I think that probably neither Professor Lowie nor Dr. Benedict would, at the present time, maintain this view of the nature of culture" (Radcliffe-Brown, 1935: 402). In 1940, he seems to backpedal from this position and starts talking about cultures as reified abstraction:

> In place of the study of the formation of new composite societies, we are supposed to regard what is happening in Africa as a process in which an entity called African culture comes into contact with an entity called European or Western culture, and a third new entity is produced, or is to be produced, which is to be described as Westernized African culture. To me this seems a fantastic reification of abstractions. European culture is an abstraction and so is the culture of an African tribe. I find it fantastic to imagine these two abstractions coming into contact and by an act of generation producing a third abstraction. There is contact, but it is between human beings, European and African, and it takes place within a definite structural arrangement.
> RADCLIFFE-BROWN, 1940: 10–11

The mention of culture as 'reified abstraction' is toned down in his book, published in 1952, which brings together, among others, the two articles mentioned, in the same year as a paper by Lévi-Strauss rebuking the original text. Radcliffe-Brown, in this work, returns to his own 1935 view, closer to Lévi-Strauss, who is himself very clear about his objection to those who seek to weaken the concept of culture:

> anthropologists usually reserve the term 'culture' to designate a *group* of discontinuities which is significant on several of these levels at the same time. That it can never be valid for all levels does not prevent the concept

of 'culture' from being as fundamental for the anthropologist as that of 'isolate' for the demographer. Both belong to the same epistemological family. On a question such as that of the positivistic character of a concept, the anthropologist can rely on a physicist's judgement; it is Niels Bohr who states that "the traditional differences [of human cultures] in many ways resemble the different equivalent modes in which physical experience can be described".

LÉVI-STRAUSS, 1963: 295–96

Similarly, Fredrik Barth (1956) innovatively draws on the concept of the niche, adopting, on the heels of Kroeber, an ecological perspective in which a group's relationships are analysed from their relations with natural resources and with competing groups, generating patterns of interaction that go from the symbiotic to the rivalrous. In his seminal article, "Ethnic Groups and Boundaries", the author refines his approach to ethnicity, registering the difficulties of dealing with the subject from controversial premises such as that of geographical isolation.

Barth shows that ethnic borders persist in spite of contact, the mobility of people and the flow of information between cultures, and they are often maintained precisely because of dichotomized ethnic statuses. It can also happen that one ethnic group can occupy multiple different ecological niches, without losing its cultural unity and basic ethnicity, even if it might present differences in institutionalized behavior. It is possible for interethnic relations to stabilize just as, through contact, it is possible for the differences between groups to be now reduced—by the creation of a congruence of values—and now accentuated—by the formation of poly-ethnic social systems.

Barth suggests the adoption of an ecological viewpoint for analysing the interdependency between ethnic groups that make up, complementarily, an all-encompassing social system, in which case the groups can occupy different niches, with the minimum amount of fighting for resources; they can monopolize separate territories, competing more intensely especially in the border zone; or occupy reciprocal and, nevertheless, different niches, but in close interdependence.

Obviously, we should not lose sight of the fact that ecological equilibrium always depends on demographic equilibrium. Barth also draws attention to one last question that is worthy of note, including ethnicity and stratification. Ethnic diversity does not necessarily imply stratification, and stratification doesn't necessarily imply the existence of ethnic groups. The Indian caste system, in which the borders between castes are defined by ethnic criteria, forming a stratified poly-ethnic system, is one very particular case.

These approaches to continuity and discontinuity of cultures, notwithstanding the progress, do not break away from a dyadic view of the problem. They are compatible with the idea of superspecies, but they do not raise the possibility of a semispecies speciating, in which case dialectical triadic relationships can be established. And here is it worth returning to the argument between Radcliffe-Brown and Lévi-Strauss on the subject.

For Radcliffe-Brown, social structure is based on a network of dyadic social relations of person to person, while for Lévi-Strauss something entirely different happens, since, for him, dyadic social relations are just the leftover of a preexisting structure that is more complex in nature. For the former, the structure is constant flow, organic movement of the order of empirical observation; to the latter, it is a reality that is hidden, unconscious, which unfurls over time.

Lévi-Strauss, quite clearly, feels like he is missing a *third element*, but believes he has found it in this hidden structure, common to all spirits, ancient and modern, that impose forms upon a content. He turns, for this, to Trubetzkoy and Jakobson's structural linguistics to apply procedures analogous to those of phoneme analysis to social and cultural systems, but with the same intention of examining in kinship systems, in mythology, in rituals, etc. the formal properties of these structures in their own terms.

However, as Noam Chomsky observes,

> the structure of a phonological system is of very little interest as a formal object; there is nothing of significance to be said, from a formal point of view, about a set of forty-odd elements cross-classified in terms of eight or ten features.

He continues:

> Furthermore, the idea of a mathematical investigation of language structures, to which Lévi-Strauss occasionally alludes, becomes meaningful only when one considers systems of rules with infinite generative capacity. There is nothing to be said about the abstract structure of the various patterns that appear at various stages of derivation. If this is correct, then one cannot expect structuralist phonology, in itself, to provide a useful model for investigation of other cultural and social systems.
> CHOMSKY, 2006: 66

Curiously, both Radcliffe-Brown and Lévi-Strauss cite Gregory Bateson's *Naven* (1936) in support of their arguments, though, for the French structuralist, the author had already gone beyond the level of pure dyadic relations on which

English structural-functionalism is based. Bateson does, in fact, position himself somewhere beyond dyadic relations, but not in the sense that Lévi-Strauss suggests. I am referring not so much to Bateson's treatment of the concepts of structure and function, which generated such controversy among Radcliffe-Brown and Malinowski's disciples, but to his presentation of the concept of schismogenesis, understood as a process of differentiation.

Bateson (1958) distinguishes two types of schismogenesis: complementary and symmetrical. In the case of the first, the groups' behavior and aspirations are different, but they reinforce each other mutually, with the possibility, absent any moderating restrictions, of leading to a rupture. The assertive attitude of one group that provokes submission on the part of another can encourage some new assertion, which is responded to with still more submission, until a schism occurs. In the second, the behavioral pattern of the two groups in contact is the same, symmetrical, altering only by degree, over the course of time, until the rupture, as in the case where one group responds to the other's bragging with more bragging, without any stabilizing mechanisms coming into play.

When two groups of individuals with entirely different cultures come into contact, three possible results should be considered:

(1) the complete fusion of the two groups;
(2) the elimination of one or both groups;
(3) the persistence of both groups in dynamic equilibrium as differentiated groups in a single major community.
BATESON, 1958: 184

This list does not consider the subjugation of one group by the other, which limits the scope of the analysis. Indeed, slavery, for example, does not fit into the hypotheses listed. This is not exactly a matter of fusion, elimination or dynamic equilibrium, although it contains elements of all three of these possibilities without being identical to any one of them.

It is understandable that Bateson suggests that the then unsettled and unstable political conditions—remember that he was writing shortly before the outbreak of the Second World War—are characterized by two schismogeneses: (a) symmetrical schismogenesis of international rivalries and (b) complementary schismogenesis of the class struggle. Bateson does not realize the connection between them, however, and the excluded third, which structures the dyadic relations *from the outside*, is not revealed.

The concept of schismogenesis has endured, surviving in the work of contemporary writers such as Roy Wagner (1981), Marilyn Strathern (1990, 2017) and Viveiros de Castro (2002), among others. But it was Graeber and Wengrow (2021), in their recent book, who took a step in the direction that interests us, considering processes in which groups of humans can idealize or exaggerate points of difference between them so as to resemble one another as little as possible. In our study, the concept of schismogenesis is radicalized to the point of contemplating the possibility of cultural speciation, in which groups see themselves as antagonistic cultural species in which annihilation or subjugation become concrete possibilities.

Bateson failed to consider the forming of dialectical triadic relationships. This is why he, a participant in the famous Macy Conferences, will find support for the development of his highly original ideas in the concept of *feedback* and move closer to cybernetics.

The idea of feedback, used by Clerk Maxwell in his analysis of the steam engine with a governor and by Claude Bernard's pioneering work on the constancy of the internal environment, followed by Walter Bradford Cannon, who developed the concept of homeostasis, was crucial for the appearance of cybernetics. As we know, cybernetics, rather than working with linear chains of cause and effect, explains biological and social phenomena using circular causal chains, which either seek a state of dynamic equilibrium or are modified in exponential progression, a movement that is generally limited by finite energy resources or by some kind of external constraint.

Cybernetics, however, are very limited when it comes to explaining biological and social phenomena. Feedback is a determining factor for explaining the stability of systems, but not their evolutionary (or r-evolutionary) dynamics, which is why Bertalanffy tries to add cybernetics, which deals with closed systems, into the bigger picture of the general systems theory, which is beginning to work with the idea of open systems to explain the dynamics of biological and cultural systems.

We are especially interested in the connection that Bertalanffy establishes between Jakob von Uexküll's biology and Benjamin Lee Whorf's linguistic relativism. Before discussing that, however, I should mention Marshall Sahlins' contribution to the debate. In an attempt to overcome the dichotomy between universalism and relativism, within the theory of evolution, he offers a few critical elements that will be useful to us in composing the general schema of our argument.

In *Evolution and Culture*, Sahlins and his colleagues return to a few coinciding intuitions developed by Tylor and Spencer, and also observed by Durkheim, to propose an original synthesis of the apparently conflicting perspectives of Leslie White and Gordon Childe, on the one hand, and Julian Steward, on the other, around the unilinearity or multilinearity of the evolutionary process in the field of culture. Sahlins reasserts the idea of progress without entirely breaking with the idea of relativism.

For him, there are two aspects of the total evolutionary process that are not always well contained by the theory: one adaptive aspect, and a progressive one. Evolution involves both advance and divergence, both progress and variation. These two moments demand, for analytical purposes, that a distinction is drawn between specific evolution, which creates phylogenetic diversity by adaptive modification, and general evolution, which produced—without reference to phylogenesis—superior forms that surpass the inferior forms both at an organizational level and, reciprocally, in exploitation of energy, or, in other words, on the level of integration.

Biological evolution and cultural evolution, to Sahlins and Service, respect this same logic, unfolding, equally, on both these axes, the specific and the general.[2] One of the noteworthy similarities is that the most recent specific forms—biological and cultural forms—are not necessarily the highest general ones: "The stages or levels of general development are successive, but the particular representatives of successive stages need not be" (Sahlins and Service, 1960: 33).

There are, however, equally noteworthy differences. Although it is possible to draw a parallel between mutation and gene flow, on the one hand, and innovation and diffusion, on the other, the authors observe that diffusion does also occur among different cultural species, a phenomenon impossible in biology, given the irreversibility of the process of speciation. Unlike separate biological lineages, different cultural traditions can converge through coalescence, diffusion or acculturation.

In the view of Sahlins and Service, this seems to support Fredrik Barth, who is responsible for adopting the idea of the ecological niche to depict a cultural group's environment as the totality of resources available and the surrounding cultures and respective patterns of intercultural relationship and level of development. Convergence, therefore, is as common among cultures as divergence which, following along the lines of biological evolution, happens through variation and selection.

---

2 Do note, however, that the theorists of the two disciplines followed different paths, the biologists adopting an initial position that was relativist, in line with specific evolution, the sociologists and the anthropologists adopting an initial position that was progressive, in line with general evolution. In the 20th century, relativism gained an increased presence in the humanities, while the idea of progress in biology, with the exception of Julian Huxley, has few followers today.

Each axis of biological or cultural evolution, specific or general, has a corresponding form of dominance that carries the same name. Specific dominance responds by vertically specialized adaptation adhering to a given environment, while general dominance responds by growing adaptability to a laterally expanded ecological horizon.

Unlike biological evolution, however, whose species vary proportionately to an unlimited number of ecological niches, cultural evolution, according to Sahlins and Service, gives rise to a reduced number of cultural types. This combined with the fact that cultural diffusion occurs by mechanisms that are not genetic but are very fast, means we see two trends that are only apparently contradictory.

On the one hand, superior cultures tend to dominate and reduce the variety of cultural systems, including by extermination, colonization or mere threat; on the other, a greater homogeneity is observed among cultures capable of changing level. Cultures, according to Sahlins and Service, can thus converge as regards general evolution, but remain differentiated as regards specific evolution, relegating inferior cultures, from the perspective of general evolution to ever more restricted geographical spaces.

This does not eliminate the possibility of a super-specialized culture, not yet very developed, dominating a very specific niche, at least for a time. Proof of this is in the fact that hunting and gathering, in certain historical situations, can, in more generous environments, produce more energy than agriculture or raising livestock and, as a result, prevent their introduction.

It is important to note that, thus far, Sahlins and Service have remained fans of the idea of cultural evolution, even if they have distinguished general evolution from specific evolution. They add little, therefore, to the efforts to clarify the dialectic of the cultural dynamic more precisely. Nevertheless, despite their explanations allowing no space for the role of contradiction in the historical process, their few observations about the diffusion of culture bring an argument into the anthropological debate that suggests an alternative path, which the authors do not explore.

At a certain point in their explanations, they state that there are obstacles to the general evolution of cultures. On the one hand, a more technologically sophisticated culture seeks, in general, to delay the diffusion of practical knowledge, while promoting the propagation of its institutions (customs, religion, ideology, law, etc.) in the broad sense of Thorstein Veblen's institutionalist thinking. On the other, if this culture, though superior, is very specialized, its potential to change from one level to a different, higher one can be less than the potential of an inferior and less specialized culture which can, by virtue of its greater flexibility, surpass the former.

Thus, the model incorporates an argument from Soviet Marxism about the Leninist-Trotskyist law of unequal and combined development, according to which the new form can result from more delayed forms:

> Specific evolutionary progress is inversely related to general evolutionary potential. It is important to remember that because of the stabilization of specialized species ... over-all progress is characteristically irregular and discontinuous rather than a direct line from one advanced species to its next descendant.
> SAHLINS and SERVICE, 1960: 97-98

Despite the illusions of Soviet Marxism, which even goes against the forecasts of classical Marxism, the benefit of Sahlins and Service's study is less the separation between general evolution and specific evolution, which deserves much comment, so much as having refined the theory of diffusionism through the distinction between technical diffusion and institutional diffusion. This allows anthropology to be in dialog with contemporary economic schools of thought, of various shades, that seek to explain the non-convergence of economies toward a common level of development, most of them using neo-institutionalist arguments.

In a passage from the work of Douglass North that is not very often mentioned, for example, he points out that:

> recent neoclassical models of growth built around increasing returns (Romer, 1986) and physical and human capital accumulation (Lucas Jr., 1988) crucially depend upon the existence of an implicit incentive structure ... At the other extreme are Marxist models or analytical frameworks initially inspired by Marxist models that do crucially depend on institutional considerations. Whether they are theories of imperialism, dependency, or core/ periphery they have in common institutional constructs that result in exploitation and/ or uneven patterns of growth and income distribution. To the extent that these models convincingly relate institutions to incentives to choices to outcomes they are consistent with the argument of this study. And *because much of human economic history is a story of humans with unequal bargaining strength maximizing their own well-being, it would be amazing if such maximizing activity were not frequently at the expense of others.*
> NORTH, 1990: 134; italics by the author

Although North recognizes Marx as the precursor of a vision that separates and integrates technological change and institutional change, via an original conception of the development of the productive forces—a technique together with the social relations of production (institutions)—the contemporary economic debate over cultural diffusion and cooperation between human beings took another path, toward a rapprochement of economics and biology that passes through the Nelson and Winter's evolutionary economics to reach Fehr's neuro-economics, through Bowles and Gintis. This is not the place, however, for dealing with these lines of research.

Even though the conclusions of our study could offer some input into a debate with this tradition, since its intention is precisely to assess its assumptions, this task would divert us from our purpose. We shall remain with Sahlins, then, in the field of anthropology, trying to respond to a concern expressed by one of his first inspirations, the archeologist Gordon Childe, about "why man did not progress straight from the squalor of a 'pre-class' society to the glories of a classless paradise, nowhere fully realized as yet" (Childe, 1965: 236). We find an answer to the question, indirectly, in North himself: "[Marxist theory] entails a fundamental change in human behavior to achieve its results, and we have no evidence of such a change" (North, 1990: 132). Who knows if we shouldn't be asking whether there already was, in the distant past, some change in human behavior in this deep sense, though in the opposite direction.

Twelve years after *Evolution and Culture*, Sahlins published *Stone Age Economics*, a book clearly inspired by the economic anthropology of Karl Polanyi, whose critical appraisal will allow us to advance the aims of this study. I would like to stress, first of all, that the book begins by questioning the assumption of Gordon Childe's provocation about 'pre-class' society: the alleged *Paleolithic poverty*. What meaning can be assigned to that expression? I would propose that the distinction between the two meanings of economics, the formal and the substantive, which were suggested by Polanyi, even if it explores interesting alternative paths, is insufficient to tackle the problem. Sahlins goes further, but, even so, in the light of this study's preliminary observations, his conclusions need to be partially re-evaluated.

According to Polanyi, the formal meaning of economy has its basis in the means-ends relationship and refers to the aim of obtaining as much as possible with the resources available, which leads, logically, to the concept of scarcity. The substantive meaning comes from man's dependency in relation to nature and refers to human subsistence. To Polanyi, the fusing of these two concepts can only be justified in a market society where the satisfying of material needs and choice, in the midst of scarcity, are inevitably linked. This conceptual fusion only happens in a particular institutional set-up which does not apply to societies characterized by other types of integration, as has been pointed out, in line with what has come to be called *non-market economics*, by Karl Bücher and Richard Thurnwald.

Customs and tradition, Polanyi argues, in certain situations eliminates choice and, when choice does need to be made, it is not always induced by the limiting effects of scarcity of resources. Everything depends on how the economy has been established. A market society, only one of the historical forms of economic institution, makes certain assumptions that aren't always recognized by the theory: choice presupposes insufficient means with alternative uses, along with competing aims arranged on a scale of preferences.

Seen from a different angle, this suggests that, in such conditions, scarcity is a corollary of the market society; it is the result rather than the cause of a certain kind of institutional organization.[3] Other forms of economic institution, however, are possible and have proved stable, with a discovery, not in the exchange but in the reciprocity and the redistribution, of alternative patterns of integration. Reciprocity, explains Polanyi

> describes the movement of goods and services ... between corresponding points of a symmetrical arrangement; redistribution stands for a movement towards a center and out of it again; and exchange represents a movement in a similar sense, but this time between any two dispersed or random points in the system.
> POLANYI, 1977: 36

These pure types cohabit within the same society, generally in a subaltern relationship, with one of them dominant over the rest. The predominance of one form of integration is seen, according to Polanyi, in the way in which land and labor are integrated into the society: in primitive groups, by kinship links, which define their use; in feudal society, by vassalage, which determines their fate; in current society, by the transformation of the land and labor into commodities.

The forms of integration, however, do not represent stages of development. Redistribution, to take one example, happens on all levels of civilization, with hunters depending on cooperation, without which the horde would

---

3   I will not go into the debate, at this point, about the critique of the substantive approach to economic anthropology which, for good or ill, is at the root of the methodological argument between Carl Menger and Gustav von Schmoller and which might, perhaps, have compelled the former, after the heated argument, to write four extra chapters for his book *Principles of Economics*, published posthumously fifty years after the first edition.

disintegrate, and ever more present in modern industrial societies, with the substantial increase of public budgets. On the other hand,

> although market institutions ... are exchange institutions, market and exchange are not coterminous. Exchange at set rates occurs under reciprocative or redistributive forms of integration; exchange at bargained rates ... is limited to price-making markets.
> POLANYI, 1957a: 267

Exchange, therefore, a phenomenon that is almost generalized throughout history, is not to be confused with the market, a recent dominant formation that supports a composite concept of economics in which the formal and substantive meanings coincide in practice.

The approach is an innovative one, but it doesn't get to the root of the problem we want to tackle. Polanyi's recourse to Aristotle, who is presented as being a supporter of the substantive view of economics, might have suggested taking one step further. For Aristotle, man is a self-sufficient being like any other animal. Just like animals, men find their sustenance naturally in their environment.

The desire for material abundance and physical pleasures comes from an incorrect notion of a good life, whose true elixir cannot be accumulated or physically possessed. Aristotle's economics concerns itself with domestic life (*oikos*) and with public life (*polis*), which is about the relationships of the people who make up, respectively, the family institution and the community institution, whose members are linked by bonds of affection (*philia*). The established economy is conditioned to the preservation of these bonds.

"The emphasis is altogether institutional and only up to a point ecological, relegating technology to the subordinate sphere of useful knowledge" (Polanyi, 1957b: 81). Polanyi knows that Aristotle, unlike the formalists who posit the idea of scarcity, sees no scope for it in the ancient world. He also knows that this only happens because Aristotle naturalizes slave-based relations of production: nature, of which the slave is a part, supplies the community with its sustenance.

Scarcity, however, is 'there,' in the denial of the slave as a person. The 'up to a point ecological' dimension of Aristotle's economic thought doesn't stand up, and it is precisely the transition from the ecological dimension to the economic dimension, absent from Polanyi's analysis, that we ought to investigate, making use of Sahlins' contribution.

Sahlins, at first, accepts the debate with the formalists on their own terms, without challenging the understanding of economics as the relationship between means and ends. So he begins from the basic premise that human beings can satisfy their bare necessities by producing more or desiring less. Once our irrepressible biological necessities have been satisfied, we can devote ourselves to idleness, to leisure, to games, to the theatre, to politics, to religion, etc. with the advantage that the technological advance inherent in human action can free up more and more time for non-economic activities.

Economics is, like art, politics and religion, a category of culture. You do not need to resort to substantivism to confirm that. Note that this has nothing to do with a judgment about the convenience of adopting market rules for regulating strictly economic activities; even less with assessing the consequences on the system of needs of transforming the land and labor into commodities.

Today, we have historical needs that the ancients never would have imagined. Unlike other animals, human beings have needs that are quite elastic, able to expand unlimitedly. If the criterion for measuring the affluence of a society were not quantity but the proportion of desires that are satisfied, a horde of hunters could be more affluent than a modern industrial society.

In the preface to the new edition of Sahlins' book, David Graeber states provocatively:

> Life in the Paleolithic—which, after all, is at least 90 percent of human history—was in no sense a struggle for existence. In fact, for most of our history, humans have lived a life of great material abundance. This is because 'abundance' is not an absolute measure; it means when you have easy access to large amounts of the things that you want or think you need. In relation to their needs, most hunter-gatherers are rich. Most of all, their hours of labor would be the envy of any modern wage-slave of today.
>
> GRAEBER, 2017: XI

Setting aside the difficulty that Sahlins faces in comparing such remote periods and concepts as abstract and hard-to-measure as satisfaction, wealth or happiness, I think it is no exaggeration to state that the Neolithic Revolution represents, in a way, the transition of man from an ecological plane to an economic one, via a gradual process of denaturalization. Man puts himself at some distance from nature: he objectifies it. This does not mean, of course, that Paleolithic man had no culture, but that culture and nature were not in opposition like the poles of a relationship. Maybe it would be appropriate to declare, in line with Amerindian perspectivism, the occurrence of a gradual process of dehumanization of nature. Before this change, culture was there, the subject was there, the spirit was there, because symbolic language was there, but only at the level of a presupposition; culture and nature as part of one and the same socio-cosmic field, undissociated. The split between the paradigmatic series that today are in opposition has still not been completed, it is not yet established: the pairs of subject and object, altruism and selfishness, spirit and body, culture, and nature, etc. have not yet been formed. *In that context*, it makes more sense to talk about multinaturalism than multiculturalism. Only when those pairs have been formed, through the workings of the Neolithic Revolution, can thought oscillate between "a naturalism monism (of which 'sociobiology' is one of today's avatars) and the ontological dualism of nature/ culture (of which 'culturalism' is the contemporary expression)" (Viveiros de Castro: 2002: 316).

The position of these dualities finds an expression in myths. Mythology is, at once, an expression of the man-nature unit and the narrative of its dissolution. It recounts the naturalization or de-subjectification of nature: it *posits* nature, breaks away from magic and begins the *Aufklärung*. Myths, those victims of the enlightenment, are already a product of it. But what story does mythology tell? What, after all, does the Neolithic Revolution entail?

2 The Primitive Exchange Economy

From Gordon Childe to Jared Diamond, via Robert Braidwood, archeologists and geographers emphasize the process of domesticating nature, elevating agriculture and livestock, which are taken to be the tipping-point in the Neolithic Revolution. Nomadism gives way to sedentarism; natural selection gives way to 'artificial' selection. Nevertheless, in the first place, we should emphasize, on the one hand, that agriculture and raising livestock are not, originally, sedentary activities. The exhaustion of earth and pastures demand mobility even long after the arrival of the domesticating of plants and animals. On the other hand, tribes of hunters—and especially of fishermen—were able to settle, very early, in permanent villages, with houses that are typical of sedentary populations. Graeber and Wengrow relativize the impact of the so-called 'birth of agriculture.' The authors make reference, based on archaeological evidence, to various aspects relating to the official story of this appearance, from the number of human centers where agriculture developed—far more than was thought—to the economic consequences of its development, which was not necessarily associated with a greater well-being. Most interesting, however, is the reference to what the authors describe as an 'ecology of freedom' or 'play farming,' understood as

> the proclivity of human societies to move (freely) in and out of farming; to farm without fully becoming farmers; raise crops and animals without surrendering too much of one's existence to the logistical rigors of agriculture; and retain a food web sufficiently broad as to prevent cultivation from becoming a matter of life and death.
>
> VIVEIROS DE CASTRO: 2002: 316

Secondly, agriculture and livestock are not exclusively human activities. American ants and African termites grow fungi. Leafcutter ants, for example, whose colonies can grow to two million individuals, form gigantic subterranean nests.

In the depths of these excavated locations, they sow fungi fertilized with a compost of leaves they themselves have chewed but not ingested. An agricultural activity like any other. Ants, just as they grow fungi, also raise aphids (greenfly). Aphids are more efficient at sucking the sap from plants than at digesting it, given the huge concentration of sugars in sap, compared to that in the nitrogenous compounds they need. They end up excreting honeydew, a liquid that is rich in sugars, high in nutritional value, whose benefits the ants can enjoy.

These ants, then, 'milk' the aphids, rubbing their bodies with their antennae and their legs, and protect them, making up for the loss of defensive capacity resulting from the process of 'domestication.' A typical activity of the breeders of 'ant cows,' as aphids are known.

I am shining a light on these exotic and apparently insignificant phenomena only to draw attention to the fact that, in nature, cooperation between species, mutualism, is a totally trivial occurrence and does not presuppose any process of objectification. In that sense, there is nothing artificial about the domestication of plants and animals by humans. It is very unlikely that the process of objectification of nature is a result of some practical activity, that is, of the mere interchange between species, even if one of them is the human being. Magic itself (which is not religion) has practical aims, as Marcel Mauss pointed out, by means of a mimetic interchange with nature, without getting some distance from it, as science does.

What I mean is that if this study's assumptions are correct, the human being's first object was another human being, a human being who was alienized and depersonalized. The alienization and depersonalization of one *Homo sapiens* by another, possible thanks to cultural speciation, initiate the subject/ object relationship. The objectifying relationship towards nature is derived from this primordial movement that is inscribed in myth itself. The epics of Homer and the hymns of the Rigveda, late literary expressions of distant historical patterns, recount the processes of alienization and depersonalization carried out by the subjugation of one human group by another, putting an end to nomadism by installing a social order based on territorial property. And as was demonstrated, most notably, by Orlando Patterson (1982), the concepts of property and freedom are only established at that moment, with the advent of slavery.

Let me return to Sahlins to deal with a subject that will clarify our point of view: reciprocity. Sahlins reconsiders Polanyi's schema. For him, economic transactions in the ethnographic register are divided into two types: reciprocal movements between just two symmetrical parts, commonly called reciprocity; and centralized movements, in which collection is made through the control of a center (*centricity*) for subsequent re-division among the group—which can be understood as a *system* of reciprocities. Redistribution, as a system of reciprocities, is thus a form of integration that regulates the circular economic relations *within a group*. Reciprocity, strictly speaking, is a form of integration that regulates symmetrical relations in both directions *between different groups*.

Reciprocity, therefore, is a continuum of forms in which,

> at one end of the spectrum stands the assistance freely given, the small currency of everyday kinship, friendship, and neighborly relations, the 'pure gift' Malinowsky called it, regarding which an open stipulation of return would be unthinkable and unsociable. At the other pole, self-interested seizure, appropriation by chicanery or force requited only by an equal and opposite effort on the principle of *lex talionis*, 'negative reciprocity' as Gouldner phrases it. The extremes are notably positive and negative in a moral sense. The intervals between them are not merely so many gradations of material balance in exchange, they are intervals of sociability. The distance between poles of reciprocity is, among other things, social distance.
>
> SAHLINS: 1972: 191

Sahlins, then, proposes a typology of reciprocity divided into three parts, according to the social distance between the social groups, represented by two extremes and the mid-point: the extreme of greatest solidarity, characterized by altruistic transactions of mutual aid, in an environment of generalized reciprocity where you find those whom culture defines as relatives (*kin*); the mid-point, marked by even exchanges of more or less the same kind of goods in approximate amounts, in an environment of balanced reciprocity between 'friends;' and the antisocial extreme, defined by negative reciprocity, in which the non-kin participants ("nonkin—other people, perhaps not even 'people'") fight one another with opposing interests in search of practical benefits.

I raise the following objections to Sahlins, which also apply to Polanyi. As for one of the extremes, that of generalized reciprocity, Polanyi himself states that the simplest activity, cooperative hunting, is based on redistribution as a form of integration of the group; he failed to recognize, however, that it happens equally in the hunting activities of a pack. We aren't talking about an economy exactly, at least not as a category of culture; reciprocal altruism, as we have seen, is one of the forms of cooperative animal interaction.

As for the other extreme, that of non-reciprocity, Sahlins does not realize that speaking of a continuum of forms of reciprocity only makes sense up to a point. Non-reciprocity is not one extreme pole of reciprocity, it is its negation. There's a difference of quality here, not of degree. There is, in fact, a contradiction, which is why he ends up treating *nonkin* as *nonpeople*. Now, economy is no more than the relation between *people* and *nonpeople*, between human and 'alien' groups, not between people and nature. This objection of ours to Sahlins will even be extended, in due course, to Marx himself.

Two passages cited by Sahlins should have caused him some doubt:

1) "Unto a stranger thou mayest lend upon usury; but unto thy brother thou shalt not lend usury;"
2) gain at the cost of other communities, particularly communities at a distance, and more especially such as are felt to be aliens, is not obnoxious to the standards of homebred use and wont.[4]

These passages make it clear that, just like mythology, economy is also born of the non-reciprocity between human groups who are symbolically separated. Religious needs and economic needs are two sides of the same coin, minted by the excluded third as a symbolic formation that is 'foreign' to dyadic relations, but which, through contradiction, structures them; they constitute them from outside. If we must invoke 'something behind' dyadic relations, that something is certainly alien, symbolic and dynamic. In that sense, actual economies have since the very first been a *national* economy, or tribal economy, as the main political economists of the Enlightenment knew until Smith, List and Roscher.

Economy and religion stem from the Neolithic Revolution and they r-evolve interdependently. We will not, therefore, find in human genes any 'tribal instinct' or 'religious instinct,' as evolutionary psychology claims; the needs

---

[4] Deuteronomy 23:21; Veblen, 1915: 46. Quoted by Sahlins, 1972: 191.

that correspond to these 'instincts' are manifest in another dimension, on the plane of a second nature created by symbols. Symbolic language—yes, but only symbolic language—is undoubtedly a product of natural evolution that unleashes a r-evolutionary cultural process that doesn't follow the logic of natural evolution.

We have not spoken yet about the mid-point in Sahlins' model, equidistant from the two extremes. What happens there and what is it for? Perhaps we could, in the light of what has already been said, reinterpret some ancient ceremonies that have been the subject of much attention by anthropologists. In the hope of seducing biologists to our thesis, let us resort to an analogy: the human species is a superspecies, from a biological point of view, made up of semispecies, from a cultural point of view. Unlike in biology, however, when a cultural semispecies completes the process of speciation, what is produced is contradiction, not difference. Cultural speciation does not produce a new biological species, but a cultural schism within itself.

Contradiction, which is alien to nature, is a possibility embedded in the language that is realized on the symbolic plane by the process of alienization. And as I see it, the mid-point represents the very place where the tensions between cultural semispecies are made manifest and eased to prevent them going astray. It is the place of a gift, and the gift is the total social fact, the *potlatch*, which prevents the completing of the alienization process.

One first characteristic, observed by Mauss, is that the gift is a relationship between groups, not between individuals. This is highly significant. The parties involved are distinct moral groups—families, clans and even tribes (intertribal *potlatch*)—who confront and oppose one another, exchanging (and destroying) goods and wealth, on the one hand, and pleasantries, feasts, women and military services, on the other. Refusing to give, refusing to receive, is equivalent to refusing the alliance and the communion. The flow is as genetic as it is symbolic, as natural as it is cultural. Furthermore, the *potlatch* is not only intended to produce effects on men who, in the search for peace, 'compete' in generosity and selflessness but also on nature and the spirits, in order that they continue to provide abundance.

The *potlatch* prevents alienization precisely so that those needs—economic and religious—do not assert themselves. Hence the permanent tension of the meeting: the groups fraternize and yet they remain strangers; fear and generosity exaggerated in a 'war' whose purpose is not subjugation, but communion. Hence the fact that the nascent economic and religious elements are undissociated in these meetings and that economic activities, steeped in rites and myths, have a hybrid nature, combining provision that is purely unforced and free, and exchange and production that are interested purely in what is useful.

It was only in another context, according to Mauss, that the Romans and the Greeks

> separated sale from gift (*don*) and exchange, isolated moral obligation from contract, and above all conceived the difference between rites, laws, and interests. It was they who, by way of a genuine, great, and venerable *revolution*, left behind this obsolete morality and economy of the gift (*don*), which was too risky, too expensive, too extravagant, encumbered with consideration for people, incompatible with the development of the market, of commerce and production, and, fundamentally, at that time, *antieconomic*.
> MAUSS, 2016: 157; italics by the author

At that point, though, the Neolithic Revolution had already been completed, our twin-engine was in full flight and contradiction had been established, a product of the alienization and subsequent subjugation of one community by another.

3 Alienization and Materialism

Analogies are often impoverishing and demand caution. The alienization to which we are referring might become clearer if we position it in relation to the philosophical tradition. The debate about alienation, which involved Hegel, Feuerbach and Marx, would require a whole separate work, which is unnecessary given the volume of theses already produced on the topic. A brief note on the subject, however, might be enough to distinguish this study's approach and make it more robust. The digression that follows requires some familiarity with German philosophy. It is not indispensable for understanding this book's argument, except in relation to Karl Marx and Marshall Sahlins' critique of him, which will be covered below.

We can say, schematically, that the difference between the authors cited on the matter of alienation is its 'localization' in the general schema of each one's thinking: in Hegel, alienation pertains to the relationship between Creator and creature, the world 'created' understood as the Spirit alienated from itself which, through intellectual work, returns to itself, dialectically; in Feuerbach, alienation pertains to the relationship of man with the 'Creator,' but as projection of the man alienated from himself who comes around via the materialist critique of religion; and in Marx, alienation pertains to the relationship of man and nature, mediated by labor which, freed from the bonds of a class society, will promote a dialectic reconciliation. In Hegel's idealism and Marx's materialism, the process is historical and contradictory. Feuerbach's materialism is contemplative and, as it were, inactive.

Hegel's philosophy is theological and teleological. Contradiction, banned from mythology by logic—logic as pure, externalized thought, which abstracts nature and the human—only reappears in Hegelian philosophy, which is no more than religion brought into thought (theology), as a sublationed moment (teleology) of the phenomenology of the spirit, as a negation of the negation. Hegel, in Feuerbach's view, begins with the infinite, from the abstractly universal, from religion (thesis), only then to deny it, by an assertion of the finite, of the particular, of the real (antithesis) and, subsequently, going back to assert it, as a negation of the negation, restoring religion (synthesis).

Feuerbach, meanwhile, understands the negation of the negation not as a movement, but merely as a 'formal' contradiction of religion with itself, and his own reading of the Hegelian dialectic leads him to disregard the active side of idealism, precisely the side valued by Marx. Hegel, however, wants to save God from philosophy through philosophy, particularly from what he interprets as the 'pantheism' of Benedictus de Spinoza, which drives him to resort to contradiction as driving and generative principle only to dissolve it in the final reconciliation prompted by *spiritual labor* (the only kind Hegel recognizes), of which his philosophy is the last word, and the preceding philosophy, isolated moments of thought.

Hegelian idealism, therefore, does not abstract nature and the human being, objectivity, but takes them as an externalization of the alienated spirit *in* objectivity which, through knowledge, as the only active behavior, supersedes the externalization and recovers objectivity *within itself*. Knowledge has opposed itself to a nullity (nullity because, outside knowledge, there is no objectivity), something that only has the *appearance* of an object, but which is the externalization of the knowledge itself.

If Hegel turns to contradiction to get away from the pantheist identity, which affirms objectivity through the suppression of the subject—a type, therefore, of inverted atheism—, Feuerbach, in a materialistic key, sees pantheism as a corollary of the reason that takes anthropotheism further from religion:

> The understanding is universal, pantheistic, the love of the universe; but the grand characteristic of religion, and of the Christian religion especially, is that it is thoroughly anthropotheistic, the exclusive love of man for himself, the exclusive self-affirmation of the human nature, that is, of subjective human nature.
>
> FEUERBACH, 2012: 40

Religion only extracts the essential qualities from inside man himself, abstracted from his own limitations, and deifies them, bringing them together in one single being, as in monotheism, or keeping them separate in distinct beings, as in polytheism. The development of religions follows the same course as the development of cultures, a process in which the less ancient religions consider the older ones idolatry. What used to be adored comes to be considered human by the religion that follows, which, by adoring a different object, believes itself, mistakenly, exempt from the necessary laws that are the basis for all religions, which are different from one another because the people who conceive them are different as are the virtues that each value most.

However, religion is invariably the splitting of man from himself, with his own essence, since God is the essence of man, who projects and objectifies himself in Him, and the consciousness of God is the first indirect awareness that man has of himself. Unity with man is, by the way, the very condition of divinity. A being that does not possess personal intelligence, personal consciousness, is not God to man, just as a being without wings could never be God to a bird.

The concept of divinity is therefore dependent on the concept of personality, but a personality whose existence is outside and above man, like another being, like a super-human personality essentially distinct from ours, a quality through which man transforms his own alienated essence into an essence that is estranged from himself. It is only when the predicates of God are thought of abstractly by philosophy that the distinction arises between existence and essence, and the illusion is established that a de-anthropomorphized metaphysical subject, the objective essence of reason, is something other than its predicates.

Now, in Hegel—and this is where, in Feuerbach's eyes, the main problem of his philosophy resides—the awareness that man has of God is the self-awareness of God; so human consciousness is itself divine consciousness:

> Why then dost thou alienate man's consciousness from him, and make it the self-consciousness of a being distinct from man, of that which is an object to him? Why dost thou vindicate existence to God, to man only the consciousness of that existence? God has his consciousness in man, and man his being in God? Man's knowledge of God is God's knowledge of himself? What a divorcing and contradiction! The true statement is this: man's knowledge of God is man's knowledge of himself, of his own nature.
>
> FEUERBACH, 2012: 189

In order to establish materialism, Feuerbach turns Hegel upside-down and takes religion to be a mere projection of the alienated man; but in so doing, he takes reality and the sensible world not as a historical product, not as *human sensible activity*, but as a form of the object or of passive contemplation. For Marx,

> Feuerbach certainly has a great advantage over the 'pure' materialists since he realises that man too is an 'object of the senses.' But apart from the fact that he only conceives him as an 'object of the senses,' not as 'sensuous activity,' because he still remains in the realm of theory and conceives of men not in their given social connection, not under their existing conditions of life, which have made them what they are, he never arrives at the actually existing, active men, but stops at the abstraction 'man' and gets no further than recognising 'the actual, individual, corporeal man' emotionally, i.e., he knows no other 'human relations' 'of man to man' than love and friendship, and even then idealized.
> MARX and ENGELS, 1970: 63–64

In theoretically dissolving the religious essence into the human essence, Feuerbach does not notice that human essence is a group of social relations, religious feeling, a social product; religious self-alienation is not an abstraction intrinsic to generic man, since individuals belong to particular historical forms of society. Materialism that is merely contemplative cannot understand that it is not enough to dissolve the religious world into its worldly basis, but that the worldly basis can itself only be truly grasped through its material contradictions.

Hegel's greatness, according to Marx, consists precisely in taking man's self-realization to be a process in which he is the result of his own work, even if he apprehends the work merely as the essence of the man who is confirmed, not as work that is alienated. This is the active dimension, contradictory and abstractly developed by Hegelian idealism, which Marx keeps in order to formulate new materialism. For him, man's self-realization immediately appears both as a natural relationship, man's relationship to nature, and as a social relationship, a relation of men between them, since it presupposes the cooperation of a number of individuals.

Language, the material expression of the spirit as a real, practical consciousness, which exists for others and for oneself, is born out of the need for human interaction. Consciousness (which takes the place of instinct or is a conscious instinct) is, from the start, simultaneously an awareness of the nature that presents itself to men as a strange power, omnipotent and unshakeable, with which mankind relates in an animal way, and gregarious consciousness, faced with men's need to form bonds with those they live with. This gregarious or tribal consciousness develops continuously with the growth in productivity, the increase in needs and the growth of the population.

A space opens up for the development of the division of labor, initially resulting only from natural gifts, including sexual ones, toward the division between material work and intellectual work, which firmly establishes an alienated relationship between men and the product of their labor. Only then is consciousness in a position to emancipate itself from the world and launch itself into the developing of pure theory, theology, philosophy, morality, etc.

> But even if this theory, theology, philosophy, ethics, etc. comes into contradiction with the existing relations, this can only occur because existing social relations have come into contradiction with existing forces of production.
> MARX and ENGELS, 1970: 52

For Marx, through the development of productive forces and the corresponding social relations of production, men oppose nature as being a constituent force, adapting it to their own desires and, at the same time, transforming their own nature as men. Like every living organism, man is a corporeal, sensitive being, who endures and suffers, dependent and limited like any plant or animal.

> But man is not only a natural being; he is a *human* natural being; *i.e.* he is a being for himself and hence a *species-being*, as which he must confirm and realize himself both in his being and in his knowing. Consequently, *human* objects are not natural objects as they immediately present themselves, nor is *human sense*, in its immediate and objective existence, *human* sensibility and human objectivity. Neither objective nor subjective nature is immediately present in a form adequate to the *human* being.
> MARX, 1992: 391

Would nature be immediately available in an adequate form to non-human organisms? The question does not arise. Non-human organisms are not beings for themselves. They have biological necessities, and not the needs and desires of a symbolic animal for whom nature, taken abstractly, in isolation, means nothing. Labor itself is a symbolic activity—it presupposes human language, therefore—which imprints upon nature a project that was consciously and conceptually in view, and therefore which ideally already existed in the head of whoever conceived it.

And language, according to Marx, just like consciousness, is born from man's need for exchange with other men. Our needs and desires, meanwhile, have no relation with the objects that serve their gratification, but have their origin in culture and it is in relation to that that we measure them. From this point of view, all needs and desires are symbolic, derived from the differential relations between people. Even what a society understands as a level of subsistence is determined not merely by biological necessities, but also by needs that are cultural, historical and moral, as Marx acknowledges in *Das Kapital*.

However, as Sahlins (1976) observed regretfully in *Culture and Practical Reason*, there is a second aspect to Marxist theory that became dominant. From this other perspective, the historical mediation between man and nature is not carried out by culture; on the contrary, culture appears more as a consequence than as a structure of productive activity, transforming materialism into the reverse of the cultural. Sahlins identifies two inter-related weaknesses in historical materialism.

The first derives from the fact that Marx expands the concept of production to such an extent that it starts to encompass not only material production in the strictest sense, the interchange between man and nature, but the production of the institutional structure in which the production occurs, the interchange of humans with each other. Mankind produces the productive forces and the relations of production that constitute the economic base, as well as the judicial and political superstructure that rises above it and to which certain philosophical, religious and artistic forms of social consciousness correspond.

Compared to modern neoclassical economic theory, the benefits of this formulation are noteworthy. As Douglass North observed,

> Marx's early elaboration of the productive forces (by which he usually meant the state of technology) with the relations of production (by which he meant aspects of human organization and particularly property rights) was a pioneering effort to integrate the limits and constraints of technology with those of human organization.
>
> NORTH, 1990: 132

However, as concerns anthropology, the distance could not be greater, since culture, in this formulation, finds itself totally subsumed into the paradigm of production. Particularly in the famous preface to *A Contribution to the Critique of Political Economy*, historical materialism establishes a relationship—a largely deterministic one—between the economic base and the ideological forms of social consciousness. As Sahlins points out, a real about-turn occurs

> as opposed to a fundamental appreciation on Marx's part that men transform nature, produce, according to a construct ... all conception now tends to be banished from the infrastructure to reappear as the construct of its material transformations.
> SAHLINS, 1976: 139

The second weakness, which is harder to deal with, derives from the fact that the paradigm of production is itself exclusively grounded in labor. According to Sahlins,

> [the] decisive grounding of historical materialism in work, and of work in its material specifications, robs the theory of its cultural properties and leaves it to the same fate as the anthropological materialism.
> SAHLINS, 1976: 134–5

Taking work as the mediator between human subjectivity and the objective world, Marx makes culture a consequence of the nature of things, erected on the facticity of nature and of technical means. In *The Poverty of Philosophy*, for example, Marx states that

> social relations are closely bound up with productive forces. In acquiring new productive forces men change their mode of production; and in changing their mode of production, in changing the way of earning their living, they change all their social relations. The hand-mill gives you society with the feudal lord; the steam-mill, society with the industrial capitalist. The same men who establish their social relations in conformity with the material productivity, produce also principles, ideas, and categories, in conformity with their social relations. Thus the ideas, these categories, are as little eternal as the relations they express. They are *historical and transitory products*.
> MARX, 1963: 109

Passages like this, as Sahlins himself acknowledges, can be relativized by others that move in the opposite direction. So much so that Sahlins speaks of two Marxisms, without identifying where exactly the crux of the question is to be found. Indeed, for Marx, labor is not a purely instrumental category, as in Habermas's frankly incorrect reading of him; for Marx, human labor possesses an obvious intersubjective dimension. The conscious cooperation between men, ever since primitive communities, is the basis for labor, for language, and for the very ownership of the land as a primeval laboratory. This is not where the problem is. *The crucial issue is that, for historical materialism, language very often appears as an instrumental category.*

Similarly, Marx writes:

> Men and animals also learn to distinguish 'theoretically' the external objects which serve to satisfy their needs from all other objects. At a certain level of later development, with the growth and multiplication of men's needs and the types of action required to satisfy these needs, they gave names to whole classes of these objects, already distinguished from other objects on the basis of experience. That was a necessary process, since in the process of production, i.e. the process of the appropriation of objects, men are in a continuous working relationship with each other and with individual objects, and also immediately become involved in conflict with other men over these objects.[5]

Although Marx did not formulate a theory of language, language does seem to fulfil, within the framework of his theory, a functionalistic role. We have already emphasized that language, for him, is a precondition of human labor; and there is no consciousness without language. Nevertheless, it is human labor that fulfils the driving, generative, active and creative role of historical development.

> Marx arrives in this way at a truncated view of the symbolic process. He apprehends it only in its secondary character of symbolization ... — the model of a given system in consciousness, while ignoring that the system so symbolized *is itself symbolic*.
> SAHLINS, 1976: 139

To put it another way, historical materialism does not start from the evidence that what distinguishes humans from other animals, their unique quality, is precisely the fact that they experience the world symbolically right away. Sahlins therefore feels compelled to state that Marx was a pre-symbolic social theorist. The argument undoubtedly merits some consideration. Nevertheless,

---

5 Marx quoted by Schmidt, 2014: 110.

a useful dialog with historical materialism demands that one recognise that anthropology, as a discipline, remains at a pre-dialectic stage.

4 Marxism and Anthropology

What does this mean? Would a dialectic anthropology be possible? Symbolic activity does not only produce identity and difference. Symbolic activity also produces contradiction. Identity, difference and contradiction are the symbolic threads with which we weave—according to what we tend to call 'free will'—the threads of our social life. This free will of ours is, therefore, a 'prisoner' to these dynamic attributes of symbolic language.

Marx, to my eyes, seems to have positioned contradiction somewhere different to where it originally was. The contradiction between man and nature is not originary. The statement that "neither objective nor subjective nature is immediately present in a form adequate to the human being" (Marx, 1992: 391) sounds incompatible with the empirical evidence from the Pleistocene, which, as Graeber notes, accounts for 90% of human history. One of the merits of a certain anthropology (I am thinking about Marcel Mauss and, more recently, Viveiros de Castro (2002), Philippe Descola (2013), Tim Ingold (2021), among others) was to have paved the way for a recognition of the historically dated character of the subject-object relation, something, by the way, insufficiently understood by fundamental ontology and by post-structuralism. This lack of comprehension also leads to the difficulties of the Marxist anthropology of Maurice Godelier or Claude Meillassoux (1986), of wanting to overlay the concept of mode of production onto ecological societies, in which economics was simply not posit.

Anthropology went even further, to recognize that dyadic relations do not support themselves. They need a third element, which Lévi-Strauss, for example, went looking for, mistakenly, in the unconscious *structure*. However, structural anthropology, in my view, failed to take one further step: incorporating contradiction into their repertoire. They failed to understand the relationship between the advent of symbolic language and its relationship with temporality.

The symbol is what frees humans from immediacy, to which all non-human organisms are prisoner, and it allows them to *project themselves forward*. Without a symbol, there is no projection; without projection, there is no contradiction. The symbol suspends time, creating a new temporality; it transforms the present from a simple moment into a reference-point for the past and the future. And what applies to the individual, applies even more to the group with whose members historical time weaves the symbolic net of relationships that unites them around one particular culture with its own physiognomy, idiosyncrasy and projection—and potentially different or antagonistic ones. This is what free will means: freeing ourselves from the immediacy of the present to fall into the warp and weft of symbolic language. There is no analogue in biology that resembles this.

What do we mean when we say that symbolic language produces contradiction? How can we situate this proposition in relation to the theories of alienation we have discussed? Let us quote one last time from the *Paris Manuscripts*:

> religion, wealth, etc. are but the estranged world of human objectification, of man's essential powers put to work and that they are therefore but the path to the true human world—this appropriation or the insight into this process appears in Hegel therefore in this form, that sense, religion, state power, etc. are spiritual entities; for only mind is the true essence of man, and the true form of mind is thinking mind, the logical, speculative mind. The human character of nature and of the nature created by history—man's products—appears in the form that they are products of abstract mind and as such, therefore, phases of mind—thought-entities.
> MARX, 1992: 385

Now, Hegel situates contradiction in the relation between spirit and nature. Hegelian idealism, as we have said, takes nature and the human being as externalizations of the alienated spirit in objectivity which, through knowledge, supersedes the externalization and recovers objectivity *within itself*. If we now situate contradiction, as we suggest, not between the spirit and its externalization, but in the relationship between *human spirits* (culture) and each other (hence the recourse to Freud's *Unheimliche*), this same passage from the *Manuscripts* takes on a new significance.

Economics and religion come to be an expression of the alienization between cultures, mediated through language. The phenomena analysed by Feuerbach and Marx come to be seen as phenomena derived from a more fundamental process, in which language recovers its pre-eminence, without lapsing into idealism and, as a driving and generative principle, not dispensing with contradiction, which is lacking from contemplative materialism.

Let us remain, then, in the field of historical materialism, incorporating the anthropological perspective. Anthropology, for its part, gains an argument, the dialectics, which, once incorporated into its repertoire, obstructs biologizing readings of culture. Anthropologizing materialism and making anthropology dialectic: that is what this book is proposing.

We should add one last note, an important one for our argument, about historical materialism. Marxism has the great merit of presenting a reading that is 'anthropological,' up to a point, of the Industrial Revolution, though without having done this for the Neolithic Revolution. Let me explain. Just as archeologists and geographers tend to consider the domesticating of plants and animals as the determining factor of the Neolithic Revolution, pure economists tend to consider the introduction of machines as the determining factor of the Industrial Revolution.

Hicks, for example, states that "it is at the point when fixed capital moves, or begins to move, into the central position that the 'revolution' occurs" (Hicks, 1969: 142). It is clear that these same economists recognize the effects of the introduction of machines on labor relations. According to Hicks, there are, historically, two ways of acquiring labor: buying the worker directly, as a slave, or hiring out their services, as a salaried worker. Machinery, which affected agriculture and mining as much as it did industry, favored the replacement of slave labor by 'unforced labor', precisely because in these new conditions, salaried labor became cheaper.

Marx sees something much more radical in this process. We have said that the Neolithic Revolution, in a way, establishes the subject-object relation. The process of alienization of cultures opens up the possibility of objectifying man and, later, nature. Economic (and religious) needs are born from this estrangement. Meanwhile, unless you can imagine men selling themselves as slaves, primordial slavery cannot be the product of commerce.

Slavery occurs through the subjugation of one human group by another, which reduces the dominated group to a part of the inorganic conditions of reproduction of their masters, a situation in which alienization, which is internalized, is converted into depersonalization. It is only then that the buying and selling of slaves becomes possible. Meanwhile, the hiring of a worker's services is only possible when he is freed from slavery but remains deprived of means of production: freed from his master and dispossessed of the land and the tools of labor. In such a case, he hires himself out.

In Hicks's terms, we can state that the subjugation of the salaried worker is different from the subjugation of the slave to the same extent that hiring is different from buying, with the difference that the hiring of the worker by himself appears to be a free, spontaneous action, without coercion. The manner of the depersonalization alters.

The transformation of labor into a commodity undoubtedly brings with it a great cultural impact, about which much has already been said; but an equally important change happens elsewhere: the Industrial Revolution also alters the relationship of the 'new masters' with one another. At first, when it was still only the proto-industrial age, industry was set up in the countryside, making use of the rural family's free time to get around the non-compete rules of the urban trading corporations whose production was geared toward local trade.

With the introduction of machines, however, the increase in productivity from labor made it possible to produce for the 'foreign' market in totally new conditions. Transport costs are won over, falling thanks to the technical progress in logistics. Gradually a system of competition is produced in which the productive units compete with each other via the adoption of ever more efficient machines, which save labor. At a certain point, the machines come to be produced by other machines.

Human labor becomes an appendix to the process insofar as the worker only carries out those movements that the machine, owing to its technological limitations, has not yet been made able to do. With each cycle of innovation, however, new operations are mechanized, up to the limits of automation. According to Marx:

> to the degree that large industry develops, the creation of real wealth comes to depend less on labor time and on the amount of labor employed than on the power of the agencies set in motion during labor time, whose 'powerful effectiveness' is itself in turn out of all proportion to the direct labor time spent on their production, but depends rather on the general state of science and on the progress of technology, or the application of this science to production.
>
> MARX, 1973: 705–6

Salaried work, in this way, is continually reduced to pure abstraction and it disappears into the process of production. As for the owners of fixed capital or their representatives (when these withdraw into rent-seeking), they are transformed, by inter-capitalist competition, into supports for the process of accumulation of capital, which becomes a real automatic subject, taking control of the process. Everything is back-to-front, the object assuming the position of subject, and the subjects, that of object.

This inversion provokes a cultural transition just as important as the Neolithic Revolution. If the Neolithic Revolution launches the economy, the Industrial Revolution turns that economy upside-down. Marx again:

> In all its forms, [wealth] appears in the form of objects, whether of things or of relationships by means of things, which lie outside of, and as it were accidentally besides, the individual. Thus, the ancient conception in which man, in spite of his various narrow national, religious or

> political determinations, still nevertheless appears as the aim of production, seems very superior to the modern world where production appears as the aim of man and wealth the aim of production.
>
> MARX, 1973: 387

If economic needs are no longer the aim of production; if production is now the goal of the human being, and accumulation the goal of production, the system's dynamics necessarily imply a process of feedback based on the continual creation of new needs.

> In bourgeois economics—and in the epoch of production to which it corresponds—this complete working-out of the human content appears as a complete emptying-out, this universal objectification as total alienation, and the tearing-down of all limited, one-sided aims as sacrifice of the human end-in-itself to an entirely external end. This is why the childish world of antiquity appears on one side as loftier. On the other side, it really is loftier in all matters where closed shapes, forms and given limits are sought for. It is satisfaction from a limited standpoint; while the modern gives no satisfaction; or, where it appears satisfied with itself, it is *vulgar*.
>
> MARX, 1973: 488

In the modern world, to use the terminology of neoclassical economic theory, the marginal utility of consumption is growing, and consumerism, a true addiction, is only one of the many consequences of this paradigm shift. We go from being unsatiated humans, to become insatiable ones.

In these circumstances, it sounds optimistic to subscribe to the theory that, under capitalism, the dynamic between productive forces and the relations of production will remain the same as that seen in previous economic formations. The idea that, at a certain stage of development, productive forces necessarily become at odds with relations of production, which become an obstacle, giving way to new social relations, seems not to apply when faced with the new situation where the subject-object relation is reversed.

The second nature is now in charge, with human beings who are reified and a first nature that has been nullified; hence also the difficulties in conceiving of something like a green or ecological capitalism. Parenthetically, it is worth considering that the sociology of Niklas Luhmann, who came to this same conclusion, is merely an attempt to biologize and naturalize this movement of the subject-object inversion and the nullifying of the first nature, by incorporating into systems theory the concept of autopoiesis developed by Humberto Maturana and Francisco Varela.

Notwithstanding the extraordinary value of historical materialism in deciphering the real meaning of the modern revolution, the fact is that, despite the brutal development of the productive forces, there is no sign on the horizon of a change in the capitalist relations of production, which keep being replaced by technological advancement, even when they exacerbate distributional conflicts and provoke environmental disequilibria.

Moreover, labor's loss of centrality in the productive process, as foreseen by Marx himself, represents an even greater challenge to historical materialism, as it compromises the classic view of the contemporary class struggle and its desired outcome. Perhaps that was why Marx did not include within his magnum opus, even if unintentionally, the repercussions resulting from his thought, developed in the *Grundrisse*, which, if properly understood, call the political dogmas of common Marxism into question.

While still on the relationship between historical materialism and anthropology, there is one more question to consider, if we want to advance our study. From what we have written so far, the reader might be left with the mistaken impression that the triadic relationship to which we referred has come apart in the modern world. The inversion of the subject-object relation would have created, under capital, a 'global culture', a universal way of life. There would not really be an excluded third; everything would be subsumed to the dyadic logic of accumulation. The question, then, should be asked: does the subject-object relation imply doing without a third element? The answer is clearly *no*. Even without expanding on the matter, an author not particularly familiar with dialectics could understand that, without that third element, the relationship cannot be sustained. As Max Weber points out, in *General Economic History*:

> [The] perpetual struggle for power in peace and war ... created the largest opportunities for modern western capitalism. The separate states had to compete for mobile capital, which dictated to them the conditions under which it would assist them to power. Out of this alliance of the state with capital, dictated by necessity, arose the national citizen class, the bourgeoisie in the modern sense of the word. *It is the closed national state which accorded for capitalism its chance for development—and as long as the national state does not give place to a world empire, capitalism also will endure.*
>
> WEBER, 1981: 337; italics by the author

Let us look at the genesis of this process in the terms proposed by Marxist historian Perry Anderson, which incorporate the contributions of Max Weber's comprehensive sociology. The modern state was born in the heart of pre-industrial society, when the owners of the fundamental means of production were the owners of the lands who had never found themselves stripped of the commanding of political power until the advent of the bourgeois revolutions. In fact, the lack of distinction between economy, politics and religion is the hallmark of that period.

Despite the gradual emancipation of the forms of forced labor, through the exchange of personal obligations for monetary income—which would weaken the power of the nobility—, aristocratic property ownership remained an obstacle to the free market in the countryside and to a real mobility of manpower. The nobility found itself facing an impasse, which was resolved through a "displacement of politico-legal coercion upwards towards a centralized, militarized summit—the Absolutist State. Diluted at village level, it became concentrated at 'national' level" (Anderson, 1974: 19).

This new state machinery, whose permanent political function was the repression of the rural poor and the masses, would soon show itself, by its nature, to be a coercive force able to discipline individuals and groups from the nobility itself. The basis of the nobility's power was the land, by definition an immovable property. The target of the noble rule, therefore, was territory, and the typical means of protecting it, the military. The protection offered by the lord was even the justification for the demand for the *corvée* from the peasant.

Now, the first regular national taxes, which generally fall on the poor, were created specifically to finance the first regular 'national' military units, made up initially of hired mercenaries. That is why Weber characterizes capitalism into two movements: the separation of the worker from the means of production, which led to the modern firm; and the separation of the master from the means of war, which led to the modern state and its monopoly on the legitimate use of violence. In contrast, the ownership of the land was made allodial, while strata of the nobility were incorporated into the absolutist state through the sale of 'positions'.

On the other hand, the aristocracy were facing the emerging mercantile bourgeoisie in the medieval cities, which were flourishing more freely, compared to the cities of eastern Europe, thanks to the hierarchical dispersal of the sovereignties of western feudalism. With the growth in commerce, significant areas of urban manufacturing, such as paper and textiles, grew during the feudal depression. A second antagonist to the aristocracy was formed, now in the cities, which was also incorporated into the absolutist state. The integration of the bourgeoisie into the state apparatus occurred by the same means, the acquisition and inheriting of public posts, but its assimilation was always subordinate to an order in which the nobility sat at the top of the social hierarchy. The structure of the absolutist state thus derives from a double determination:

> [It] was fundamentally determined by the feudal regroupment against the peasantry, after the dissolution of serfdom; but it was secondarily *over-determined* by the rise of an urban bourgeoisie which after a series of technical and commercial advances was now developing into pre-industrial manufactures on a considerable scale.
> ANDERSON, 1974: 22

From the economic perspective, this absolutism was not limited to the sale of posts and the levying of taxes. Mercantilism, its economic doctrine, sought to establish an internal national market, that is, a unified domestic market, whose aim was to increase the power of the state as well as the wealth of the nation, which required two measures to be taken: on the one hand, the suppression of particularist barriers to commerce within the realm and, hence, a confrontation with the autonomy of the cities and their corporate policies (internal *laissez-faire*); and on the other, the establishing of barriers in relation to all other states, through the stimulating of the exportation of goods and the restricting of gold and silver exports (external protectionism).

"Mercantilism", says Perry Anderson,

> was precisely a theory of the coherent intervention of the political State into the workings of the economy, in the joint interests of the prosperity of the one and the power of the other.
> ANDERSON, 1974: 16

It is worth noting that, at that stage in the process of formation of the modern state, one should not speak about nationalism, a concept alien to the nature of mercantilism.

The 'communitarian nature' of the absolutist state appears more like a negative unit turned outward (an entity that essentially has no truly communitarian nature) than something culturally constituted and spiritually genuine. A state conceived as patrimony of the monarch, whose legitimacy resides in dynasty rather than territory, and certainly not in the people, could not count on a national halo that wasn't contingent and borrowed.

Mutatis mutandis, something of this nature happens to those cultural processes described by Edward Said through which "European culture gained in strength and identity by setting itself off against the Orient as a sort of surrogate and even underground self" (Said, 1979: 3).

Actual nationalism arises at the end of the 18th century. But as the political theorist Tom Nairn asserts, and not without justification, "the *theory* of *nationalism* represents Marxism's great historical failure" (Nairn, 1975: 3). Benedict Anderson (2006), on whose work I will be relying for what follows, prefers to call it an uncomfortable anomaly for Marxist theory, which chose to avoid it.

If the subject was already troubling the 19th-century communists, the contemporary conventional wars of one revolutionary Marxist regime against another, involving Vietnam, Cambodia and China, for example, made things even more awkward. The interest prompted by *Imagined Communities* stems from the fact that its author treats nationalism as a cultural product which, to my mind, is in harmony with the 'anthropological' transition described by Marx, concerning the inversion of the subject-object relation, establishing a dialectical triadic relationship that sustains it.

It might be said that, at the same time as the Industrial Revolution, capitalism was completed with the advent of nationalism. It is in that sense that we endorse the Weberian thesis that, without a plurality of nation-states competing with one another, it would be hard for capitalism to survive, with the difference that we do not take the nation-state in its instrumental sense, but beginning with its spiritual substratum, the cultural equivalent of what evolutionary psychologists mistakenly call 'tribal instinct'.

Benedict Anderson defines a nation as an imagined political community that is limited and sovereign. Imagined, because its members will never know most of their fellows, nor do they share a common origin—as indeed is the case in any community bigger than a primeval village. In addition, a nation is limited, since it does not seek to possess the full extent of humanity, and sovereign, a concept formulated by the Enlightenment at the moment when revolutions were destroying the legitimacy derived from the divinity of dynastic kingdoms made up of a heterogeneous community of subjects who lived in territories whose borders were porous and, quite often, discontinuous.

> Finally, it is imagines as a *community*, because, regardless of the actual inequality and exploitation that may prevail in each, the nation is always conceived as a deep, horizontal comradeship.
> ANDERSON, 2006: 7

Nationalism does not count as an ideology, alongside liberalism or fascism; rather, it is a concept that should be treated the same way as kinship or religion, to the point of its being rashly considered by Carlton Hayes as their substitute.

Religion has an impulse that is alien to nationalism, the impulse toward conversion. Nevertheless, just like religion, nationalism is interested in the bonds with those who have come before, the dead, and those who will come afterward, the as yet unborn, that is to say, in the mystery of regeneration. That is why, although modern states are considered new and historic phenomena, "the nations to which they give political expression always loom out of an immemorial past" (Anderson, 2006: 11).

The idea of the nation, therefore, brings with it an anachronistic view of the imagined community's past and, I would add, a teleological vision of its future, even if the memory of what has already happened and the anticipation of what has not yet come are both in reference to the present.

In an original reading of Erich Auerbach and Walter Benjamin, Benedict Anderson underlines the difference that the idea of simultaneity takes on in religion, on the one hand, and nationalism, on the other. In the former, time is conceived of as 'messianic time' (Benjamin), with its simultaneity of past and future in a present that is *instantaneous*, so that the relevant events are not joined either temporally or causally (Auerbach). Only divine Providence establishes the link between events and supplies the key to their historical understanding.

> What has come to take the place of the medieval conception of simultaneity-along-time is, to borrow again from Benjamin, an idea of 'homogeneous, empty time,' in which simultaneity is, as it were, transverse, cross-time, marked not by prefiguring and fulfilment, but by temporal coincidence, and measured by clock and calendar.
> ANDERSON, 2006: 24

Now, for Benedict Anderson, the nation is exactly this, a *sociological organism* that passes chronologically through a time that is empty and homogenous, and imagined with the help of the technical means that are suited to represent it, the novel and the newspaper, which promote a vernacularization of the written language. The book was the first industrial commodity to be mass-produced, in the Ford style, and as such, it demanded the tireless search for ever broader markets.

There was no other way of reaching this goal without the publishing market promoting a rapid migration away from works in Latin, a language limited to the educated elite, to cater to a broader market of the monoglot masses. This was only possible through the assembling of written languages that were related to the greater possible diversity of spoken languages, an assembling made easier by the natural arbitrariness of sign systems in relation to their corresponding sounds.

The publishing success of the Bible, translated and printed in a German that was both well-wrought and accessible, which sealed the alliance between the protestant Reformation and 'industrial' capitalism and definitively shook the foundations of a church that was irremediably fragmenting, was only a portent of what was to come. Gradually, the Romance languages were also becoming nationalized, creating a community of readers who did not always understand each other in speech. It was these printed languages that, in taking on their more fixed modern forms around the 17th century, laid the groundwork for the national consciousness.

Thus, the book and labor, reproduced as commodities, preconditions of the modern state and of capital, respectively, rebuild the dialectical triadic relationship in the midst of the Industrial Revolution, just as much as writing and slavery did at the height of the Neolithic Revolution. In modernity, this triadic arrangement is only disrupted, albeit briefly, when the process of alienization overlaps with the process of depersonalization, typical in colonialism, in Simone Weil's shrewd argument. The metropole-colony relationship, from the colony's perspective, is dyadic and, as such, always unstable, however enduring it might prove.

Unsurprisingly it is there, in the colonial system, that the anti-imperialist 'revolutionary' movements appear that break away from the metropole with the aim of reaching it by internal means, usually despotic ones, of development of their own productive forces in a process of primitive accumulation. Yet it is always a case of national emancipation movements and not, as was intended, human emancipation movements.

Frantz Fanon grasped, as few others have, the tension between these two possibilities and denounced the action—internal and external—of groups that resisted the more radical contours of the emancipatory movements who did not want to be restricted to the frameworks of nationalism. Fanon notes that these groups reestablish the conditions of neo-colonial practices:

> Colonialism, which the birth of African Unity had trembling on its foundations, is now back on its feet, and now undertakes to break this will to unify by taking advantage of every weak link in the movement. Colonialism will attempt to rally the African peoples by uncovering the existence of 'spiritual' rivalries.
>
> FANON, 2005: 107

CHAPTER 4

Symbolic Language and the Time of Culture

> In analysing the historicality of *Dasein* we shall try to show that this entity is not 'temporal' because it 'stands in history,' but that, on the contrary, it exists historically and can so exist only because it is temporal in the very basis of its Being.
> MARTIN HEIDEGGER

∴

Well before B. Anderson, Edward Sapir had already pointed out a significant alteration to the relationship between language, race and culture that came with the advent of nationalism. Anthropology provides us with ample demonstration that no relationship between these elements is necessary. When, in the distant past, sparse populations have occupied vast territories and contact between them, geographically and historically isolated as they were, was only episodic, it was likely that racial, linguistic and cultural differentiation, according to Sapir, could evolve in parallel and synchronously.

Nevertheless, no sooner did these populations come into prolonged contact, than the races and cultures tended to assimilate, while contiguous languages, according to Sapir, assimilated only in a casual fashion. Races and cultures mixed in a way that was different to languages. The latter propagated, invading the territories of other races and cultures far beyond their own base.

In the United States, for example, English is spoken by representatives of three white European races: the Baltic, the Alpine and the Mediterranean. In this case, the language community presupposes the same cultural community. Even if we recognize that the U.S. and Great Britain share a common Anglo-Saxon heritage, which alleviates difficulties in mutual understanding, we should not disregard the fact that there are other cultural factors that contribute to a differentiation in the opposite direction.

On the other hand, the Hupa, the Yurok and the Karok, indigenous peoples of the U.S. territory, while they speak different and unconnected languages, belonging to three different language groups, commune with the same culture and the same rituals, even if, in more primitive societies, according to Sapir, the "secondarily *unifying* power of the 'national' ideal does not arise to disturb the flow of what we might call *natural distributions*" (Sapir, 1921: 227–28).

But everything changed with the rise of nationalism, which was consolidated 200 years ago. Race, language and culture came to be seen as facets of a single social unit. The fact that nationalities overlap with different racial and linguistic groups does not avoid the sociological fact that the concept of the nation came to shape the behavior of the people it involves. Sapir highlights the role of language in this process:

> The important thing to hold on to is that a particular language tends to become the fitting expression of a self-conscious nationality and that such a group will construct for itself, in spite of all that the physical anthropologist can do, a race to which is to be attributed the mystic power of creating a language and a culture as twin expressions of its psychic peculiarities.
> SAPIR, 1963: 29

Sapir also mentions the curious cases of the Croatian and Serbian languages: while they are essentially the same, the first is written in Latin characters, the other in Cyrillic, an entirely external difference that serves as a strategy for these people, who maintain great similarities with each other, to demarcate each group's different feelings and their particularities.

The national question actually refers back to the origins of Herder and Humboldt's linguistics, at the very dawn of nationalism. Humboldt, whose contribution, as we shall see, influenced writers as diverse as Sapir and Chomsky, understands that language, although it is a self-creation of individuals, present in the human mind through its own activity, is linked to and dependent upon the nation to which it belongs, which, in turn, just like a person, should be considered an individual following its own internal spiritual path, the language being the mental exhalation of the national life which emerges from everybody's simultaneous activities.

Herder, similarly, considered 'nation' to be the association of users of a language, who share traditions and a particular way of being in the world. Although reason is a universal human potential, it is realized through the acquisition of language, which opens up the possibility of separating universal reason, on the one hand, from its national cultural manifestations, on the other, which develop in the most appropriate way for their own particular environment, their history, their traditions and their understanding of the world. Since nature is diverse, the forms of expression of reason are diverse, which does not mean that the truth is relative—it is universal—but that its means of expression are linguistically and culturally determined.

That is why Herder criticizes "the unnatural expansion of States, the savage mixing of humanity's types and nations under one scepter." As a critic of the way European expansionism was taking place, he called Columbus, in a poem, an 'assassin,' for destroying the beauties, the customs and the youthful vigor of the New World, eventually stating that for the good of humanity, Europe should perish:

> Our part of the world must be called, not the wise, but the *presumptuous, pushing, tricking* part of the earth; it has not cultivated but has destroyed the shoots of peoples' own cultures wherever and however it could.
> HERDER, 2012: 382

His position did not fail to prompt sharp responses such as that from Kant, who, in his review of *Ideas on the Philosophy of the History of Mankind*, clearly adopted the view of which Herder most disapproved:

> If the happy inhabitants of Tahiti, never visited by more civilized nations, were destined to live in their peaceful indolence for thousands of centuries, it would be possible to give a satisfactory answer to the question of why they should exist at all.
> KANT, 1970: 220

In his *Essay on the Origin of Language*, Herder even sketches out a naïve genealogy of what, in this study, I have called the process of alienization. It is not economic necessities, such as hunger and thirst, that set two human groups into combat, but a feeling of honor, of pride in a group to which one belongs and in its superiority. The same inclination that, when turned inward into the group, united everybody into one, when turned outward constitutes the force of discord. The basis of this hostility, says Herder, is not so much a contemptible vice as a noble human weakness.

At the very beginning, when humanity possessed more active forces than accumulated goods, discrimination between tribes occurred through comparisons of the virtues and bravery of their noteworthy men, who express, so to speak, the condition of the whole tribe. "Hence the slogan soon became natural: *Whoever is not with and of us is beneath us*! The foreigner is *worse* than us, is a *barbarian*" (Herder, 2012: 152).

Later, when it became a matter of self-interest and of the defense of property, the idea of hating one's neighbor for his weakness was less well-founded.

Nevertheless, the silent delight at that fact—being a feeling that is common to both tribes—wounds the honor of both and readies them for war. "And there the second synonym was ready: Whoever is not with me is against me. Barbarian and spiteful one! Foreigner, enemy!" Herder concludes:

> The third thing followed immediately: complete *division* and *separation*. Who wanted to have anything in common with such an enemy, the contemptible barbarian? No familial customs, no remembrance of *a single* origin, and least of all *language*. For language was actually *"characteristic word of the race, bond of the family, tool of instruction, hero song of the fathers' deeds, and the voice of these fathers from their graves."* Language could not possibly, therefore, remain *of one kind*, and so the same *familial feeling* that had formed a single language, when it became national hatred, often *created difference, complete difference* in language. He is a *barbarian*, he speaks *a foreign language*—the third, so usual synonym.
> HERDER, 2012: 152–3

The reasoning is superficial at first glance, but it contains a good dose of lessons to be learned. In the first place, the idea that it is not the economy that creates disagreement between human groups, a statement that is compatible with our understanding that it is alienization that sets off the economy (and religion), or, to be more precise, alienization is material (and spiritual) need. Secondly, the idea that it is not the diversity of languages that creates discord; rather, it is discord that creates 'difference, complete difference in language:' (Herder, 2012: 153) a half-truth, since only the first passage is true, but not its reverse.

There is not necessarily any relation between the diversity of languages and cultural speciation between groups, which becomes clear when the distinction is drawn between language in general and individual languages (tongues). Language can create difference and contradiction even within groups who speak the same tongue, and it can create identity among groups who speak different tongues, as we have just seen. What matters is cultural speciation.

The flaw in Herder's reasoning is his building of the process of radical differentiation on a family feud when, in truth, the difference that exists between a human group and a mere herd is the fact that a human group is a *project*, precisely because the human group has an anachronistic vision of its past and a teleological vision of its future, both of them with reference to the present.

This is also the place where we find the challenge in dealing with cultural differences from an ecological perspective, since the different projects of different human groups cannot necessarily be made to harmonize, and can possibly, at the extreme, be antagonistic.

While promising, this fledgling theory of alienization of Herder's, which he calls the 'third natural law,' had no ramifications. None of his illustrious readers—Kant, Hegel, Feuerbach, and Heidegger, to mention just a few—gave it any consideration. Feuerbach dismissed it, for example, understanding that Christianity allows the human being to objectify his human essence in God, freed from the barriers of nationality. But that assertion brings huge problems with it. The first is that religion forms human groups just as any nation does—the former responding to spiritual needs, the second to material ones.

These processes are contemporaneous with each other, rooted in alienization, and it is only with this in mind that we can assert *religious* need as being a part both of the *expression* of the material need and simultaneously of the *protest against* material need. And here, please note, the reverse is true. Nevertheless, it is necessary to consider that, over the course of history, these intertwined processes live their own lives, as Weber notes. With the mutual distancing of these processes, an exact overlap between nation and religion becomes increasingly unlikely.

We are interested now in Herder's 'first natural law', which fared better among linguists and anthropologists: "The human being is a freely thinking, active being, whose forces operate forth progressively. Therefore, let him be a creature of language!" (Herder, 2012: 127). Comparatively stripped of instincts, the human would be permanently subject to being preyed upon by stronger and more instinctive animals, were reflection not a character trait of his species; and since it is impossible for any reflective action to take place without a verbal signal, then the first moment of consciousness was also the moment of the inner birth of language.

For Herder, language does exist in the non-human animal world. However, he makes two significant observations. In the first place, he states that the smaller an animal's sphere of action, the less it needs language, and it can even be deaf if the universe that it is in is very restricted. In compensation, the smaller the circle to which it belongs, the stronger its other instinctive abilities. So, a smaller circle corresponds to extremely sharp senses; while a larger circle, and consequently a more varied lifestyle, corresponds to a weakening of the sensorial organization. In this way, non-human animal language can be understood, according to Herder, as a *mechanical* representation of sensorial representations which, being so strong, become instincts compatible with a limited sphere of action.

Secondly, Herder underlines the difference between animal language and human language. Humans do not have a uniform, narrow sphere of activity; on the contrary, the forces of the human soul have been spread across the entire world. Lacking a focus to which to direct their representations, the human lacks instinctive aptitudes and capability. They have senses for everything, but since these are not honed in one specific direction, they are weak and dull. To a human being, then, what good is the typical language of animals?

Animal language is neither rich enough nor distinct enough to adapt to humans' organization of the senses and directing of representations.

> *What language* (besides the earlier mechanical one) *does the human being possess as instinctively as each animal species possesses its language in, and in accordance with, its own sphere?* The answer is short: none!
> Herder, 2012: 80

Since it was without instincts, including the mechanical language of animals, nature granted the human species a specific gift, a language of its own, conscious, reflective and rational. In the void left by the absence of instinctive aptitudes, nature compensated the human with something that is as essential to them as instincts are to animals:

> Let one name this whole disposition of the human being's forces however one wishes: understanding, reason, taking-awareness [*Besinnung*], etc. It is indifferent to me, as long as one does not assume these names to be separate forces or mere higher levels of the animal forces. It is the "*whole organization of all human forces; the whole domestic economy of his sensuous and cognizing, of his cognizing and willing, nature.*" Or rather, it is "*the single positive force of thought,* which, bound up with a certain *organization of the body*, is called *reason* in the case of human beings, just as it becomes *ability for art* in the case of animals, which is called *freedom* in the case of the human being, and in the case of animals becomes *instinct*." The difference is not in levels or the addition of forces, but in a *quite different sort of orientation* and *unfolding of all forces*.
> Herder, 2012: 82–83

Herder had a major influence on the development of philosophical anthropology, especially that of Arnold Gehlen, one of his most sophisticated representatives. The opposition between symbolic language and instincts, suggested by Herder, takes on particular contours in Gehlen's anthropology. Gehlen establishes a decisive line of demarcation with evolutionary psychology, which is of the greatest relevance to the contemporary debate, since, for the latter group (following William James, as we shall see), symbolic language is an instinct, which—as will become clear—goes against this study's assumptions.

In his most important piece of work, Gehlen (1988), in line with Herder's philosophy, treats the human being as a biological problem with special characteristics. The usual statement that the human species derives from the animal is one that he finds misleading, since, due to his unique characteristics, man must be understood beginning from himself, as the unequivocal object of a general anthropology, albeit never losing sight of the connection of these characteristics to his biology. According to him, anthropology's failure, thus far, has two causes. The first is that the approaches, both monist and dualist, to the mind-body problem do not offer a satisfactory ontological response to get over this antinomy.

Gehlen turns to Nicolai Hartmann's ontology, in which he finds permeable categories that allow for the joint existence of strata, based on which the world is structured. The lower strata, the inorganic layers, are the strongest, being indifferent to the existence of the upper layers and defining their space of development. The upper layers are dependent, since the organic layer presupposes the inorganic one, and the spiritual layer, above them, presupposes both. Despite being feebler, because they are dependent, the upper layers do contain new structures and protophenomena that cannot be derived from the lower ones, making them freer and more autonomous.

The second reason is that, if we take human traits separately, whether their physical constitution, the production of artefacts, social life, means of communication, etc. we will find nothing that is specifically human, precisely because what is specifically human is found in the whole, which requires an interdisciplinary approach that tackles characteristics all together—like reason, the opposable thumb, upright bearing, language, etc. There is no causal relationship between these characteristics; they mutually presuppose each other, forming a single system.

Biological thinking is wrong, then, when it seeks to make man descend directly from the animal, and wishes to perceive the spiritual element from outside, from the corporeal. Though supposedly biological, this approach actually misses what is essential about the biological perspective: the recognition that the human is an entirely unique project in nature, requiring its own mode of study, an anthropobiology, which analyses man's particular corporeal arrangement along with his complex interiority, that is, the link between the corporeal and the spiritual.

This implies dropping the idea that there are just a number of 'steps' separating animal intelligence or language from that of humans, or separating animal sociability from human institutions, and recognizing that nature, in the case of man, took an evolutionary direction that had previously not existed, creating an altogether new organizing principle.

From a morphological perspective, the human being is determined by *lack*: the lack of fur, the lack of natural organs of fight and flight, the lack of sharp senses, and specially, the lack of authentic instincts—the latter understood as modes of behavior that are innate, typical of the species, brought into play by 'signals' emitted by suitable 'objects', found around them, like their companions, their prey and predators, their sexual partner and their children, etc. In this respect, man's essential quality actually consists in a reduction of instincts. Desperately lacking in means and instincts, the human makes up for this lack through his capacity for work or the gift of action. The same nature that denied him instincts gave him the reason and free will to "to develop his potential, and [face] the challenge of interpreting his own existence" (Gehlen, 1988: 27).

Thus the 'deficient being,' from an organic point of view, is, for this very same reason, open to the world. Being unable to live in a concrete fragmented setting, the lack of an environment is their conceptual expression. Subjected to a plethora of stimuli and impressions that flow toward them and which they need to master, humans have no way of dealing with them via instinct; rather they must overcome, through prediction and through the taking of measures, the burden provoked by the organic necessities, making use of entirely new means of guiding their life. Discharge (*Entlastung*) means exactly that: a suspension of immediate contact with the world, through which man orders these stimuli and impressions, and masters them.

We have arrived, at last, at Gehlen's concept of culture. The human ...

> acts because he is unspecialized and deprived of a natural environment to which he is adapted. The epitome of nature restructured to serve his needs is called *culture*.
> Gehlen, 1988: 29

Like second nature, 'anti-natural' culture is nothing but the result of the action of one unique being, who is similarly 'anti-natural,' who produces their own environment that is already, from a merely optical point of view, a highly symbolic world.

The common root that exists between knowledge and action is plain to see, as is that between the capacity for direction in the world and the steering of actions, and the role of language in the suspension of immediate contact with the world, without which there is neither knowledge nor action, since man, as a deficient being, must act in order to survive, and in order to act, he needs to know. Now, the symbol is what makes it possible to represent a thing in its absence. It is the condition for any theoretical behavior that does not immediately produce any real change but is a prerequisite for all action that is planned.

In this way, language frees man from the cycle of immediacy in which all animals are trapped, and without the deferral that it allows him, the human species would not have the capacity to turn toward the future and thus act opportunely, which is what ensures his survival. The same reduction in instincts that dismantles direct automatism, then, frees a system of behavior unencumbered by the pressure of instinct, whereby thought and non-innate action patterns react to variations in their surroundings.

Man, thus, has a constitutional surplus of impulses, conceived as "the internal aspect of an unspecialized, organically helpless being who suffers chronic pressure from internal and external stresses" (Gehlen, 1988: 47). In contrast with animals, whose instincts are adapted to their environment and follow the 'time' of nature, as regards migration, mating, hibernation, etc. man must contribute to the formation of lasting impulses and, by creating institutions, to the organization of a well-targeted architectural impulse system.

We should not, then, confuse animals' instinctive behavior, which is predictable and relates to a natural and subordinated environment, with human behavior acquired in the face of a strung-together cultural sphere. Without institutions, the behavior of a deficient being like man would be marked by unpredictability and insecurity. Human behavior as something predictable, secure, almost automatic, which appears in the place of animals' genuinely instinctive behavior, is stabilized only through institutions.

Through a predicting action, man creates for himself, in any concrete external conditions, his cultural sphere, which is made up of the totality of the representative material means, objective techniques and mental techniques, including institutions, which constitute the *natural conditions of life* of this deficient being. For Gehlen, culture is, because of all this, an anthropological concept, and man, by definition, a cultural being.

At this point, we are interested in Gehlen's counterpoint to the approach of Uexküll, who in 1934 published *A Foray into the Worlds of Animals and Humans*, a book that was translated into countless languages and which popularized his theory. It contains a description of the lifecycle of a tick, which became famous. The little creature comes out of the egg 'incomplete', with just one pair of legs and no reproductive organs, but already capable of attacking cold-blooded animals it spots from the tip of a blade of grass. It reaches its adult phase, after shedding its skin several times, when it acquires those organs that it had been lacking.

The female then mates, and, with her four pairs of legs, she climbs a shrub up to a height from where she can drop down onto hot-blooded animals. Being blind, she allows herself to be guided by the photosensitivity of her skin. Being deaf, she trusts her sense of smell to detect the scent of the butyric acid that emanates from every mammal's skin, and she launches herself at them. The tick's refined heat sense allows her to recognize her prey in contact with their body. With the endeavor successfully achieved, all the parasite needs to do is find an area of the body with the least amount of hair to suck their blood and live happily. Finally, she will allow herself to drop back down onto the ground to lay her eggs, and then die.

Now, to Uexküll, every organism, in accordance with its anatomy, has a receptor system, through which it receives external stimuli, and an effector system, through which it reacts to them; together, they form a closed unit: its surrounding world (*Umwelt*). Such considerations allow Uexküll to propose a return to Kant to extend his scope. According to him, by emphasizing the conditions *a priori* of all experience, Kant focused only on the analysis of the most basic forms of sensitivity: space and time. He leaves open the analysis of the forms that vary according to each organism's anatomy, the starting point for learning about the reality experienced in different ways by different organisms. In the introduction to his densest book (*Theoretical Biology*, 1920), Uexküll makes his purpose clear:

> The task of biology consists in expanding in two directions the results of Kant's investigations: — (1) by considering the part played by our body, and especially by our sense-organs and central nervous system, and (2) by studying the relations of other subjects (animals) to objects.
> UEXKÜLL, 1926: XV

We have seen how Cassirer received Uexküll's contribution. Between the receptor system and the effector system—both of which are found in all species—Cassirer proposes the incorporation of a third link: the symbolic system. By representing an entirely new method of adapting to the environment, the symbolic system qualitatively alters man's functional circle in comparison to that of animals, shifting human life into a new dimension.

Gehlen adds to the discussion, with another decisive argument for our purposes. Uexküll compares the safety with which an animal and a man move in their respective surrounding worlds, but transposes, without the due mediations, what Gehlen considers a fruitful approach from zoology onto the human world, stating, through an inappropriate analogy, that a forest is not the same forest for a poet, a hunter or a madman.

So Uexküll does not realize that culture, understood as second nature, is not merely the world surrounding humans but that it is also *continuously transformed* by human societies *according to a project*, which, according to Gehlen, in going against the biological theory of niche construction mentioned in this study, does not apply to zoology. Animals do not transform their surrounding worlds in the same way humans create and transform theirs. Human beings do not live in the same temporality as other organisms. According to Sidarta Ribeiro:

> we are the only species who travel in time, because of our use of the neural circuit called the default mode network, which allows us to weave (auto-) biographical narratives and to have empathy; and it's no coincidence that this is the neural circuit involved in dreaming and daydreaming.[1]

Symbolic language, as I conceptualize it, is precisely the biological evolution that allows humans to travel in time and take on cultural perspectives that assume a r-evolutionary dynamic. We shall see, in the concluding part of this study, how this combines beneficially with François Jacob's biological approach.

For now, let us look at how this whole digression helps with our analysis of the appropriating of Uexküllian theory carried out by Bertalanffy, who combined it with Whorf's linguistic hypothesis. Kant's universalism is once again called into question, now not only in order to determine the difference in the ways of apprehending the world between species that are anatomically distinct, but to determine the difference in ways of apprehending the world themselves.

Right away, we ought to ask: if all men, as a species, have the same anatomical characteristics, in which other characteristics would the differences in their apprehension of the world reside? According to Kant, the forms of intuition, 'space' and 'time', and the categories of the intellect impose themselves on every rational being. Nevertheless, Bertalanffy recalls, even these forms of intuition, represented by Euclidian space and Newtonian time, are only adequate for the physical world on an intermediate scale.

As soon as we place ourselves in the astronomical dimension or the atomic one, we need to operate in spaces that are non-Euclidian or multidimensional. In the theory of relativity, for example, time is 'transformed' into one coordinate of a four-dimensional manifold. In quantum physics, meanwhile, the

---

[1] Correspondence between Sidarta Ribeiro and the author, 24 January 2022.

determinism of classical physics is replaced by the indeterminism of subatomic laws of a statistical nature.

We must also remember that man's receptor system is completely altered by the use of artificial means of perception. The theory of relativity would not have been formed without the development of instruments for measuring the speed of light; and gravitational waves, a hypothesis arising from that theory, would not have been detected without the development of new techniques of perception.

In the field of biology, the relativity of the categories also stands out. As we have seen, according to Uexküll, any organism extracts, from the multiplicity of objects surrounding it and according to its receptor system, a reduced number of characteristics, to which it reacts via its effector system. Each organism, then, perceives the world and reacts to it according to its psychophysical organization, which demarcates the world around it, including its perception of time and space.

The 'instant', for example, understood as the smallest unit of perceptible time, varies from organism to organism. For man, an instant corresponds to $1/18$ of a second, since impressions that are any shorter are not perceived separately. Whereas the fighting fish does not recognize its image in the mirror unless, using a mechanical device, the image is shown to it at least thirty times a second, when it then attacks it as if it were an adversary. Bertalanffy notes that, here too, forms of intuition are not universal, but depend on the psychophysical conditions and physiological conditions of each animal, the human included.

With the help of Whorf, Bertalanffy will add—in line with what Cassirer and Gehlen had done already—a new element to Uexküll's schema. To sum up: the human being, according to Cassirer, has an exclusive system for adapting to the environment, located between the receptor system and the effector system, that is, the symbolic system. Gehlen, then, argues that the world surrounding man, unlike the world surrounding animals, is culture, produced and constantly transformed by man himself according to a plan that he develops. Bertalanffy takes the Uexküllian schema and adds the cultural diversity of the categories:

> Our perception is essentially determined by our specifically human, psychophysical organization. This is essentially von Uexküll's thesis. Linguistic, and cultural categories in general, will not change the potentialities of sensory experience. They will, however, change apperception, i.e., which features of experienced reality are focused and emphasized, and which are underplayed.
> BERTALANFFY, 1968: 235

To put it another way, since the psychophysical endowment of humans, as a species, is universal, the same can be said of humans' perception of the surrounding world. This, however, does not happen with conceptualization, which, being dependent on symbolic systems that are largely determined by linguistic factors, is subject to cultural diversity.

Thus, a new relativity principle is introduced, which suggests that the same pieces of physical evidence can lead to different pictures of the universe if the observers have different linguistic origins that cannot be calibrated with one another. According to Whorf:

> When linguists became able to examine critically and scientifically a large number of languages of widely different patterns, their base of reference was expanded; they experienced an interruption of phenomena hitherto held universal, and a whole new order of significances came into their ken. It was found that the background linguistic system (in other words, the grammar) of each language is not merely a reproducing instrument for voicing ideas but rather is itself the shaper of ideas, the program and guide for the individual's mental activity, for his analysis of impressions, for his synthesis of the mental stock in trade. Formulation of ideas is not an independent process, strictly rational in the old sense, but is part of a particular grammar, and differs, from slightly to greatly, between different grammars.
>
> WHORF, 2012a: 272

Although he is attuned to Whorf's point of view, Bertalanffy criticizes him for not having been sufficiently clear that the relationship between language and a view of the world is not unidirectional. According to Bertalanffy, if you could say, with Whorf, that the structure of language seems to determine which features of reality will be extracted and what form the categories of thought will take, it should then also be stated, reciprocally, that 'how' the world is seen determines and shapes language.

At this point we should emphasize that it would be a mistake to imagine that this movement is in dialogue with the perspective proposed in this study. The same mediations regarding biology and anthropology now need to be carried out in the field of linguistics, if we hope to conclude our journey usefully. The subtleties are even greater in this field, which is why we have left this struggle for last. Whorf's linguistic relativism, as it should be clear, only seems to resolve our problem satisfactorily.

We have already seen, with Sapir, that according to the anthropological evidence, there is not necessarily any relationship between culture and language.

Whorf, meanwhile, declared himself "the last to pretend that there is anything so definite as 'a correlation' between culture and language" (Whorf, 2012b: 179). Peoples who speak different languages can share the same culture; peoples who speak the same language can create different cultures. This would be enough to cast some doubt on the association of Sapir's name with Whorf's as regards the hypothesis that language determines man's perception and how he thinks of the world and that, therefore, human groups who use different linguistic systems would have different views of the world.

There are passages in Sapir's work that corroborate this linkage with Whorf's. In "The Status of Linguistics as a Science," Sapir argues that man is at the mercy of the particular language that has become his community's means of expression, not only as a way of solving specific problems of communication and reflection, but as the foundation upon which his linguistic group unconsciously constructs their real world (Sapir, 1929). However close they may be, there are no two languages that can express the same social reality, just as, however close they may be, two societies are two different worlds, not simply the same world with different labels.

Sapir acknowledges the relativity of concepts, or, to be more exact, the relativity in the form of thinking. Seen all together, though, his writing actually suggests a greater rapprochement with the approach taken by his master, Franz Boas, than with that of Whorf, his pupil, who points in a different direction.

Far from being a biolinguist, it is worth noting that Sapir, on the contrary, situates linguistics in the field of social sciences, not without first pointing out those facts that bring it close to biology, namely, linguistic behavior's dependence on adjustments of a physiological nature and, more importantly, the regularity and typicality of the linguistic processes that contrast with human beings' freer behavior when analysed from a strictly cultural point of view. Behind the apparent disorder of the cultural world, there are regularities that are as real as those observed in the physical one, albeit infinitely less rigid.

If, on the one hand, the morphology of known languages varies, in a surprising way, more than any other kind of cultural pattern, on the other hand, the grammar of any one language, defined as "the sum total of formal economies intuitively recognized by the speakers of a language" (Sapir, 1963: 9), has a high degree of fixity. Its regularity and its formal development reside in aspects of a biological nature, but this does not make it into an adjunct area of biology or even of psychology.

What is striking, however—and this is the point of closeness shared by Sapir and Boas that distances them from Whorf's perspective—is the fact that, for Sapir, every language has a *formal completeness*. This evidently has nothing to do with the wealth of its vocabulary; rather it is about the fact that the speaker of any language, no matter what he might wish to communicate or how bizarre his ideas might be, is able to use it without needing to create new forms or to force new directions from the constant forms of its structure.

The universe of linguistic forms is a complete system of reference, and moving from one language to another is as possible as moving from one geometric reference system to another. New words can be created, and the meaning of existing ones expanded, other words might be borrowed from foreign sources, etc. But none of this will affect the form of the language, just as the incorporating of new objects into a particular bit of space does not affect its geometric shape.

Out of this flows one of languages' remarkable properties. In order to explain it, Sapir proposes an unsettling exercise: would it be possible to translate the *Critique of Pure Reason* into an indigenous language? Sapir responds thus:

> There is nothing in the formal peculiarities of Hottentot or of Eskimo which would obscure the clarity or hide the depth of Kant's thought—indeed, it may be suspected that the highly synthetic and periodic structure of Eskimo would more easily bear the weight of Kant's terminology than his native German. Further, to move to a more positive vantage point, it is not absurd to say that both Hottentot and Eskimo possess all the formal apparatus that is required to serve as matrix for the expression of Kant's thought. If these languages have not the requisite Kantian vocabulary, it is not the languages that are to be blamed but the Eskimo and the Hottentots themselves.
> SAPIR, 1963: 154

This reply could not be more in line with Franz Boas's position. In *The Mind of Primitive Man*, Boas's own focus on the subject is almost exactly the same, as the following passage shows:

> Thus it would seem that the obstacles to generalized thought inherent in the form of a language are of minor importance only, and that presumably language alone would not prevent a people from advancing to a more generalized form of thinking, if the general state of their culture should require expression of such thought; that the language would be molded rather by the cultural state. It does not seem likely, therefore, that there is any direct relation between the culture of a tribe and the language they speak, except in so far as the form of the language will be

molded by the state of culture, but not in so far as a certain state of culture is conditioned by morphological traits of the language.

BOAS, 1938: 219

Whorf's hypothesis is a radicalization of partial observations from Boas and Sapir, but a radicalization that does little to help understand the cultural dynamic. The idea that profound linguistic differences determine differences in the way we perceive the world has been the object of many empirical studies, with contradictory results.[2] The aim is not to deny the possibility that language, on its own, shapes scenarios that promote religious, aesthetic and even cognitive experiences and concepts, which are not easily translated. There are many examples, meanwhile, of 'unification' of languages that have promoted greater understanding between members of a nation or a religion.

The work of B. Anderson, cited above, offers a number of references on the subject. The hypothesis, however, that a diversity of languages can be an obstacle to mutual understanding, in any aspect of the world, seems a huge exaggeration. Extrapolating the argument, it is as if, in order to think of or perceive the world in the same way, we would all need to speak the same specific tongue, although already having the same biological capacity for language. Bertalanffy's conclusions are more unsettling still: everything happens, in his Uexküll-Whorfian system, as if each particular language corresponded to a particular *Umwelt*; as if different languages transformed us into different organisms.

1   Philosophies of Language and of Culture

So, the line drawn by Whorf, beginning from Boas and Sapir, seems to lead us to a dead end, as far as the purposes of this study are concerned. Another possible path, and a more promising one, starts with Wittgenstein. I propose that we approach three authors, each of them differently influenced by his later work, who make very impactful contributions to the debate that we're interested in, beginning with the analytic philosophy of W.V.O. Quine, moving on to Peter Winch's philosophy of social science, and finally arriving at Clifford Geertz's interpretative anthropology.

In *Word and Object*, Quine issues a warning about Whorf's hypothesis (which he also associates with the names of Sapir, Cassirer and Dorothy D. Lee): what

---

2   Cf. references in Lenneberg (1967) and Tomasello (2019).

is normally at play, where translation is concerned, is the indeterminacy of the correlation between languages, given that, the further we go from our home turf, the more fragile the basis of comparison between them. However, the issue, he suggests, is not an uncommon one, even between compatriots. The problem arises in relation to any two people. Two individuals, faced with all possible sensory stimuli, can adopt strictly the same verbal behavior and yet the ideas expressed in their utterances can still diverge radically.

There is some advantage to dialog between compatriots; it arises from the fact that deviations can compensate for each other by virtue of context, so as to preserve the global pattern of associations. You might say that there is also an advantage when translation involves two languages that are related, which are able to benefit, potentially, from a common etymology, or languages that are not related which, also potentially, can benefit from a shared evolution.

The question becomes more obvious when we consider the hypothesis of a translation from the language of an isolated people, as yet uncontacted, without the help of interpreters. This is *radical* translation which, according to Quine, refers to what he calls the 'indeterminacy of translation' principle. Quine's hypothesis is that translation handbooks can be set up in different ways, compatible with the totality of verbal arrangements, though incompatible with one another, allowing the opportunity for translations with no kind of plausible relationship of equivalence.

Even if we recognize that the case of radical translation makes the questions raised more complex, using it is a mere expedient for shedding light onto problems that we face daily in any context, which distance's Quine's exercise from other approaches that opened the way for a reconsideration of problems in the anthropological field.

Quine's thesis is too contentious, especially if we consider his analysis of the causes explaining the failure to grasp the indeterminacy of translation. One of these causes is sufficiently drastic as to attract notice. Let us imagine somebody truly bilingual. Let us suppose they are in a position to correlate phrases exceptionally correctly between the languages they have mastered. This assumption can also be reinforced uncritically by a mentalist hypothesis according to which each phrase and its respective translation express identical ideas in the bilingual's mind. Well, on this matter, Quine's conjecture is disturbing:

> Another bilingual could have a semantic correlation incompatible with the first bilingual's without deviating from the first bilingual in his speech dispositions within either language, except in his dispositions to translate.
> QUINE, 1960: 74

Note that for Quine, translation can be right, and it can be wrong, but what matters is that, according to his argument, two *right* translations can still diverge.

We are not interested, at present, in running through the whole great controversy that this conjecture generated (Raatikainen, 2005). Quine might have wanted to call into question the very idea of meaning. In that case, it would not be a matter of indeterminacy of translation but indeterminacy of meaning. But this does not seem to be so. He could, alternatively, have wanted to reinforce, by going down this path, his behaviorist view of language, and there are several passages in his work to support this.

It is important, first of all, to understand the place and scope that Quine reserves for behaviorism. He has no trouble in admitting that an *aptitude* for language is innate, but the same cannot be said about the *learning* of language, since this involves intersubjectively observable characteristics of human behavior. It is in this rather limited sense that Quine states: "The linguist has little choice but to be a behaviorist at least qua linguist" (Quine, 1968: 278).

This, then, is a behaviorism limited to linguistics, required by the way language is learned, or, more precisely, a behavioral linguistics based on the reflex of language acquisition:

> Each of us learns his language by observing other people's verbal behavior and having his own faltering verbal behavior observed and reinforced or corrected by others.
> QUINE, 1987a: 5

The learning of meanings should therefore be based on observation, or, to put it another way, meaning is determined by observable use.

> Language is a skill that each of us acquires from his fellows through mutual observation, emulation, and correction in jointly observable circumstances. When we learn the meaning of an expression, we learn only what is observable in overt verbal behavior and its circumstances.
> QUINE, 1987b: 130

Secondly, however, we should investigate a path that Quine did not take, but which it is perfectly possible to espy if we begin from his dispute with Rudolf Carnap, in which he launches a set of formulations that outline something that goes beyond linguistic behaviorism. In order to understand this, let us start with Quine's critique of the distinction, so dear to logical positivism, between analytic truths and synthetic truths.

In the case of the former, a statement is considered true exclusively by virtue of the meaning of the words it contains. Logical or mathematical truths, for example, are analytical truths, requiring no theoretical justification and depending entirely on the choice of language. In the latter, however, the statement makes reference to extra-linguistic facts, and it can only be recognized as true through the evidence revealed by experience. Scientific truths, therefore, are synthetic truths. Thus, within a given language, for each specific subject there is one single correct theory, and in order to know which theory is correct, one makes use of the rules of a language and experience.

However, it is not possible to adopt a similar procedure when we choose one given language, because, in doing so, we are choosing its own rules. It would fall to philosophy, in analyzing the language of science, to suggest, potentially, alternative languages, but not to prescribe them, as one cannot talk about a correct language. This idea came to be known as the Tolerance Principle. It presupposes the distinction between analytic truths and synthetic truths, which, according to Carnap, rest on entirely different epistemological foundations.

Quine denies the existence of an epistemological difference between philosophy and science. For him, philosophy does not enjoy any methodological or epistemological advantage over science. Just like synthetic truths, analytical truths can be refuted, and the reasons that lead us to reject a synthetic truth are of the same nature as those that lead us to propose a change in the language. Just as an isolated word cannot be understood out of the context of its proposition, so a proposition can only be understood in the context of the language. This makes it practically impossible to set the border between philosophy and science within language.

We should stress right away that the choice of language is not theoretically neutral, as Carnap acknowledges, but, more importantly, the correctness of a proposition is hard to prove only by its isolated relation to experience, without considering broader aspects of the theory, if not the theory as a whole. Considered in isolation from the theory of which it is a part, a proposition does not stand up on its own. Logic and mathematics, according to the Tolerance Principle, seem to be necessary and independent of experience. They would enjoy special status due to not being subject to refutation by evidence supplied by experience.

For Quine, however, a good part of our knowledge does not come directly from experience; on the contrary, a proposition's adherence to experience is almost always indirect, because it presupposes a theoretical framework. The more 'basic' this theoretical framework, the closer to the center of our web of beliefs, the more it seems to be a piece of *a priori* knowledge.

Giving up logic or mathematics would mean letting go of a complete system of knowledge in favor of an alternative system that nobody today is capable of glimpsing. However, according to Quine, there's nothing to rule out the possibility that we might do this if the course of experience shows us that logic and mathematics have become completely useless. But as long as this entirely abstract possibility is not on the horizon, logic and mathematics will continue to be seen as *a priori*.

Quine, in this way, recognizes the notion of analyticity in its useful application, but highlights its insignificance from an epistemological point of view. Any statement we do not believe that we can reject is subject to revision, and we only accept it for the contribution it can make to the success of a theoretical framework as a whole, as an efficient method for dealing with experience. Other factors come into play with the acceptance of propositions that contribute to the effectiveness of the theory as a whole.

Carnap himself suggested that pragmatic factors play their role, but only in the choice of language, as external factors of change. In rejecting the separation of analytic and synthetic truths, Quine undermines the basis of epistemological difference between them and adopts a more comprehensive pragmatism that also affects the internal changes.

Now, this perspective might have suggested to Quine that Whorf's hypothesis is not a mere illusion resulting from the indeterminacy of correlation between substantially different languages. In tackling the issue of radical translation in this way, Quine positions it in the same order of problems that can be confronted on the domestic plane, and which pertain, for example, to the identical verbal behavior of people with different neural connections and different personal histories, cases in which it makes no sense to imagine semantic differences between them.

"It is ironic", Quine suggests, "that the inter-linguistic case is less noticed, for it is just here that the semantic indeterminacy makes clear empirical sense" (Quine, 1960: 79). But we should ask whether the inter-linguistic case is a simple matter of semantic *indeterminacy* or whether it transcends this sphere. The indeterminacy of translation can be, at its most extreme, a case of incommensurability of a whole system of beliefs, given the impossibility of delimiting the epistemological border between philosophy and science.

Wittgenstein, it seems to me, took a step in this direction. In *Philosophical Investigations*, he stated that "to understand a sentence means to understand a language" (Wittgenstein, 2009: §199). Anyone who is willing to translate a truth of the synthetic type, like the famous theory of relativity ($E = mc^2$), into the language of an uncontacted people would need to invent words or distort the meaning of existing indigenous words until they have concluded that the indigenous peoples do not have the necessary concepts for carrying out the translation owing to the limited knowledge of physics. This does not mean, as Quine said, that there is anything linguistically neutral in the proposition that we catch and that the indigenous person does not.

Anybody who communicates symbolically has the capacity to follow a rule, mainly that of the use of symbols. Nevertheless, as Wittgenstein recalls,

> to *think* one is following a rule is not to follow a rule. And that's why it's not possible to follow a rule 'privately'; otherwise, thinking one was following a rule would be the same thing as following it.
> WITTGENSTEIN, 2009: §262

Following a rule, then, cannot be reduced to a simple empirical regularity; rather it depends on intersubjective validation, since its meaning owes its identity to a regulation of a conventional type. As a result, following a rule is not something that a person can do just on their own; "that's why 'following a rule' is a practice" (Wittgenstein, 2009: §262).

Let us take a closer look at what this means. Wittgenstein explains:

> In the practice of the use of language one party calls out the words, the other acts on them ... We can also think of the whole process of using words in as one of those games by means of which children learn their native language. I will call these games '*language-games*' and will sometimes speak of a primitive language as a language-game ... I shall also call the whole, consisting of language and the activities into which it is woven, a 'language-game'.
> WITTGENSTEIN, 2009: §7

On some occasions, Wittgenstein suggests that language is part of a form of life: "The word 'language-*game*' is used here to emphasize the fact that the *speaking* of language is part of an activity, or of a form of life" (Wittgenstein, 2009: §23). On other occasions, he uses the word 'language' as a synonym for the expression 'form of life', when, for example, he states that "to imagine a language means to imagine a form of life" (Wittgenstein, 2009: §19). In *Brown Book*, he prefers to use the word 'culture' in the place of 'form of life': "Imagine a use of language (a culture)," and right after this: "We could also easily imagine a language (and that means again a culture)" (Wittgenstein, 1964: 134).

In the same vein, in *Lectures and Conversations on Aesthetics, Psychology and Religious Belief*: "What belongs to a language game is a whole culture" (Wittgenstein, 1967a: 8). Obviously, the plane on which these questions are raised, although they are located in the context of what can be called 'semantic holism', is not the right one for the discussion of radical translation. In reality, these formulations of Wittgenstein's open up space for a *culturalist concept of language* that is very different from Whorf's perspective, which, as we have seen, proposes something like a linguistic conception of culture.

This positioning is established with a bit more clarity in Wittgenstein's notes that were gathered into book form, entitled *On Certainty*. Here the author approaches a subject which, beyond the question of translatability between languages with unrelated roots, deals with the *incommensurability of belief systems or propositions*. A person's 'image of the world'—their culture, you might say—is seen as a backdrop inherited from the tradition whose correctness is not certified by it. The propositions that describe this image of the world, according to Wittgenstein, resemble the rules of a game, and it is based on these rules, and from them, that true and false are differentiated.

The refutation or confirmation of an assumption, then, happens *within* a system that is not itself a doubtful point of view, but rather a vital element of the argument itself. Anybody who wanted to doubt everything, would not even get to doubting something, since the very game of doubting does itself presuppose certainty. In reality, before doubting an isolated proposition, we do already believe in a whole system of propositions, in a totality of opinions that support each other and serve as reference for us (Wittgenstein, 1969).

It has not gone unnoticed that there do also exist certain supposed points of contact between Wittgenstein's approach and Whorf's.[3] This perception was strengthened by the way the two of them use the term *grammar*, an ambiguous word that has received increasing attention in modern linguistics. For Whorf, as we have seen, the grammar of a language—which he defines as the background linguistic system—shapes ideas and the process of idea formation varies from one human group to another depending on the distance between their respective grammars. For Wittgenstein, in a similar vein, "the harmony between thought and reality is to be found in the grammar of the language" (Wittgenstein, 1967b: §55). Like Whorf, Wittgenstein does not take the word *grammar* in its trivial sense, understood as an idealized external system that defines how a word is employed within the construction of a phrase; rather, he understands it also as the rules of the *ordinary* language that describe how we use words to justify and critique our particular expressions. Not as an abstraction, then, but as part of an activity or even of a form of life.

In this sense, he says:

---

3 See Chatterjee (1985); Kienpointner (1996).

> In the use of words, one might distinguish 'surface grammar' from 'depth grammar.' What immediately impresses itself upon us about the use of a word is the way it is used in the construction of the sentence, the part of its use—one might say—that can be taken in by ear.—And now compare the depth grammar, say of the word, 'to mean,' and what its surface grammar would lead us to expect.
>
> WITTGENSTEIN, 2009: §664

For Wittgenstein, however—and this is a fundamental difference—the relevant depth grammar is not the grammar of languages, as Whorf suggests, but the *grammar of the forms of life*, a theory that comes close to the perspective of this study.

It is from this depth grammar of forms of life that Peter Winch develops his point of view. If, for Quine, philosophy does not enjoy any epistemological advantage over science, Winch argues for a theory that is even more surprising: that scientific thought cannot be considered more intelligible than magical thought. The 'indistinction' between analytic truths and synthetic truths gains a new significance, given that Winch relativizes the very concept of rationality: "To say of a society that it has a language is also to say that it has a concept of rationality" (Winch, 1964: 318).

For him, in a primitive society, the acceptance of new verbal expressions and actions occurs, in general terms, the same way as in any other society: any new verbal expression or action should be intelligible to the other members, in the light of everything that has already been said and done before, but it is through a community's *own grammar* that the meaning of proposed new ways of speaking and acting is understood, not through some universal pattern of rationality.

The new ways of speaking and acting can even involve modifications to the depth grammar, but the new rule ought to be related intelligibly to its predecessor. That means that a bit of speech or an action can seem rational to somebody only in the terms of their own understanding of what is or is not rational. So, it makes no sense to judge somebody's behavior as irrational if we do not share their conception of rationality.

This does not mean that we abandon the idea that a person's formulations and actions should not be, in any context, verifiable by reference to reality, but this procedure, according to Winch, is not exclusive to science, which mistakenly believes that its 'method' alone guarantees utterances that are in accordance with it. Because even the concept of reality ought to be problematized.

For Winch,

> reality is not what gives language sense. What is real and what is unreal shows itself *in* the sense that language has. Further, both the distinction between the real and the unreal and the concept of agreement with reality themselves belong to our language.
> WINCH, 1964: 309

Not even scientific thinking escapes this rule, since, according to Winch,

> the general nature of the data revealed by the experiment can only be specified in terms of criteria built into the methods of experiment employed, and these, in turn, make sense only to someone who is conversant with the kind of scientific activity within which they are employed.
> WINCH, 1964: 309

Winch means that scientists have a grammar just like sorcerers have theirs. Archaic man understands witchcraft as the power to do somebody harm by mystical means. He knows, just like modern man, that wild animals, insects, fire, etc. can harm a person. No special procedure is needed to understand somebody's death that's been caused, for example, by an elephant attack.

It is not the job of witchcraft to explain, then, *how* the harm was caused, which we get immediately from the perception of the event in question, but rather to inform us about *why* the harm occurred. The revelation of the *why* is mediated, and it occurs through consultation of the oracles. And thus, the question arises: "Is it wrong for them to consult an oracle and be guided by it?" asks Wittgenstein. "If we call this 'wrong' aren't we using our language-game as a base from which to combat [the game of those who do consult it]?" (Wittgenstein, 1969: §609). By what criterion, asks Winch, could we call this practice irrational, mistaken, meaningless or unintelligible?

Science responds that magical thought is possible to dismiss, pointing out that it is shrouded in contradiction. It suggests two ways of demonstrating this: (1) two oracular pronouncements can contradict one another directly; (2) an oracular pronouncement can be contradicted by future experience. Oracular consultation among the Azande, for example, is done by the ritualistic administering of a substance (an oracular poison) to a chicken whose death or survival is associated, respectively, with a yes or no response to the question formulated.

In the former case, where two responses are contradictory, many 'explanations' can be offered: the poor quality of the poison, the impurity of the operator of the oracle, an incorrectly formulated question, the influence of witchcraft on the consultation itself, etc. In the latter, where some future experience contradicts the pronouncement, it should be understood that, to primitive man, the oracular response is not equivalent to what a scientist considers subject to empirical confirmation or refutation. Oracular revelations are not hypotheses for confirmation, but expressions of the way in which members of a primitive community decide how to act.

Mystical notions are therefore interrelated through a group of logical bonds that give coherence to the formulations and actions of that form of life.

> Zande notions of witchcraft do not constitute a theoretical system in terms of which Azande try to gain a quasi-scientific understanding of the world. This in its turn suggests that it is the European, obsessed with pressing Zande thought where it would not naturally go—to a contradiction—who is guilty of misunderstanding, not the Zande.
> WINCH, 1964: 308-9

Despite Azande not having categories that allow them to differentiate between the scientific and the non-scientific, they do have a clear understanding of what separates the technical from the magical: so much so that their practical activities, aimed at the material reproduction of the community, follow a coherent pattern of action and cooperation. According to Winch, however, what ought to be in play in the study of other cultures are not the different technical possibilities for doing things, but the different ways of giving meaning to human life as a whole:

> My aim is not to engage in moralizing, but to suggest that the concept of *learning from* which is involved in the study of other cultures is closely linked with the concept of *wisdom*.
> WINCH, 1964: 322

Winch draws attention to the fact that we judge different cultures according to our own culture's benchmarks. There are reasons for this. We have said above that the Neolithic Revolution established the subject-object relation, and that the Industrial Revolution reversed that relationship. Remember that pre-Neolithic magic practices ignore, in a way, the distinction between the non-human world (nature) and the human world (culture), that is, between the objective world and the social world.

An analogous confusion also develops between culture and the subjective world. Non-objectified nature corresponds to a preconceived language (and a tautological one, if you like), that impedes the formation of the concept of the (objective) external world and the concept of the (subjective) internal world. This does not only mean that the objective, social and subjective worlds get confused in magical practices, but that, more radically, the very differentiation between language and world is shown to be impaired.

Magic undoubtedly bears some resemblances, as Mauss teaches us, to technique and to science. Magic, crafts and science respect certain rules, and they aim to produce effects. In craft, the artisan, just like the magician, performs regulated actions in a uniform way, but in the case of technique, "the effects are conceived as produced mechanically"; meanwhile, in magic,

> this is the realm of the occult and of the spirits, a world of ideas which imbues ritual movements and gestures with a special kind of effectiveness, quite different from their mechanical effectiveness.
> MAUSS, 2005: 25

Unlike religion, a collective phenomenon in all its parts, magic, technique and science all have a different affinity. These activities

> are not collective in every single essential aspect, and, while they may have social functions and society is their beneficiary and their vehicle, their sole promoters are individuals.
> MAUSS, 2005: 111

Mauss, however, thinks it difficult to assimilate magic to the sciences and the arts, as he cannot assert in magic what is present in crafts and science, a 'creative or critical activity of individuals' (Mauss, 2005: 35).

In short, magical thought does not establish the semiotic distinctions between the sign substrate, the semantic content, and the referent to which the linguistic expression relates, which only happens in the wake of the historical process of desocialization of natures and denaturalization of society. This is the essence of the Neolithic Revolution, which establishes the subject-object relation. The Industrial Revolution, in turn, inverts that relationship. As we have already indicated, historical materialism's great contribution was to show that, in modernity, the second nature took on the command of the social process, faced with reified human beings and a nullified first nature.

The disruptive combination of the machine and salaried labor brought about the subjectification of the second nature, as it transformed human beings into supports of a process that they simply do not control. The subjectification of the second nature corresponds, therefore, to the objectification of society: subjects become objectified, and first nature loses its place. The so-called ecological crisis is just a corollary of the material reversal produced by the Industrial Revolution.

In view of this, it sounds 'understandable' that modern man should look at pre-modern societies with an air of superiority, given the current technical and scientific domination of nature when compared to any other period in history, even if, for this, one must abstract the environmental damage and the subjective damage caused by the rationality of modern society as a whole. Winch's suggestion is precisely that we study other cultures beginning with a concept that, in a way, transcends the concept of rationality.

Winch seems to suggest—and this is, in my opinion, his great contribution to the debate—that the *rationalities* (*ontologies*, nowadays) of Paleolithic, Neolithic and modern societies are different and cannot be compared in their own terms. Within the framework of this study, one need only think about the subject-object relation in the context of each of these types. While in Paleolithic societies, the subject-object ratio is not even structured, in Neolithic and modern societies, numerator (subject) and denominator (object) are in reversed positions, when compared to each other.

Since, according to Winch, there is no quantitative hierarchical relationship between these rationalities (Paleolithic society is neither more nor less rational than modern society), he links a culture's process of learning to the concept of *knowledge*. Knowledge, however, over the course of history, has not served to contain the process of alienization, extermination and subjugation that has characterized cultures' r-evolutionary dynamic, their destinies being determined by each one's firepower, especially in relation to archaic societies.

Clifford Geertz begins, like Winch, from the Wittgenstein of *Philosophical Investigations*, of which he declares himself a disciple, to argue for a semiotic conception of culture in which man is seen as an animal tied to symbolic webs that he has himself woven, with it falling to anthropology to transform itself not into an experimental science searching for laws, but into an interpretative science searching for meaning.

The anthropological description of cultures should thus be developed in terms of the constructions that, it is imagined, the subjects involved build over the course of their lives and the formulas that they use to define what happens to them. For Geertz,

> there are three characteristics of ethnographic description: it is interpretive; what it is interpretive of is the flow of social discourse; and the interpreting involved consists in trying to rescue the 'said' of such discourse from its perishing occasions and fix it in perusable terms.
> GEERTZ, 1973: 20

The semiotic approach aims, therefore, to assist the anthropologist to access an unfamiliar conceptual world inhabited by the subjects whose form of life he is to interpret.

Geertz is quite clearly aware of the risks of this proposal lapsing into subjectivism or into a kind of sociological aestheticism, losing contact with the hard surfaces of the classifying realities of economics and politics, as well as of the biological necessities and historical needs on which they rest. His 'model', however, breaks with what he calls the *stratigraphic conception* of man, according to which he is a composite of superimposed 'levels', which are complete and irreducible, as if, under the forms of culture, one would find the structures of social organization; beneath them, the psychological factors; and at the base of the whole edifice of human life, the biological foundations, whether anatomical, physiological or neurological.

Geertz, meanwhile, proposes a synthetic conception, in which all these factors—biological, psychological, sociological and cultural—can be treated as variables within the same system of analysis. From this perspective, cultures stop being seen as complexes of behavioral patterns and are considered a group of control mechanisms, or, to be more specific, as computational programs for governing human behavior.

According to this conception, the human being is precisely that, an animal characterized by the dependency on organized systems of significant symbols of extra-genetic control, without which their behavior would be ungovernable, a meaningless chaos of emotional explosions. Since man, according to Geertz, was given innately only extremely general capacities for response, which simultaneously have the advantage of plasticity and the disadvantage of non-specificity, then culture, as the accumulated totality of symbolic control systems, is the essential condition for human existence and the basis of its uniqueness.

As for evolutionary psychology, the comparison becomes easy. Geertz is in agreement with Cosmides and Tooby as to the need to assume a large number of specialized mechanisms to explain human beings' high performance, without which we would not have the competencies we need to survive. A generic capacity to respond, however sophisticated, does not provide the conditions for processing information at the speed necessary for obtaining effective results.

The more complex the problems to be faced, the greater the need for specific rules of domain of relevance, specialized procedures and prior hypotheses for setting them in motion. Nevertheless, for evolutionary psychologists, these mechanisms already exist in the evolved human brain. To them, the brain is not a general-purpose computer; rather, it is composed of a group of specialized mental organs which, far from liberating us from instincts, has incorporated new ones.

For Geertz, however, the innate human capacities are generic; it is cultures, as a group of symbolic systems of extra-genetic control, situated 'outside the skin', that stabilize the human being's behavior and gives him a ready capacity to respond.

There is no way, at this point, that we could help but notice the similarities, albeit with some significant nuances, between Geertz's interpretative anthropology and Gehlen's philosophical anthropology. As we have seen, for Gehlen, without culture, humans' behavior would be characterized by insecurity and ungovernability. Institutions, created by man himself, operate precisely as an impulse system that ensures the predictability and almost automaticity of human reactions to any external conditions. Moreover, Gehlen, in his own way, also breaks with what Geertz calls the stratigraphic conception of man. To do this, he has recourse to Hartmann's ontology, which accepts the joint existence of *permeable* strata from which the world is structured.

Geertz, in turn, welcomes three scientific advances about the understanding of the emergence of *Homo sapiens*. In the first place, everything suggests that we should discard the sequential view of the relations between the biological and cultural advance according to which the first, the biological one, was completed before the second, the cultural one, had even begun, as if a marginal genetic change to a species made it capable, all of a sudden, of producing culture.

For Geertz, the empirical evidence suggests that no such moment existed, and he embraced the theory that the process involved a large number of marginal genetic changes in a sequence that was long and complex. "What this means", he argues,

> is that culture, rather than being added on, so to speak, to a finished or virtually finished animal, was an ingredient, and a centrally ingredient, in the production of that animal itself.
> GEERTZ, 1973: 47

Secondly, we should consider that the majority of the biological changes that produced modern man happened in the brain.

The small-brained proto-human *Australopithecus* gave way to the large-brained *Homo sapiens*. Geertz observed a process of feedback over the course of this progression:

> Between the cultural pattern, the body, and the brain, a positive feedback system was created in which each shaped the progress of the other, a system in which the interaction among increasing tool use, the changing anatomy of the hand, and the expanding representation of the thumb on the cortex is only one of the more graphic examples.[4]
>
> GEERTZ, 1973: 48

For Geertz, so-called human nature does not exist independent of culture. Without significant symbols, working merely from our few useful instincts, we would be incapable of directing our behavior and organizing our experience. Symbols are, therefore, prerequisites of our very biological, psychological and social existence. Finally, Geertz underlines man's incomplete and unfinished nature in physical terms, which is the condition that obliges him to learn in order to function; learning, then, is less a faculty than a necessity.

And this is where one striking characteristic of Geertz's interpretative anthropology appears: "[We] finish ourselves through culture—and not through culture in general but through highly particular forms of it" (Geertz, 1973: 49). There is no such thing, for him, as a 'universal cultural pattern' (Wissler), 'universal institutional types' (Malinowski), 'common denominators of culture' (Murdock) or 'universal categories of culture' (Kluckhohn). The so-called 'cultural universals' are, in practice, 'fake universals', in Kroeber's phrase, since they are such general concepts that any explanatory power that they might possess simply evaporates amidst the generalization.

> If we want to discover what man amounts to, we can only find it in what men are: and what men are, above all other things, is various. It is in understanding that variousness—its range, its nature, its basis, and its implications—that we shall come to construct a concept of human nature that ... has both substance and truth.
>
> GEERTZ, 1973: 52

According to Geertz, anthropological research suggests that mankind's mindsets do not genetically precede culture. According to him, cultural accumulation was already in motion before the organic development stopped, with culture playing an active role in the latter stages of the process, especially as

---

4 The development of the opposable thumb in ancient hominids, associated with the manipulating of complex objects such as tools, led to an expansion of the area of the cerebral cortex (the outermost area of the brain) responsible for the control of this digit.

concerns the actual expansion of the brain, a phenomenon that followed, and did not precede, the beginnings of culture.

Human nature, in this way, seems as much a cultural product as a biological one, forged in a period of quick environmental variation, in which the perfect conditions appeared for a rapid evolutionary development of mankind, the Pleistocene, following which the cultural environment came increasingly to supplement the natural one in the process of selection.

Biology and culture share some coevolution, then, but unlike what the biologists of coevolution believe, it is limited to the process of anthropogenesis. When this is completed, the link between cultural change and organic change is weakened, if it does not break altogether.

Geertz acknowledges his doubts that an infrahominid primate could have possessed a *true culture*, in the sense of an ordered system of meanings and symbols, but he asserts that *monkeys are social creatures* capable of acting through imitative learning and developing collective social traditions that are transmitted from generation to generation as non-biological inheritance, and which play a significant role in the process of anthropogenesis. Here Geertz is simply confusing the social with the cultural. It is one thing to say that social practices preceded the appearance of symbolic language, in evolutionary terms; it is another to claim that there was culture where there were no symbols.

Finally, Geertz concludes that his position does not imply any denial of the doctrine of the psychic unity of mankind, since

> phyletic differentiation within the hominid line effectively ceased with the terminal Pleistocene spread of *Homo sapiens* over nearly the whole world and the extinction of whatever other *Homo* species may have been in existence at that time. Thus, although some minor evolutionary changes have no doubt occurred since the rise of modern man, all living peoples form part of a single polytypical species and, as such, vary anatomically and physiologically within a very narrow range.
> GEERTZ, 1973: 69

It should be noted, at this point, that on this journey that goes, on the one hand, from Uexküll to Bertalanffy, via Whorf, and on the other, from Gehlen to Winch and Geertz, via Wittgenstein, the subject suggested by this study of alienization as a structuring process of dialectical triadic relationships appears in the universe of linguistics with the same timidity as in the anthropological debate. Among biologists, the situation is understandable.

There is no contradiction in nature simply because, in the non-symbolic dimension, there is no historical temporality. It sounds reasonable, then, even for a biologist who acknowledges the existence of a symbolic dimension that is relatively detached from genetics, still to want to apply the variation-selection binomial to cultural evolution, too. Culture, however, does not evolve. Nor does it develop; at least, not in the sense in which sociology (cf. Habermas) seeks to transpose onto the phylogenetic plane those ontogenetic concepts from the theory of cognitive development (Piaget) and moral development (Kohlberg). *Culture r-evolves*.

In the fields of anthropology and linguistics, it might have been a different story. Herder could have followed through on his 'third natural law', an entirely possible path, especially if he had lived long enough to encounter the young Hegel's Jena lectures. Or Gehlen, a diligent reader of them both. Whorf could have realized that the central question was not of the relativity of individual languages (tongues), but the properties of symbolic language itself, properties that would remain active even if we all communicated in Esperanto. Winch and Geertz could have expanded the argument that Wittgenstein did not develop very far, which appears in *On Certainty*, where he imagines what a conflict between two different forms of life would be like:

> Where *two principles* really do meet which cannot be reconciled with one another, then each man declares the other a fool and a heretic. §612 I said I would 'combat' the other man,—but wouldn't I give him reasons? Certainly; but ... at the end of reasons comes persuasion. (Think what happens when missionaries convert natives).
> WITTGENSTEIN, 1969: §611–12

It would have been enough for Winch and Geertz to have thought, in Wittgenstein's wake, about what happens when conquerors convert indigenous people into depersonalized beings and treat foreigners as alienized heretics. But for this, they could not have gotten around the problem of the contradiction: in the case of Winch, accepting the different 'rationalities' as one of the sources of alienization; in the case of Geertz, seeking not only the meaning of the symbolic webs woven by man, but the direction (in time) of the symbolic projection of human groups, which considers antagonistic projects.

Linguistics, however, thanks to biology, took a different path and deflected attention onto a very unpromising argument. We have already said it elsewhere: excluding those instincts that, as biological beings, we share with other mammals, the 'instincts' that evolutionary psychology attributes to humans are a result of the historical process, whether it be the tribal 'instinct' or the religious 'instinct.' Our study has shown that economy and religion are ramifications of the process of alienization which has symbolic language as prerequisite—the latter, due to its intrinsic properties, projecting human groups in temporality. Even Lévi-Strauss's structuralism encounters this question when he states that

> from birth onwards, a thousand conscious and unconscious influences in our environment instil into us a complex system of criteria, consisting in value judgments, motivations and centers of interest, and including the *conscious reflection upon the historical development of our civilization which our education imposes.*
> LÉVI-STRAUSS, 1952: 25; italics by the author

Now, Lévi-Strauss recognizes then that the movement of the 'historical development' *between* different cultures depends on the "*quantity of information* able to 'pass' between two individuals or groups, as a function of the greater or lesser diversity of their respective cultures" (Lévi-Strauss, 1976: 341). The foundations were laid for a leap beyond structuralism, which never happened. Lévi-Strauss failed to admit that this 'degree of difference between cultures' can be of such an order that the word *difference*, in many cases, no longer has any explanatory power. It is here that dialectics imposes itself, exposing the inadequacy of structuralist thinking which, as Tremlett (2011) has already pointed out, maintains some affinities with evolutionary psychology. The shift from stationary history to cumulative history might have suggested a path that would have avoided this undesirable approach.

This is why we have intentionally left till last what, to my mind, is the 'instinct' that demands the greatest care, precisely because it provides an opportunity for the greatest mistakes. Treating symbolic language as an instinct is simply incorrect. Of course, one can resort to the argument that everything depends on which definition of instinct you are using. As a word that is given to controversies, the arguments around this subject tend to remain inconclusive.

Konrad Lorenz (1937), for example, devoted a lengthy essay just to refuting the inaccurate conceptions put forward by major theoreticians of instinct, though without, naturally, putting an end to the discussion.[5] Evolutionary psychology, however, turned unwittingly to William James (1890) to extract—from

---

5   See also. Lehrman (1953), a critique of Lorenz recently revived by developmental systems theory.

a side observation in his *The Principles of Psychology*—an assumption about the nature of language.

In this work, James makes the mistake that, to my mind, is at the root of the errors of evolutionary psychology. At a certain point in the book, he begins from the reasonable premise that 'every instinct is an impulse', to deduce from it the false conclusion that, reciprocally, every impulse is an instinct. He does this with a rejection of the usual definition according to which instinct is the faculty of acting to achieve certain aims that are unforeseen or without prior training.

This more contained view, which James rejects, limits the concept to those reflex actions—blind and invariable—of preservation of oneself and one's descendants, among others of this kind. In this context, the human being is seen as someone almost entirely without instincts (Herder, Gehlen), who makes up for the lack of instincts with what we call reason. If, however, we widen the concept of instinct, as James would like to, to look at all impulses, whatever they may be, even the impulse to act on the idea of a distant fact, it would be impossible to limit them to those actions performed without the prediction of any aim. In this case, according to James, the situation would be radically reversed in favor of the human who has access to a much larger variety of impulses than any other animal.

All impulses, according to James, are as blind as the most basic of instincts, but, due to a human being's memory, to his power of reflection and inference, as soon as he allows himself to be led by these impulses and experiences their results, he comes to sense them in connection to those results that had been foreseen. Reason and experience lead him to 'see' further ahead. As a result, there is no conflict between reason and instinct, since reason cannot itself inhibit an instinct, merely neutralize—through the exciting of the imagination—one instinct by the activation of another. Nor is this any kind of compensation on the part of evolution: more reason in exchange for fewer instincts. We are, according to James, simultaneously more instinctive *and* more rational than other animals.

This is where an argument of William James's that is less explored by evolutionary psychology joins the story, which in a way reveals the aporias in his approach. Without seeking to ignore the specific conditions of human life that do not exist in nature, James incorporates them into the psyche, naturalizing them through his theory of instinct. According to him,

> *nature implants contrary impulses to act on many classes of things*, and leaves it to slight alterations in the conditions of the individual case to decide which impulse shall carry the day, Thus, greediness and suspicion,

> curiosity and timidity, coyness and desire, bashfulness and vanity, sociability and pugnacity, seem to shoot over into each other as quickly, and to remain in as unstable equilibrium, in the higher birds and mammals as in man. They are all impulses, congenital, blind at first, and productive of motor reactions of a rigorously determinate sort. *Each one of them, then, is an instinct*, as instincts are commonly defined. But they contradict each other—'experience' in each particular opportunity of application usually deciding the issue. *The animal that exhibits them loses the 'instinctive' demeanor and appears to lead a life of hesitation and choice, an intellectual life; not however, because he has no instincts—rather because he has so many that they block each other's path.*
>
> JAMES, 1890: 392–3

Just as evolutionary psychology shows sympathy with some premises of Malinowski's functionalist anthropology, it also allows itself to be inspired by the functional psychology of William James. In treating human impulses as instincts, however, functional psychology not only has to deal with the outlandish hypothesis that 'contradictory instincts' can throw behavior off course, which seems to go against the very idea of instinct, but it is also just a step away from considering symbolic language—seen as an impulse to speak—to be an instinct. The hypothesis would find support in the work of Darwin himself (of whom James was a follower), when he states that,

> language is an art, like brewing or baking; but writing would have been a better simile. It certainly is not a true instinct, for every language has to be learned. It differs, however, widely from all ordinary arts, for man has an instinctive tendency to speak, as we see in the babble of our young children; while no child has an instinctive tendency to brew, bake, or write.
>
> DARWIN, 1871: 55

The inference is incorrect, however. This misstep is taken by Steven Pinker (2015). In *The Language Instinct*, Pinker first questions Whorf's hypothesis about linguistic determinism, which, as we have seen, suggests that an individual's thoughts are determined by the categories of his language's grammar or, to put it another way, the world is understood through different existing linguistic systems, according to the patterns of each language. Pinker returns to the objections to Whorf raised by Eric Lenneberg, among others, to defend the translatability of any thought from one language to another.

For him, recognizing the existence of different ways of speaking is not equivalent to recognizing the existence of different ways of thinking. We know, in any language, that 'Socrates is a man', not because we have some neural pattern that associates each word in the sentence to a group of neurons corresponding to its subject, verb and object in the language in question; as a matter of preference, we use some other code for concepts of representation and their reciprocal relationship, a language of thought or Mentalese, through which thinking is transformed into strings of words; that is, we do not think in English but in Mentalese, a language that can be translated into any other. The connection between Mentalese and instinct is made by recourse to Noam Chomsky's generative grammar.

The argument between Chomsky and Skinner's behaviorism is well known. For the latter, behavior is explained by a limited group of laws of learning based on a repertoire of possible responses to environmental stimuli whose probability of recurring in similar contexts either is or is not reinforced in light of the positive or negative consequences for the organism's survival. Chomsky makes a forceful objection. For him, language is not a limited repertoire of responses; rather, it functions as a mental grammar that produces an unlimited set of sentences from a finite list of words.

This being so, the premise of behaviorism is weakened. The strongest evidence to support this hypothesis is the behavior of children who, even without any formal instruction, develop this complex grammar that enables them to give consistent interpretations for phrases they have never encountered before. This capacity for language, according to Chomsky, can only be innate: and the acquisition of a cognitive structure like language should be studied in a similar way to our study of a complex organ of the body.

In Pinker's terms,

> language is not a cultural artifact that we learn the way we learn to tell time or how the federal government works. Instead, it is a distinct piece of the biological make-up of our brains. Language is a complex, specialized skill, which develops in the child spontaneously, without conscious effort or formal instruction, is deployed without awareness of its underlying logic, is qualitatively the same in every individual, and is distinct from more general abilities to process information or behave intelligently. For these reasons some cognitive scientists have described language as a psychological faculty, a mental organ, a neural system and a computational module. But I prefer the admittedly quaint term 'instinct'.
> PINKER, 2015: 18

Note that there are two kinds of argument which could perhaps be confused: defending the innate character of language and defending its instinctive nature. As we will see in greater detail below, Chomsky argues that language is a biological 'artefact', not a cultural one. Pinker and Bloom (1990) contradict him, arguing, through an orthodox Darwinism, that language is instinctive—a direct product of natural selection and not a side-effect of other evolutionary forces, whether an exaptation (pre-adaptation) or a spandrel.[6]

Arguing for the instinctive character resorts to arguments—which do not conflict with innatism—that look at children's capacity to reinvent language when the situation requires, not because they are smart, not because they have been taught, or because language is useful to them, but because they simply cannot help doing it, as in those cases of the formation of Creole languages, created from a contact language (a pidgin), via a process in which children inject grammatical complexity where previously no grammar existed.

We should note that, for Pinker, the complete proof that language is an instinct would also require locating an identifiable space for it in the brain, and, perhaps, a group of genes responsible for 'situating' it in the correct place. Although he acknowledges that no such organ of language or gene for grammar has yet been located, Pinker states that promising research shows that severe intellectual impairments do not necessarily limit a fluent grammatical language, which reinforces the perspective of evolutionary psychology.

Finally, it is worth saying that for evolutionary psychologists there is not, in fact, any profound divergence between Skinner's radical behaviorism and Chomsky's innatism, since both argue for the existence of universal evolved psychological mechanisms without which the learning itself could not happen. The argument is about how general or specific these mechanisms are: "Skinner proposes conditioning mechanisms that apply to all situations, while Chomsky proposes specialized mechanisms particularly designed for language" (Tooby and Cosmides, 1992: 37).

Learning, in this context, is not, therefore, an alternative to innatism, since behaviorists themselves acknowledge that there are premises for learning that cannot themselves be learned. "This is why it is no paradox to say that flexibility in learned *behavior* requires innate constraints on the *mind*" (Pinker, 2015: 417).

Pinker concludes his book by listing, in the manner of William James, the specifically human 'instincts' (including language) that he understands to be associated with specific computational cerebral modules that are particular to the species, a perspective from which we already distanced ourselves when

---

6   See Gould and Lewontin (1979); Gould and Vrba (1982).

we discussed supposed tribal and religious 'instincts'. Let us focus, then, on the 'language instinct'.

In a review of Pinker's book, Tomasello offers some quite convincing objections, about the inappropriateness of characterizing language as an instinct:

> In the common understanding of both scientists and laypersons alike an instinct is a behavioral competency, or set of behavioral competencies, that: (a) is relatively stereotyped in its behavioral expression, and (b) would appear in ontogeny even if an individual was raised in isolation from its species-typical set of experiences.
> TOMASELLO, 1995: 132–33

What Tomasello seeks to present is a less rigid alternative to the theory of language acquisition—not in the Chomskyan form of linguistic structures preformed in the human genome—without, however, dispensing with the recognized biological foundations of language. Chomsky resorted to strong, non-verifiable hypotheses to argue his perspective: the hypothesis that the module of innate syntax contains the basic plan (*bauplan*) of all possible languages; and the hypothesis that linguistic structures are not learned, but merely triggered by linguistic inputs.

It is worth noting that the difference between Tomasello and Chomsky is not about whether or not humans are biologically prepared to acquire language; rather it is a question of whether or not they come into the world equipped with "an innate linguistic module that contains from the outset linguistic structures of the Generative Grammar kind" (Tomasello, 1995: 137).

Thus, the universal fact that all cultures have a language does not imply the existence of specific language genes, just as the fact that we cook our food and eat with our hands does not imply that any corresponding genes exist, even though all these abilities are inscribed in the human genome somehow. Pinker, as we have seen, invokes the existence of so-called *linguistic savants*—people with very low IQs who are capable of producing complex grammatical sentences—to advocate the autonomy and innatism of syntax.

However, according to Tomasello, in the empirical cases reported, the adolescents analysed did have a mental age of between four and six, that is, the age when a human being, according to Pinker himself, acquires the linguistic competencies of an adult. Tomasello reinforces this same objection with the following argument:

> It is now well known, and Pinker documents, that there is significant variation in the human population with respect to the localization of

language functions in the brain, with a fair proportion of the left-handed individuals showing atypical localization patterns, and that brain damaged children quite often develop language functions in atypical portions of the brain.

TOMASELLO, 1995: 143

The idea of a dedicated brain module just for language sounds flimsy in the light of these considerations.

Other objections from Tomasello sound less strong to me, such as those relating to the mastery by children of grammatical rules as relating to their own language or to the role they play in the formation of Creole languages. It is notoriously difficult logically to formulate a question beginning from a sentence with two auxiliary verbs. Children, however, do it relatively naturally. The sentence 'The man who is running is bald' corresponds to the question 'Is the man who is running bald?' and not 'Is the man who running is bald?'. That example suggests that the human is born equipped with some innate linguistic components.

For Tomasello, however, there are many reasons why children do not adopt the second formulation; for example, the fact that they have never heard the word 'who' followed by a gerund. In the case of Creole languages, Tomasello argues that we do not know the exact social conditions for learning in which where languages were formulated and, therefore, what the children involved actually heard. He concludes:

> There is no question that language acquisition is a robust and well-canalized developmental phenomenon. Human children acquire basic skills of linguistic competence in a wide variety of circumstances. But this robustness by itself does not tell us the nature of the developmental mechanisms involved. Walking is a developmental function perhaps even more heavily canalized than language, but recent research has shown that it is not controlled by a specific genetic program that specifies muscle movements or other specific components of walking itself.
>
> TOMASELLO, 1995: 148

Tomasello's considerations do not take any of the power away from the Chomskyan revolution, at least not from the perspective that interests us in this study. In one of his latest books, Chomsky adopts a less demanding approach to argue his point of view. In partnership with Robert C. Berwick, he seeks to explain what he calls the basic property of language, or the fact that "every human language is a finite computational system generating an infinite array of hierarchically structured expressions" (Berwick and Chomsky, 2019) (a formulation previously found in Humboldt), which requires some notion of recursiveness, relating to semantic-pragmatic systems (thought) and sensory-motor systems that are not exclusively human (sound).

Chomsky is willing to confront the disagreement, mentioned above, between Darwin and Wallace. Wallace found it hard to approach human language starting from a conventional adaptationist treatment. Pinker, as we have seen, adopts Darwinian adaptationism. Chomsky proposes a synthesis of Darwin and Wallace. For Darwin, natural selection only acts through the use of successive small variations, and not by leaps, unlike Wallace, whose concerns find backing in the empirical evidence brought to light in Eric Lenneberg's seminal book.

Chomsky praises Lenneberg for a number of reasons, among them the fact of having discovered that language acquisition can occur despite serious pathologies; of grasping the dissociation of syntax from other cognitive faculties; of supplying evidence, from the analysis of families with a language deficit, that language has a genetic component; and, just as important, of observing that, despite this, there is no need to conceive of 'genes for language'.

Lenneberg, moreover, would have sided with the theory of discontinuity in the evolution of language, which would suggest some kind of 'leap', starting from the evidence that "the identical capacity for language among all races suggests that this phenomenon must have existed before racial diversification" (Lenneberg, 1967: 266).

If the biological differences between races are minimal, by any criterion at all, in relation to the capacity for language, they are non-existent. The theory of discontinuity also implies rejecting the results of recent studies (Bornkessel-Schlesewsky et al., 2015) that the basic computational biological pre-requisites for human language are already present in non-human primates. For Chomsky, the mechanisms identified by these studies are insufficient for what is found in human language.

The way out that Chomsky found was to abandon the deterministic Darwinian paradigm of the theory of evolution by natural selection and accept a stochastic (statistically random) process—of contingency and chance, in which "[every] cog in the evolutionary engine—fitness, migration, fertility, mating, development, and more—is subject to the slings and arrows of outrageous biological fortune" (Berwick and Chomsky, 2016: 16).

In incorporating Mendel's discovery into Darwin's theory, in order to save it from its internal inconsistencies, the founders of the Modern Synthesis—Wright, Fisher and Haldane—show how the former's laws of heredity led to a change in the way of seeing how the frequency of features in populations alters from generation to generation, showing how aptitude itself is a random variable, since the fittest of a general population might not leave any offspring. This characteristic of the evolutionary process is even more striking precisely when genuinely new characteristics appear, such as the evolution of language, in which the new variants of genes must escape from what Chomsky calls the 'stochastic gravity well'.

Evolution, then, both crawls and proceeds by leaps. Were this not the case, it would be very hard to understand the phenomena described by Maynard Smith and Szathmáry that they call major transitions. From the origin of linear DNA, through sexuality, up to the origin of symbolic language, almost all transitions seem to be confined to one single lineage, and some are due to genetic introgression, such as the appearance of eukaryotes. Through these examples, Chomsky seeks to escape from the rigid choice between micro-mutationism and what looks like genuine leaps, including the appearance of symbolic language. The only one of the founders of the Modern Synthesis who seems to have shown any openness to this hypothesis was J.B.S. Haldane, perhaps owing to the admiration he harboured for Engels's dialectics of nature which, while incorrect, might have served to broaden his horizons.

According to Chomsky, the paleo-archeological record for the *Homo* lineage corroborates the non-gradualist view of the appearance of human language. The making of the first unequivocally symbolic artefacts, for example, dates back just 81,000 years. At that moment, modern man was living alongside Neanderthal man, who appeared around 400,000 years ago and became extinct 28,000 years ago. Both species derived from a common ancestor, *Homo heidelbergensis*, and they lived side by side following *Homo sapiens*' migration to Eurasia.

The Neanderthals have a large portion of their DNA that is similar to the sequences in modern humans, whose own sequencing even shows a gene flow between them through hybridization. Although many authors state that the Neanderthals had language,[7] Chomsky is skeptical toward that hypothesis, following those authors, like Ian Tattersall and Svante Pääbo, who note the weak evidence for Neanderthals' symbolic behavior, such as the lack of figurative art, among other absences, which suggests the faculty for language being an autapomorphic feature of the anatomically modern human beings from southern Africa, before their exodus to Eurasia, a feature which thus far has remained unaltered and uniform through the human population.

---

7   See Dediu and Levinson (2018).

According to Chomsky, then, this curious biological object, language, appeared on Earth very recently, and from a biolinguistic perspective, should be considered an 'organ of the body', of the same order of complexity as the visual or immunological system, or a 'mental organ' (if by *mental* we understand certain aspects of the world), common to all the individuals of the human species.

But if that is the case, how are we to explain the huge diversity and variety of languages? At first sight, an observer might actually appear to be facing a myriad of languages that differ from one another in ways that are unpredictable and unlimited. This perception is strengthened by the flourishing of anthropological linguistics, whose proposal is that each language should be studied with no previous schema of how a language should be, a conception that, as we have seen, can be attributed with only slight reservations to Franz Boas.

In view of this, both the American structuralism of a Zellig Harris and the European structuralism of a Nikolai Trubetzkoy seek, respectively, 'methods' or 'phonological patterns' in order to reduce the data of the unlimited variation of languages into a relatively organized form. It was what seemed to be to hand, given the approaches of Saussure, who saw language as "a storehouse of word images in the minds of members of community", which "exists only by virtue of a sort of contract signed the members of a community", or of Bloomfield, for whom "language is an array of habits to respond to situations with conventional speech sounds, and to respond to these sounds with actions" (Berwick and Chomsky, 2016: 95–96).

The picture, then, resembled what has happened to biology itself since 1830, when Cuvier got the better of Geoffroy by emphasizing not what was common to life, but the almost infinite variety of forms that had evolved and continue to evolve, a perspective that would be reinforced not long afterward by the authority of Darwin himself.

Chomsky, as we know, took a different route:

> Reconciliation of the apparent diversity of organic forms with their evident underlying uniformity—why do we see this array of living things in the world and not others, just as why do we see this array of languages/grammars and not others?—comes about through the interplay of three factors, famously articulated by the biologist [Jacques] Monod: First, there is the historically contingent fact that we are all common descendants from a single tree of life … ; second, there are the physio-chemical constraints of the world, necessities that delimit biological possibilities … ; third, there is the sieving effect of natural selection [on] a pre-existing menu of [biological] possibilities.
> BERWICK and CHOMSKY, 2016: 59

Along those same lines, Chomsky observes that the proponents of the 'new evo-devo science' (evolution and development), Sean Carroll (2006) and Gerd Müller (2007), among others, in tune with the propositions of the Extended Evolutionary Synthesis, seek to show, starting from the discovery of complex circuits for gene regulation and for development, that beneath the apparent infinity of forms that evolved, one finds chemical structures that are noticeably uniform. From this point of view, if alien scientists happened to come down to Earth, they would very probably see the organic world as a single organism, with only small apparent superficial variations.

Chomsky sees François Jacob as the precursor of the understanding that,

> it was not ... biochemical innovation that generated the diversification of organisms. In all likelihood, things worked the other way around. It was the selective pressure resulting from changes in behavior or in ecological niches that led to biochemical adjustments and changes in molecular types. What distinguishes a butterfly from a lion, a hen from a fly, or a worm from a whale, is much less a difference in chemical constituents than in the organization and distribution of these constituents.
> JACOB, 1989: 395

It was exactly this model that inspired Chomsky to develop the 'principles and parameters' approach to language, based precisely on the assumption that "languages consist of fixed and invariant principles connected to a kind of switchbox of parameters" (Berwick and Chomsky, 2016: 68). He thus seeks to make it easier to separate what is universal in language from what is contingent: the universal is what emerged suddenly in evolutionary terms, probably as a result of a mutation, that is, the generative procedure emerged that supplies the principles; while the diversity of languages arises from the fact that "principles do not determine the answers to all questions about language, but leave some questions as open parameters" (Berwick and Chomsky, 2016: 69).

From this new perspective, the above-mentioned alien scientists (the ones who would see our organic world as a single organism with apparent superficial variations) could now conclude that there is only one language, with small dialectal variations.

Universal grammar, for Chomsky, is precisely the theory of the genetic component of the faculty for language. It was the capacity for language that evolved and that remains unchanged since our forefathers left Africa. Languages themselves, meanwhile, change, but they do not evolve. Non-biological evolution 'is not evolution at all' (Berwick and Chomsky, 2016: 92). And what evolved should be quite simple, consisting of basic computational principles that operate in computationally efficient conditions that produce an infinite set of hierarchically structured expressions.

In general, any computational system incorporates an operation through which, from two already-formed objects, a third is constructed. The 'Merge' of objects is basically an operation for forming sets. Language is based on this recursive generative process, which takes basic elements and applies this procedure repeatedly to produce unlimited structured expressions. Note that, within this framework, there is no space for protolanguages, since the discrete infinity of human language requires the same recursive process, whether for a single-word phrase or an infinitely long one.

What is remarkable about the human computational system, among other things, and which also differentiates it from any other computer language, is the fact that human language has paradoxical properties of great computational efficiency that children handle easily without assistance, which would be one piece of evidence for the innateness of this system.

The Chomskyan theory, as we can see, decisively calls into question Whorf's hypothesis and, consequently, Bertalanffy's approach and, in a way, recovers, via Uexküll, Kant's universalism, with reinforcement from Konrad Lorenz's concept (around which Chomsky maintains some reservations) of 'biological a priori' (for Lorenz, a pure science of the forms of human thought, independent of experience, is possible), and C.S. Peirce's concept of 'abduction' (Pierce took an interest in the study of the rules that limit the class of possible theories).

As 'dialects' of human language, individual spoken languages do not alter the surrounding world (*Umwelt*) which corresponds to the nature of that biological being that is the human. In a largely overlooked passage from *Language and Mind*, Chomsky notes that:

> For the present, it seems that most complex organisms have highly specific forms of sensory and perceptual organization that are associated with the *Umwelt* and the manner of life of the organism. There is little reason to doubt that what is true of lower organisms is true of humans as well. Particularly in the case of language, it is natural to expect a close relation between innate properties of the mind and features of linguistic structure; for language, after all, has no existence apart from its mental representation. Whatever properties it has must be those that are given to it by the innate mental processes of the organism that has invented it and that invents it anew ... [which] are associated with the conditions of its use.
>
> CHOMSKY, 2006: 83

There is, of course, the possibility—also via Uexküll—of bringing Chomsky's theory closer to Cassirer's philosophy, so long as due care is taken not to confuse the former's universal grammar with the latter's symbolic system, which allowed Cassirer to expand the categories by which Kant thought about science to include all forms of human activity such as the mythic, the aesthetic and the social. This argument, about the precedence of the grammatical or the symbolic, persists to this day.

Despite the significance of the debate about the biological foundations of language, I think that the relevance of François Jacob's work, which evidently inspired Chomsky in his 'principles and parameters' approach of the 1980s, lies in a development of Jacob's thinking that was not much explored by Chomsky, and whose consequences have not been properly examined. Let us recall that Chomsky always emphasized the creative aspect of language use.

He actually opens his *Cartesian Linguistics* with the observation that Descartes was convinced that non-human animals behave like automata, while man, thanks to his unique abilities, most notably language, cannot have his behavior explained mechanically.

According to Chomsky, the Cartesian view understands that

> in its normal use, human language is free from stimulus control and does not serve a merely communicative function, but is rather an instrument for the free expression of thought and for appropriate response to new situations.
>
> CHOMSKY, 1966: 65

In general, the Cartesian linguists did not see human language as an instinct, and, in the above-mentioned case of Herder, it was even considered a consequence of human instincts' weakness. Schlegel, meanwhile, notes the independence of ordinary language from immediate stimulation and its eventual liberation from practical purposes, and underlines its poetic quality, stating, for example:

> The greatest things as well as the least significant, the greatest marvel never before heard—indeed the most impossible and unthinkable things—slide off our tongues with equal ease.[8]

---

8 Schlegel quoted by Chomsky (2009: 68).

However, nobody has emphasized the creative aspect of language use more strongly than Humboldt, who characterized it as *energeia* (activity), preferable to *ergon* (product, artifact), having as a fundamental property "its capacity to use its finitely specifiable mechanisms for an unbounded and unpredictable set of contingencies."[9] Underpinning this activity, only the laws of generation are fixed and immutable, its form as a systematic structure and generative principle that supplies the means and determines the scope of the creative process.

According to Chomsky's reading, Humboldt, on the one hand, remains within the Cartesian linguistic universe in considering language primarily a means of thought and self-expression, but, on the other hand, he moves away from it in suggesting that, despite the universal properties of language, which are specific to the human intellect, each particular language, taken individually, plays a role in determining the mental process, itself providing a thought world and a point of view that are unique. There is, then, a distinction between the form of a language, which is fixed and invariable, and the character of a language, which can be modified and enriched by individuals as means of expressing their specific culture, without affecting the grammatical structure. This point is where Chomsky's main objection to Humboldt's linguistics is to be found:

> For all his concern with the creative aspect of language use and with form as generative process, Humboldt does not go on to face the substantive question: what is the precise character of 'organic form' in language. He does not, so far as I can see, attempt to construct particular generative grammars or to determine the general character of any such system, the universal schema to which any particular grammar conforms.
> CHOMSKY, 2009: 75

We know that the path taken by Chomsky was a different one. He extols a Cartesian tradition that is not highly valued, known as philosophical or universal grammar, whose object of study was not grammar as 'natural history' but grammar as philosophy, or even as 'natural science'. In line with modern generative grammar, the Port-Royal *Grammar* and *Logic* take an interest in the hidden organizing principles of language which cannot be detected in 'phenomena', whether superficial or profound, and nor can they be derived from them, even through the method of European or North American structuralism.

---

9 Humboldt quoted by Chomsky (2009: 70).

Hence, as we have seen, the recourse to the 'principles and parameters' approach for providing the basis for universal grammar.

For the purposes of this study, however, taking a neglected aspect of the work of the same François Jacob who inspired the 'principles and parameters' approach, we can sketch out a critique that, to my mind, will bring greater clarity around the perspective argued here. I am referring to the question of temporality.

The various approaches analysed above are still prisoners to two different notions of temporality: the Newtonian one, which is physical, mechanical and eternal; and the Bergsonian, which is vital, creative and cumulative. The biological, anthropological and linguistic schools of thought, as a general rule, align themselves with one or other of these conceptions. Ingold's monumental effort (which drew my attention to the problem) in his *Evolution and Social Life* (1986), was largely frustrated by these ties. Biologizing thought, which we analysed at the start of our journey, falls victim to this same vice. Interdisciplinary approaches are no exceptions to the rule: vitalism, biocybernetics, biosemiotics, system theory, biolinguistics, etc.

Well, François Jacob offers us a reflection that adds a third notion of temporality. Let us go, in turn, through the three notions of temporality from Jacob's perspective. We begin with the temporality of physics. For Jacob,

> curiously enough, there is no arrow of time in the basic theories of physics. In the physical world, there are some asymmetries with respect to time, such as the expansion of the universe or the spherical electromagnetic waves that propagate outward from their source. Until rather recently, however, the fundamental laws of physics, quantum mechanics and electromagnetism, were considered time symmetric, and they are still believed to be nearly so.
>
> JACOB, 1989: 407

Unlike physics, biology incorporates time as one of its most important parameters, according to Jacob:

> The arrow of time can indeed be found throughout the whole living world, which results from an evolution in time. It can also be found in every single organism, which changes incessantly during its life. The future and the past represent totally different directions. Every creature moves from birth to death. Every individual's life is governed by development according to a plan.
>
> JACOB, 1989: 407–8

Organisms, moreover, have biological clocks that regulate their physiological cycles; they have memory, on which they base their behavior; they have an immunological system, which functions as a memory of what has happened to the individual; and a genetic system, which functions as the memory of life in general and of the species in particular.

Jacob, however, points out a new temporality, that of culture, which within this schema could be designated a *third nature*. This is the *capacity to invent a future*, expressed in the mental creation of possible worlds, even beyond the death of the organism itself. The human brain, for Jacob, acquired the capacity to break up the memorized images of past events and recombine them, from fragments, to produce hitherto unknown representations, with a view to possible *future* events.

Language, in this context, would be neither an instinct nor an artefact. Language, in reality, is the result of a biological change that granted a certain living being the capacity to *project himself in time*. In this way, if a non-human animal *behaves* and unfolds according to a predetermined *plan*, a human being, a person, *acts* and develops according to a *project*.

From this perspective, it would be appropriate to say, in my opinion, that the appearance of symbolic language is more than a mere transition 'within' the biological dimension, in the terms put forward by Maynard Smith and Szathmáry. Its advent launched the human being into a third dimension of temporality, analogous in its importance to the one that occurred in the transition from the inorganic dimension to the organic one, or, to put it another way, from the physical temporality to the biological one. The science that studies human beings, therefore, from everything that has been said, cannot be reduced to biology, even if it cannot do without it, just as the study of biology cannot do without physics, even if it transcends it, in Monod's sense.

From the perspective of this study, François Jacob's considerations are extremely important. They allow an advantageous reconnection with Humboldtian linguistics that we believe is essential to emphasize. They also make it possible to trace a path that goes from Humboldt to Tomasello and Pääbo, via Boas and Sapir, situating, from a new perspective, the contemporary arguments between Chomsky and his current critics.

In the first place, biolinguistics ends up limiting itself to the aspect of human action related to cognition. The sphere of ethics and the sphere of aesthetics, which are only comprehensible in the light of the earlier observations about temporality, do not find any suitable place in the theory. We know, on the one hand, how much Humboldt draws attention to aesthetic factors in the construction of a language. On the other hand, the noteworthy deontological aspect of human language has always been pointed out by the best philosophical and sociological tradition.

In a recent book, for example, John Searle recognizes the distinctive feature of human language:

> In human languages we have the capacity not only to represent reality, both how it is and how we want to make it be, but we also have the capacity to create a new reality by representing that reality as existing.
> SEARLE, 2007: 41

In biological temporality, these actions are impossible. We should observe, also, that we invent worlds, but we do it collectively. And not only constrained by the laws of physics and biology, but also by those worlds collectively invented by others among us. But it would be a mistake to imagine that this approach can be assimilated to the group selection perspective, which prevents the human species from projecting itself, as a whole, as a single 'group'.

Humboldt is a critic of the attempts to construct a system of philosophical grammar underpinning all natural languages. He considers the process to be riddled with western prejudice, since it violates the nature of non-European languages, forcing them to take on categories alien to their internal structures. But at the same time as he recognizes that each language, in its structure and its character, represents a specific vision of the world, he does not reject the idea of linguistic universals.

With Kant, he believes in the universality of mental structures, and that the categories that represent the laws of thought are the same ones that govern our linguistic utterances. However, he rejects the idea of deducing from this that these structures are a kind of logical, philosophical or even natural grammar.

For Humboldt, the comparing of languages requires another procedure, similar to the one that Goethe adopts for comparing plants, which makes use of the notion of the prototype. To this end, Goethe devises the idea of a protoplant, which is not a real plant, but which incorporates the essential resources found in all existing plants. Humboldt will use the analogous concept of a linguistic prototype to the same comparative ends.

Unlike Goethe's proto-plant, however, which has some materiality, since its basic characteristics can be perceived by the senses, Humboldt's linguistic prototype is not substantive; rather it is something performative, which incorporates the group of rules that should be considered common and essential to the production of speech in all languages.

Humboldt gives special attention to the system of personal pronouns, because it is from them that one can reconstruct the manifestation of the prototypical speech situation. This 'prototype for all language' finds its expression, according to Humboldt, in the differentiation between the second and third persons, between you and he. From an exclusively grammatical point of view, it makes no difference if one were to use the first-, second-or third-person pronoun, as in each case, these pronouns (I, you, he) operates as the subject of a phrase.

But to Humboldt, a difference between 'thou' and 'he' does exist. When somebody thinks, they are not alone. For there to be thought, 'thou' are a necessity who, in any case, are a thinker like 'I'. 'Thou' is a 'not I', but only in the sphere of action and common interaction, that is, a 'not I' in direct opposition to the 'I', which refers to everything that makes up the subjective universe. 'I' and 'he' really are different entities. 'He' refers to everything that is external to the individual and corresponds to the universal designation of all beings. Only with 'I' and 'he' are all the possibilities of speech exhausted.

With this analysis of pronouns, Humboldt departs from the general grammar of his time, since, instead of taking them from a logical and purely representational perspective, in the Port-Royal tradition, the conception of the pronoun that he adopts is based on the idea that language and thought, language and the world are rooted in the *act* of speech. Personal pronouns are universals in human communication.

In the author's own terms:

> *Person-words* must have been primary in every language, and that it is an altogether wrong notion to consider the pronoun as the latest of linguistic parts of speech. A narrowly grammatical mode of conceiving the replacement of the noun by the pronoun has here supplanted the insight more deeply drawn from language. The first thing is naturally the personality of the speaker himself, who stands in continuous and direct contact with nature, and cannot possibly fail, even in language, to set over against the latter the expression of his self. But, in the I, the Thou is also given automatically, and by a new opposition there arises the third person, though since the field of the sentient and speaking has now been left behind, this is also extended to the inanimate.
> HUMBOLDT, 1999: 95

This being so, if the laws governing the power to produce languages are the same everywhere, how are we to explain their diversity? For Humboldt, the appearance of a language is due to the unpredictable and immediately creative advance of human mental power. The mental endowment of individuals, however, can differ with respect to degree of clarity and mental commitment, and generative power can vary in terms of truthfulness, intensity and regularity. Imagination and emotion are also factors that contribute to this diversity. In another passage from *On Language*, Humboldt sets out his perspective on the appearance of languages in highly original terms:

> Language arises, if the simile be allowable, in much the same way that, in physical nature, one crystal builds up upon another. The formation occurs gradually, but according to a law. This initially more predominant tendency of language, as the living creation of the mind, lies in the nature of the matter; but it is also apparent in languages themselves, which possess an ever richer abundance of forms, the more primitive they are ... Once this crystallization is at an end, the language is in effect a finished product. The instrument is at hand, and it now falls to the mind to make use of it and establish itself therein. This actually takes place; and the language acquires color and character through the various ways in which the mind employs it for self-expression. It would be a great mistake, however, to suppose that what I have here kept sharply separate for purposes of clear distinction, is equally distinct in Nature. The persistent *work of the mind* in using language has a definite and continuing influence even on the true structure of language and the actual pattern of its forms; but it is a subtle influence, and sometimes escapes notice at first sight.
> HUMBOLDT, 1999: 148

Still with reference to diversity, Humboldt emphasizes what he calls the national character of language, since diversity is connected to the mental aptitudes of nations. He understands language, as we have already seen, as the mental exhalation of a national life which emerges from the simultaneous self-activity of all its members; or, to put it another way, as the self-creation of individuals depending on the nation to which they belong, and who pursue, in turn, an internal spiritual path of their own, as if the nation were an individual. The colors and character of language are, in the Humboldtian universe, clearly associated with this national character, created and modified by the creative mental activity of its members. In this way, although Humboldt believes that language is a product of human nature, common to the whole species, and, as such, it cannot be considered an artifact produced as the mere means to obtaining a particular end, he also believes that the diversity of languages rests on the diversity of forms of language, and that the diversity of forms determines how human beings think.

I need hardly say how much these reflections of Humboldt's have echoes in far later works. We find similar developments in Sapir, strongly influenced by Boas's linguistics, and, more recently, in the work of Tomasello and Pääbo. Tomasello seems to support, with a basis in recent research, the hypothesis that the acquisition of a particular natural language affects the way human beings conceive of the world. More important than this, however, is his attempt

> to find a single biological adaptation with leverage, and thus I have alighted upon the hypothesis that human beings evolved a new way of identifying with and understanding conspecifics as intentional beings.
> TOMASELLO, 1999: 204

Along similar lines, his colleague Pääbo states: "There are genetic underpinnings to our propensity for shared attention and the ability to learn complex things from others" (Pääbo, 2014: 206). Tomasello and Pääbo's idea is that we developed and inherited a *biological* capacity to live culturally. This would have happened someplace in Africa around 200,000 years ago and allowed modern men, at the origins of his evolution, to rise above other hominids by spreading themselves across the rest of the planet.

From the mutual understanding that we maintain intentional relations with the world, we acquire the faculty for imagining, with other individuals, common perspectives and objectives. We are the only organisms capable of realizing behaviors of *joint attention*, which presupposes the capacity to understand other people as intentional agents like ourselves. It also presupposes the capacity to promote social interactions in which two people pay attention to a third thing and to the other's attention to that same third thing, a situation in which the two people involved and the entity of joint attention meet on the same conceptual plane.

Note that these behaviors are not dyadic ones—which occur, say, when a child manipulates objects, ignoring whoever is around them—but triadic, since they involve a coordination of interactions, resulting in a referential triangle in which the participants' roles are interchangeable. Tomasello additionally raises the interesting hypothesis that

> the uniquely human ability to understand external events in terms of mediating intentional/ causal forces emerged first in human evolution to allow individuals to predict and explain the behavior of conspecifics and has since been transported to deal with the behavior of inert objects.
> TOMASELLO, 1999: 24

It is as though, in his view, intersubjectivity preceded objectivity.

It is evident that the competitive advantages of intentional/ causal thinking are noteworthy: it allows for the resolving of problems in a creative and prescient way, in addition to enabling very powerful processes of cultural learning and sociogenesis, through which human beings produce a new type of ontogenetic niche, culture, which is exclusive to the species for its own development. More than this, we should also note the relationship that Tomasello establishes between intersubjectivity and temporality, which is very important for the purposes of this study.

> And so, from a meta-theoretical perspective, my claim is that we cannot fully understand human cognition—at least not its uniquely human aspects—without considering in detail its unfolding in three distinct time frames:
> – in phylogenetic time, as the human primate evolved its unique ways of understanding conspecifics;
> – in historical time, as this distinctive form of social understanding led to distinctive forms of cultural inheritance involving material and symbolic artifacts that accumulate modifications over time; and
> – in ontogenic time, as human children absorb all that their cultures have to offer, developing unique modes of perspectivally based cognitive representation in the process.
> TOMASELLO, 1999: 202–3

Tomasello and Pääbo's contributions to the current debate seem very relevant. The specifically human triadic behavior and the relation of symbolic language to 'historical' temporality are important elements of a modern linguistic theory, independently of taking of a stance around the modularity or plasticity of the human brain, the precedence of thought over communication or of grammar over symbol production, questions around which the controversies seem still to be very heated and far from being settled, although I cannot myself see the process of symbol production as totally dissociated from something that can take the name of grammar.

These authors, however, seem very attached to a conception of cultural *evolution* that is still biologizing, within the frameworks of coevolutionary theory and the theory of niche construction. It is true that Tomasello has recourse to Wittgenstein and Quine to invoke the perspective nature of linguistic symbols. According to this perspective nature, there is no algorithm for determining a person's communicative intention in a given situation, except as concerns proper names and basic nouns.

Communicative intentions, then, are based on the socio-pragmatic understanding that makes linguistic references a social act par excellence. This is the only reason Tomasello refers to the Wittgensteinian concept of 'form of life'. But here, again, there is no room for the idea that that construction of possible worlds, in François Jacob's terms, can give rise to contradictory perspectives.

The idea that the third element of the triadic relationship can be in antagonistic relation to the other two; the idea that the triadic relationship produces effects more ecstatic than static; the idea that the laws of evolutionary biology (variation/selection) do not apply to human societies, which do not evolve, but r-evolve; these ideas could restore humanities to their proper place and a critical examination of the problems that the human species is facing.

In throwing contradiction out of their repertoire, the humanities are allowing themselves to be biologized, and the specific dimension of the human is lost in a pseudo-scientism which keeps nothing of science but its appearance. Hegel, in his day, had to enthrone contradiction in the realm of logic to find God. We should re-enthrone, in a proper way, dialectics in the realm of the human sciences, if we want to clear the way to finding humanity.

References

Anderson, B. (2006) *Imagined Communities: Reflections on the Origin and Spread of Nationalism*. London: Verso.

Anderson, P. (1974) *Lineages of the Absolutist State*. London: Verso.

Bagehot, W. (1872) *Physics and Politics: Or Thoughts on the Application of the Principles of 'Natural Selection' and 'Inheritance' to Political Society*. London: Henry S. King & Co.

Barth, Fredrik (1956) Ecologic Relationships of Ethnic Groups in Swat, North Pakistan. *American Anthropologist*, 58(6): 1079–89.

Bateson, G. (1958) *Naven: A Survey of the Problems Suggested by a Composite Picture of the Culture of a New Guinea Tribe Drawn from Three Points of View*. Redwood City: Stanford University Press.

Benedict, R. (1923) The Concept of the Guardian Spirit in North America. *Memoirs of the American Anthropological Association*, 29: 1–97.

Benveniste, É. (2016) *Dictionary of Indo-European Concepts and Society*. Trans. Elizabeth Palmer. Chicago: HAU Books.

Bertalanffy, L. (1968) *General System Theory: Foundations, Development, Applications*. New York: G. Braziller.

Berwick, R. and Chomsky, N. (2016) *Why Only Us: Language and Evolution*. Cambridge: MIT Press.

Berwick, R. and Chomsky, N. (2019) The Siege of Paris. *Inference*, 4(3). Available (consulted at 26 January 2024) at: https://inference-review.com/article/the-siege-of-paris.

Blackmore, S. (1999) *The Meme Machine*. New York: Oxford University Press.

Boas, F. (1938) *The Mind of Primitive Man*. New York: Macmillan.

Boas, F. (1940) *Race, Language and Culture*. New York: Macmillan.

Bornkessel-Schlesewsky, I., Schlesewsky, M., Small, S. L., and Rauschecker, J, P. (2015) Neurobiological Roots of Language in Primate Audition: Common Computational Properties. *Trends in Cognitive Sciences*, 19(3): 142–50.

Boyer, P. (2001) *Religion Explained: The Evolutionary Origins of Religious Thought*. New York: Basic Books.

Buss, D. M. (1992) Mate Preferences Mechanisms: Consequences for Partner Choice and Intrasexual Competition. In: Barkow, J., Cosmides, L., and Tooby, J. (eds) *The Adapted Mind: Evolutionary Psychology and the Generation of Culture*. New York: Oxford University Press, 249–66.

Carroll, Sean B. (2006) *Endless Forms Most Beautiful: The New Science of Evo Devo and the Making of The Animal Kingdom*. Nova York: W. W. Norton.

Cassirer, E. (1944) *An Essay on Man: An Introduction to a Philosophy of Human Culture*. New Haven: Yale University Press.

Castro, Eduardo Viveiros de (2002) *A inconstância da alma selvagem*. Rio de Janeiro: Ubu.

Chatterjee, R. (1985) Reading Whorf through Wittgenstein: A Solution to the Linguistic Relativity Problem. *Lingua*, 67(1): 37–63.

Childe, V. G. (1965) *Man Makes Himself*. London: Watts & Co.

Chomsky, N. (1966) *Cartesian Linguistics*. New York: Harper & Row.

Chomsky, N. (2006) *Language and Mind*. New York: Cambridge University Press.

Chomsky, N. (2009) *Cartesian Linguistics: A Chapter in the History of Rationalist Thought*. New York: Cambridge University Press.

Cosmides, L. and Tooby, J. (1997) *Evolutionary Psychology: A Primer*. Santa Barbara: Center for Evolutionary Psychology, UC Santa Barbara.

Darwin, C. (1871) *The Descent of Man*. London: John Murray.

Dawkins, R. (2006) *The Selfish Gene*. Oxford: Oxford University Press.

Dawkins, R. (2012) The Descent of Edward Wilson. *Prospect* (June) 6–9.

Dediu, D. and Levinson, S. C. (2018) Neanderthal Language Revisited: Not Only Us. *Current Opinion in Behavioral Sciences*, 21: 49–55.

Dennett, D. (2017) *From Bacteria to Bach and Back: The Evolution of Minds*. New York: W. W. Norton & Company.

Descola, P. (2013) *Beyond Nature and Culture*. Trans. Janet Lloyd. Chicago: Chicago University Press.

Dobzhansky, T. (1962) *Mankind Evolving: The Evolution of the Human Species*. New Haven: Yale University Press.

Dobzhansky, T. (1973) Nothing in Biology Makes Sense except in the Light of Evolution. *The American Biology Teacher*, 35(3): 125–29.

Durham, W. H. (1991) *Coevolution: Genes, Culture, and Human Diversity*. Redwood City: Stanford University Press.

Durkheim, É. (1982) *The Rules of Sociological Method*. Trans. W. D. Halls. Glencoe: The Free Press.

Eccles, J. C. (1986) Do Mental Events Cause Neural Events Analogously to the Probability Fields of Quantum Mechanics?. *Proceedings of the Royal Society of London B*, 227(1249): 411–28.

Elsasser, W. (1966) *Atom and Organism: A New Approach to Theoretical Biology*. Princeton: Princeton University Press.

Fanon, F. (2005) *The Wretched of the Earth*. Trans. Richard Philcox. New York: Grove.

Fernald, A. (1992) Human Maternal Vocalizations to Infants as Biologically Relevant Signals: An Evolutionary Perspective. In: Barkow, J., Cosmides, L., and Tooby, J. (eds) *The Adapted Mind: Evolutionary Psychology and the Generation of Culture*. New York: Oxford University Press, 391–428.

Feuerbach, L. (2012) *The Essence of Christianity*. Trans. George Eliot. New York: Dover.

Freud, S. (2003) *The Uncanny*. Trans. David McClintock. London: Penguin.

Freud, S. (2010) *Obras completas*. v. 14. Trans. Paulo César de Souza. São Paulo: Companhia das Letras.

Geertz, C. (1973) *The Interpretation of Cultures*. New York: Basic Books.

Gehlen, A. (1988) *Man: His Nature and Place in the World*. Trans. Clare McMillan and Karl Pillemer. New York: Columbia University Press.

Gil-White, F. J. (2001) Are Ethnic Groups Biological 'Species' to the Human Brain? Essentialism in Our Cognition of Some Social Categories. *Current Anthropology*, 42(4): 515–53.

Gould, S. J. and Lewontin, R. (1979) The Spandrels of San Marco and the Panglossian Paradigm: A Critique of the Adaptationist Programme. *Proceedings of the Royal Society of London B*, 205(1161): 581–98.

Gould, S. J. and Vrba, E. S. (1982) Exaptation: A Missing Term in the Science of Form. *Paleobiology*, 8(1): 4–15.

Graeber, D. (2017) Foreword. In: Sahlins, M. *Stone Age Economics*. London: Routledge.

Graeber, D. and Wengrow, D. (2021) *The Dawn of Everything: A New History of Humanity*. New York: Farrar, Straus & Giroux.

Haldane, J. B. S. (1937) A Dialectical Account of Evolution. *Science & Society*, 1(4): 473–86.

Harris, M. (1968) *The Rise of Anthropological Theory: A History of Theories of Culture*. New York: Thomas Y. Crowell.

Heidegger, M. (2001) *Being and Time*. Trans. John Macquarrie and Edward Robinson. Oxford: Blackwell.

Herder, J. G. (2012) *Philosophical Writings*. Trans. Michael N. Forster. Cambridge: Cambridge University Press.

Hicks, J. (1969) *A Theory of Economic History*. Oxford: Clarendon Press.

Humboldt, W. (1999) *On Language*. Trans. Peter Heath. Cambridge: Cambridge University Press.

Husserl, E. (2013) *Cartesian Meditations: An Introduction to Phenomenology*. Dordrecht: Springer Netherlands.

Ingold, T. (1986) *Evolution and Social Life*. Cambridge: Cambridge University Press.

Ingold, T. (2021) *The Perception of the Environment: Essays on Livelihood, Dwelling and Skill*. London: Routledge.

Jablonka, E. and Lamb, M. J. (2014) *Evolution in Four Dimensions: Genetic, Epigenetic, Behavioral, and Symbolic Variation in the History of Life*. Cambridge, MA: MIT Press.

Jacob, F. (1989) *The Logic of Life: A History of Heredity and The Possible and the Actual*. Trans. Betty E. Spillmann. London: Penguin.

James, H. (1890) *The Principles of Psychology*. New York: Henry Holt & Co.

Kant, Immanuel (1970) Reviews of Herder's *Ideas on the Philosophy of the History of Mankind*. In: *Political Writings*. Ed. H. Reiss, trans. H. B. Nisbet. Cambridge: Cambridge University Press, 201–20.

Kienpointner, M. (1996) Whorf and Wittgenstein: Language, World View and Argumentation. *Argumentation*, 10: 475–94.

Kroeber, A. L. (1915) Eighteen Professions. *American Anthropologist*, 17(2): 283–88.

Kroeber, A. L. (1917) The Superorganic. *American Anthropologist*, 19(2): 163–213.

Kroeber, A. L. (1952) *The Nature of Culture*. Chicago: Chicago University Press.

Laland, K. N., Odling-Smee, J., and Feldman, M. W. (2000) Niche Construction, Biological Evolution, and Cultural Change. *Behavioral and Brain Sciences*, 23(1): 131–75.

Laland, K. N., Odling-Smee, J., and Gilbert, S. F. (2008). EvoDevo and Niche Construction: Building Bridges. *Journal of Experimental Zoology Part B*, 310(7): 549–66.

Laland, K. N., Uller, T., Feldman, M. W., et al. (2015) The Extended Evolutionary Synthesis: Its Structure, Assumptions and Predictions. *Proceedings of the Royal Society B*, 282(1813): 20151019.

Lehrman, D. S. (1953) A Critique of Konrad Lorenz's Theory of Instinctive Behavior. *Quarterly Review of Biology*, 28(4): 337–63.

Lenneberg, E. H. (1967) *Biological Foundations of Language*. New York: John Wiley and Sons.

Lerner, A. P. (1938) Is Professor Haldane's Account of Evolution Dialectical?. *Science & Society*, 2(2): 232–42.

Lévi-Straus, C. (1952) *Race and History*. Paris: Unesco.

Lévi-Strauss, C. (1963) *Structural Anthropology*. Trans. Claire Jacobson and Brooke Grundfest Schoepf. New York: Basic Books.

Lévi-Strauss, C. (1976) *Structural Anthropology 2*. Trans. Monique Layton. New York: Basic Books.

Levinas, E. (1991) *Totality and Infinity: An Essay on Exteriority*. Dordrecht: Kluver Academic Publishers.

Lewin, R. (1974) Accidental Career. *New Scientist*, 61: 322–25.

Lewontin, R. and Levins, R. (2007) *Biology Under the Influence: Dialectical Essays on Ecology, Agriculture, and Health*. New York: Monthly Review Press.

Lewontin, R. C. (2002) *The Triple Helix: Gene, Organism, and Environment*. Cambridge, MA: Harvard University Press.

Lorenz, K. (1937) On the Formation of the Concept of Instinct. *Natural Sciences*, 25(19): 289–300.

Lowie, R. (1920) *Primitive Society*. New York: Boni & Liveright.

Lucas Jr., E. (1988) On the Mechanics of Economic Development. *Journal of Monetary Economics*, 22(1): 3–42.

Malthus, T. R. (1985) *An Essay on the Principle of Population*. London: Penguin.

Margenau, H. (1984) *The Miracle of Existence*. Boston: New Science Library.

Marx, K. (1963) *The Poverty of Philosophy*. New York: International Publishers.

Marx, K. (1973) *Grundrisse*. Trans. Martin Nicolaus. London: Penguin.

Marx, K. (1992) Critique of Hegel's Dialectic and General Philosophy. Trans. Gregor Benton. In: *Early Writings*. London: Penguin, 379–400.
Marx, K. and Engels, F. (1970) *The German Ideology: Part 1*. New York: International Publishers.
Mauss, M. (2005) *A General Theory of Magic*. London: Taylor & Francis.
Mauss, M. (2016) *The Gift: Expanded Edition*. Trans. Jane I. Guyer. Chicago: HAU Books.
Mayr, E. (1966) *Animal Species and Evolution*. Cambridge: Harvard University Press.
Meillassoux, C. (1986) *Anthropologie de l'esclavage*. Paris: PUF.
Miller, G. F. (2001) *The Mating Mind: How Sexual Choice Shaped the Evolution of Human Nature*. New York: Anchor Books.
Monod, J. (1972) *Chance and Necessity*. Trans. Austryn Weinhouse. New York: Vintage Books.
Müller, G. (2007) Evo-Devo: Extending the Evolutionary Synthesis. *Nature Reviews Genetics* 8(12): 943–49.
Nairn, T. (1975) The Modern Janus. *New Left Review*, I(94): 3–25.
North, D. (1990) *Institutions, Institutional Change and Economic Performance*. Cambridge: Cambridge University Press.
Nowak, M. A., Tarnita, C. E., and Wilson, E. O. (2010) The Evolution of Eusociality. *Nature*, 466(7310): 1057–62.
Pääbo, S. (2014) *Neanderthal Man: In Search of Lost Genomes*. New York: Basic Books.
Patterson, O. (1982) *Slavery and Social Death*. Cambridge, MA: Harvard University Press.
Pinker, S. (1997) *How the Mind Works*. New York: W. W. Norton & Company.
Pinker, S. (2007) *The Stuff of Thought: Language as a Window into Human Nature*. New York: Viking.
Pinker, S. (2015) *The Language Instinct: The New Science of Language and Mind*. London: Penguin.
Pinker, S. and Bloom, P. (1990) Natural language and natural selection. *Behavioral and Brain Sciences* 13: 707–84.
Polanyi, K. (1957a) Aristotle Discovers Economy. In: Polanyi, K., Arensberg, C. M., and Pearson, H. W. (eds) *Trade and Market in the Early Empires: Economies in History and Theory*. Glencoe: The Free Press, 64–94.
Polanyi, K. (1957b) The Economy as Instituted Process. In: Polanyi, K., Arensberg, C. M., and Pearson, H. W. (eds) *Trade and Market in the Early Empires: Economies in History and Theory*. Glencoe: The Free Press, 243–70.
Polanyi, K. (1977) *The Livelihood of Man*. New York: Academic Press.
Quine, W. V. O. (1960) *Word and Object*. New York: MIT Press; Wiley.
Quine, W. V. O. (1968) Replies. *Synthese* (19)1–2: 264–322.
Quine, W. V. O. (1987a) Indeterminacy of Translation Again. *Journal of Philosophy*, 84(1): 5–10.

Quine, W. V. O. (1987b) Meaning. In: *Quiddities: An Intermittently Philosophical Dictionary*. Cambridge, MA: Harvard University Press, 130–31.

Raatikainen, P. (2005) On How to Avoid the Indeterminacy of Translation. *The Southern Journal of Philosophy*, 43(3): 295–413.

Radcliffe-Brown, A. R. (1935) On the Concept of Function in Social Science. *American Anthropologist*, 37(3): 394–402.

Radcliffe-Brown, A. R. (1940) On Social Structure. *The Journal of the Royal Anthropological Institute of Great Britain and Ireland*, 70(1): 1–12.

Richerson, P. J. and Boyd, R. (2005) *Not by Genes Alone: How Culture Transformed Human Evolution*. Chicago: University of Chicago Press.

Romer, P. M. (1986) Increasing Returns and Long-Run Growth. *Journal of Political Economy*, 94(5): 1002–38.

Sahlins, M. (1972) *Stone Age Economics*. Chicago: Aldine Atherton.

Sahlins, M. (1976) *Culture and Practical Reason*. Chicago: University of Chicago Press.

Sahlins, M. D. and Service, E. R. (eds) (1960) *Evolution and Culture*. Ann Arbor: University of Michigan Press.

Said, E. W. (1979) *Orientalism*. New York: Vintage Books.

Sapir, E. (1921) *Language: An Introduction to the Study of Speech*. New York: Harcourt, Brance & Co.

Sapir, E. (1929) The Status of Linguistics as a Science. *Language*. 5(4): 207–14.

Sapir, E. (1963) *Selected Writings*. Oakland: University of California Press.

Sartre, J. P. (2019) *Sartre no Brasil: A conferência de Araraquara*. São Paulo: Editora Unesp.

Schmalhausen, I. I. (1960) Evolution and Cybernetics. *Evolution*, 14(4): 509–24.

Schmidt, A. (2014) *The Concept of Nature in Marx*. London: Verso.

Searle, J. (2007) *John Searle's Philosophy of Language*. Ed. Savas L. Tsohatzidis. New York: Cambridge University Press.

Smith, J. M. (1978) *The Evolution of Sex*. Cambridge: Cambridge University Press.

Smith, J. M. (1993) *The Theory of Evolution*. Cambridge: Cambridge University Press.

Smith, J. M. and Szathmáry, E. (1999) *The Origins of Life: From the Birth of Life to the Origin of Language*. Oxford: Oxford University Press.

Spencer, H. (1867) *First Principles*. London: Williams & Norgate.

Spencer, H. (1876) *The Principles of Sociology*. London: Williams & Norgate.

Strathern, M. (1990) *The Gender of the Gift Problems with Women and Problems with Society in Melanesia*. Berkeley: California University Press.

Strathern, M. (2017) *O efeito etnográfico e outros ensaios*. São Paulo: Ubu.

Tomasello, M. (1995) Language Is Not an Instinct. *Cognitive Development*, 10: 131–56.

Tomasello, M. (1999) *The Cultural Origins of Human Cognition*. Cambridge, MA: Harvard University Press.

Tomasello, M. (2019) *Becoming Human: A Theory of Ontogeny*. Cambridge, MA: Harvard University Press.

Tooby, J. and Cosmides, L. (1989) Evolutionary Psychology and the Generation of Culture: 1. Theoretical Considerations. *Ethology and Sociobiology* 10(1–3): 29–49.
Tooby, J. and Cosmides, L. (1992) The Psychological Foundations of Culture. In: Barkow, J., Cosmides, L., and Tooby, J. (eds) *The Adapted Mind: Evolutionary Psychology and the Generation of Culture.* New York: Oxford University Press, 19–136.
Tremlett, P. F. (2011) Structure Amongst the Modules: Lévi-Strauss and Cognitive Theorizing about Religion. *Theory and Method in the Study of Religion,* 23(3–4): 351–366.
Uexküll, J. (1926) *Theoretical Biology.* Trans. Doris Livingston Mackinnon. London: K. Paul, Trench, Trubner & Co.
Veblen, T. (1915) *Imperial Germany and the Industrial Revolution.* New York: Macmillan.
Waddington, C. H. (1942) Canalization of Development and the Inheritance of Acquired Characters. *Nature,* 150: 563–65.
Waddington, C. H. (2015) *The Strategy of the Genes: A Discussion of Some Aspects of Theoretical Biology.* London: Routledge.
Waddington, C. H. (2016) *An Introduction to Modern Genetics.* London: Routledge.
Wagner, R. (1981) *The Invention of Culture.* Chicago: Chicago University Press.
Weber, M. (1981) *General Economic History.* New Brunswick, NJ: Transaction Publishers.
Weber, M. (2012) *Collected Methodological Writings.* Trans. Hans Henrik Bruun. London: Routledge.
Wheeler, W. M. (1911) The Ant Colony as an Organism. *Journal of Morphology,* 22: 307–25.
Whorf, B. L. (2012a) Science and Linguistics. In: *Language, Thought, and Reality: Selected Writings of Benjamin Lee Whorf.* Cambridge, MA: MIT Press, 265–80.
Whorf, B. L. (2012b) The Relation of Habitual Thought and Behavior to Language. In: *Language, Thought, and Reality: Selected Writings of Benjamin Lee Whorf.* Cambridge, MA: MIT Press, 173–204.
Wiener, N. (1985) *Cybernetics: Or Control and Communication in the Animal and the Machine.* Cambridge, MA: MIT Press.
Wilson, D. S. and Wilson, E. O. (2007) Rethinking the Theoretical Foundation of Sociobiology. *The Quarterly Review of Biology,* 82(4): 327–48.
Wilson, E. O. (1975) *Sociobiology: The New Synthesis.* Cambridge, MA: Harvard University Press.
Wilson, E. O. (1978) *On Human Nature.* Cambridge, MA: Harvard University Press.
Wilson, M. and Daly, M. (1992) The Man Who Mistook His Wife for a Chattel. In: Barkow, J., Cosmides, L., and Tooby, J. (eds) *The Adapted Mind: Evolutionary Psychology and the Generation of Culture.* New York: Oxford University Press, 289–322.
Winch, P. (1964) Understanding a Primitive Society. *American Philosophical Quarterly,* 1(4): 307–24.
Wittgenstein, L. (1964) *The Blue and Brown Books.* Oxford: Basil Blackwell.

Wittgenstein, L. (1967a) *Lectures and Conversations on Aesthetics, Psychology and Religious Belief.* Berkeley: University of California Press.

Wittgenstein, L. (1967b) *Zettel.* Trans. G. E. M. Anscombe. Oxford: Basil Blackwell.

Wittgenstein, L. (1969) *On Certainty.* New York: Harper.

Wittgenstein, L. (2009) *Philosophical Investigations.* Trans. G. E. M. Anscombe, P. M. S. Hacker and Joachim Schulte. Malden: Wiley-Blackwell.

Index

abundance 69–70, 75
accumulation 97
  capital 66, 87–89
  cultural 39, 122, 124
  primitive 94
adaptation 9–10, 12–14, 17, 26, 29, 33, 35–36, 43, 64–65, 100, 102–3, 131, 134, 146
  adult 12, 41, 103, 132
  cultural 25–27, 31, 33, 42, 104
  meme 20, 27
Africa 59, 72, 94, 135, 137, 146
  African culture 59
  African peoples 94
  and slave labor 53
agriculture 10, 36, 48, 65, 71–72, 86
alien 4, 50, 57, 74, 137
alienation 5, 58, 72, 79, 85, 88
alienization 4–5, 50–51, 53, 57–58, 72–73, 75–76, 85–86, 94, 97–99, 121, 125–28
allele 16, 19
allopatry 48–49
alter 4, 50
altruism 10, 13–17, 21, 30, 38, 71, 73–74
  gene 16
Americas 52, 72
Amerindian peoples 53, 95
Amerindian perspectivism 70–71
  See also Castro, Eduardo Viveiros de
anagenesis 48
  anatomy 33, 104–5
  human 26, 33, 105, 122, 124–25, 135
Anderson, Benedict 92–93, 95, 110
Anderson, Perry 90–91
animal 9, 12, 28, 30, 33, 36, 39, 45–49, 55, 57–58, 69–70, 74, 80, 83, 99–101, 103–6, 121–23, 128–29, 139, 142
  domesticated 57, 71–72, 86
  hot-blooded 104
  sexed 38
  social 34
  wild 118
Annales School 58
anthropobiology 101–2
anthropogenesis 57, 125
anthropological materialism 82

anthropology 2, 4–5, 7, 11, 17, 29, 40, 46–47, 50, 58, 60–61, 65–67, 81, 95, 101, 107, 121, 125–26, 141
  American 46
  and Marxism 84–86, 89, 92
  cognitive 26
  dialectical 46, 84–85
  economic 67, 68n3
  functionalist 129. See also Malinowski, Bronislaw
  interpretative 110–11, 123–24. See also Geertz, Clifford
  philosophical 100, 123. See also Gehlen, Arnold
  structural 53, 84
anthropomorphism 8, 16, 78
Aristotle 69
art 10, 34, 37, 48, 70, 100, 129, 135
artefact 30, 37, 47, 101, 131, 142
  language as symbolic 131, 135
Auerbach, Erich 93
Australopithecus (genus) 123

Bagehot, Walter 35
Barth, Fredrik 60, 64
Bateson, Gregory 61–63
behavior 8, 10, 13, 27, 32, 39, 77, 96, 103, 137, 139, 142, 146
  altruistic 13–14
  behaviorism 112, 130–31. See also Skinner, B. F.
  children 130
  cooperative 15
  cultural 26, 122
  human 25, 40–42, 44, 47, 60, 67, 102–3, 108, 112, 117, 122–23, 129–31, 139, 146–47
  instinctive 103
  linguistic 108, 111–12, 114, 132
  social 13–15, 46, 62
  symbolic 135
Benedict, Ruth 59
Benjamin, Walter 93
Benveniste, Émile 57
Bernard, Claude 63

Bertalanffy, Ludwig von   18, 34, 63, 105–7, 110, 125, 138
Berwick, Robert C.   133–34, 136–37
biology   2–3, 7–11, 17–19, 21, 23–25, 27–28, 31, 33–34, 38–41, 44–45, 49, 58, 63–64, 67, 75, 85, 101, 104, 106–8, 125–26, 136, 141–43
    evolutionary biology   44, 148
Blackmore, Susan   19
Bloomfield, Leonard   136
Blumenbach, Johann Friedrich   57
Boas, Franz   46–49, 51, 54, 108–10, 136, 142, 146
body   19, 21, 38, 71, 104
    human   19, 24, 40, 42, 57, 100, 104, 124, 130, 136
    mind-body interaction   101
Bohr, Niels   60
Bornkessel-Schlesewsky, Ina   134
Bowles, Samuel   67
Boyd, Robert   25–28, 45
Boyer, Pascal   45
Braidwood, Robert   71
brain   19, 20, 23, 27, 123
    and language   130–31, 133, 147
    and mind   23, 40
    human   19, 29, 31–32, 40, 43, 122–25, 142
Brazil
    Brazilian politics   1–2
brother   15, 38, 74
Bücher, Karl   68
Buss, David M.   45

Cannon, Walter Bradford   63
capital   87, 89, 94
    and state   89
    fixed   86–87
    human   66
    mobile   89
capitalism   87–90, 92
    ecological   88
    industrial   82, 94
    modern Western   89
Carnap, Rudolf   112–14
Carroll, Sean   137
Cassirer, Ernst   32–34, 104, 106, 110, 139
caste   53, 57
    in India   60

castration   37
Castro, Eduardo Viveiros de   2, 62–63, 71–72, 84
cattle-raising   48, 65, 71–72
celibacy   10
cell   21–22, 38, 55–56
    eukaryotic   27
    nerve   23
change
    organic   125
    revolutionary   17
    sub-organic   37
Chatterjee, Ranjit   116n3
chemistry   2–3, 7, 10, 11, 21–22
    biochemistry   137
    chemical structures   137
    inorganic   2, 4, 24, 37, 57, 101, 142
    molecules   55
child, childhood   9, 12–13, 26–27, 36–38, 41–42, 44, 102, 115, 129–31, 133, 138, 146–47
Childe, Gordon   63, 67, 71
choice   15, 22, 26, 29, 66–68, 129
    language   113–14
    sexual   51
Chomsky, Noam   1, 4, 7, 61, 96, 130–40, 142
Chomsky, Valéria   1
chromosome   16, 38
civilization   39–40, 47, 51–53, 59, 68, 97, 127
cladogenesis   48
clan   54, 57, 75
class   5, 10, 36, 53, 57, 62, 67, 76, 89
climate   26, 27, 36
coalition
    cultural   52–53
    organism   54
coevolution   11, 25, 27, 29, 32, 37, 125, 147
    culture   27
    gene-culture   28, 30
    mutualisms   27
colonialism   53, 94
colonization   55, 65
    of Latin America   52
colony   55, 94
    eusocial   39. *See also* superorganism
    insect   14, 24, 35, 38, 72
    selfish genes   19, 21
    vertebrates   35

INDEX 159

community 12, 62, 69, 74, 76, 92–94, 119
    and grammar 117
    and language 95, 108, 136
    cultural 95
    isolated 1
    moral 55
    political 92
    primitive 83, 119
    reader 94
    tribal 28
competition 9, 15, 17, 135, 147
    coevolutionary 27
    economic 68, 87, 89
    gene 16
    group 60
Comte, Auguste 34, 54
Condorcet, Marquis de 10
conformism 26–27
consciousness 24, 27, 45, 56, 78–81, 83, 100, 127
    national 94, 96, 99
    social 81–82
    tribal 80
continuity 58, 61
contradiction 3–6, 18, 24, 58, 65, 74–76, 84, 98, 118–19, 126, 148
    dialectic 3, 21
    in culture speciation 58
    in Hegel 77, 85
    in Marx 80, 84
    in structural anthropology 53
cooperation 15, 28, 36, 39, 68, 74, 79, 83, 119
    animal 74
    cultural 67
    gene 16, 19, 21, 29
    meme 10
    species. *See also* mutualism
Cosmides, Leda 31, 40–45, 122, 131
cosmology 1
Covid pandemic 2
culture 2, 12–13, 18–26, 28, 30–32, 37–41, 44–48, 51, 58–59, 64, 70, 73–74, 81, 95, 102, 105–6, 110, 119, 122–24, 126, 142
    acculturation 64
    African 59
    alienization 58, 85–86
    and language 107–9, 115–16
    and nature 4, 71

and race 95–96
and symbolic language 33
and taboo 51
animal 'culture' 8, 45–46
as 'second nature' 24, 27, 32, 37, 56, 75, 88, 102, 105, 120
cultural adaptation 26–27
cultural coevolution 28, 125
cultural dynamic, cultural change 3–4, 21, 25, 29–32, 34, 41, 48, 58, 66, 87, 110
cultural transmission 19–20, 26
cultural variants 25–31, 33. *See* memes
diffusion 65, 67
diversity 52–53
European 59, 91
Evolution. *See* evolution, cultural evolution
in Marx 82
incommensurability of cultures 2
intercultural relations 4–5, 52, 58, 60, 62, 64–65
isolated 52
material 47–48
primitive 48
shift from biology 3–4, 9, 11, 23–24
speciation, differentiation 4, 34, 48–50, 54, 63, 72, 75, 95, 98. *See also* alienization
Western 59
Cuvier, Georges 7, 34, 136
cybernetics 18, 21–23, 42, 63, 141
    biocybernetics 21, 34
    systems 22, 33

Daly, Martin 45
Darwin, Charles 9, 13–15, 27, 32, 35, 46–48, 129, 134, 136
Darwinism 19, 29, 33, 34, 131
    cultural 31
    social 34
Dawkins, Richard 10–11, 16–17, 19–21, 26–29, 37–38
dealienization 8, 51
Dediu, Dan 135n7
Dennett, Daniel 19
depersonalization 4–5, 57–58, 72–73, 86, 94, 126
Descola, Philippe 2, 84

determinism   42, 82
  Darwinian   134
  genetic   14
  linguistic   129
development   17, 35, 54, 64, 66, 68, 89, 101,
    134, 137, 141–42. *See also* evolutionary
    developmental biology
  agricultural   71
  animal   49
  civilization   47
  cognitive   126. *See also* Piaget, Jean
  cultural   30–32, 39, 47, 52, 64–65, 78, 96,
    126, 146
  economic, industrial, productive   47, 48,
    66–67, 76, 83, 87–89, 91, 94
  historical   45, 83, 127
  individual   42
  language   108, 130, 133
  mankind   125
  mind   44
  moral   126. *See also* Kohlberg, Lawrence
  nation   7
  new techniques   106
  organic   35, 39, 124
  organism   44
  social   35, 54
dialectics   3–5, 11, 21, 48, 50, 58, 61, 63, 76, 92,
    94, 125, 127, 148
  Hegelian   17, 77
  of culture dynamic   65
Diamond, Jared   71
difference   3–6, 27, 42, 53, 55–56, 58, 75, 84,
    105, 127
  behavioral   14, 60
  biological   134
  cultural   43, 52, 60, 98, 127
  epistemological   113
  linguistic   96, 98, 110, 114, 144
  social   57
  superstructural   51
discontinuity   8, 44, 59, 61, 66, 92, 134
dispersion, dispersal
  animal   12
  feudal   90
  human   47–48, 52, 54
divergence
  animal   49
  behavioral   14

  cultural   52, 64
  evolutionary   64
  social   54
diversity   58, 136–37
  cultural   51–53, 55, 106–7, 127
  ethnic, racial   60, 134
  linguistic   93, 96, 98, 110, 136–37, 144–45
  natural   96
  phylogenetic   45
DNA   32, 135
Dobzhansky, Theodosius   28, 33n5, 48
domination   4, 57, 65, 86
dualism   24, 40–41, 101
  mind-brain   23
  nature/culture   71
Durham, William   30n4
Durkheim, Émile   40, 54–58, 63

Eccles, John   23–24, 41
ecology   4–5, 29–31, 37, 60, 64–65, 69–72, 84,
    88, 98, 121, 137
economics, economy   4–6, 48, 66–76, 86,
    90–91, 97–98, 122, 127
  and biology   67
  and exchange   71–76
  and history   66
  and language   108
  contemporary   66–67
  development   38
  domestic   100
  economic forms   48
  economic transactions, relations   73
  evolutionary   67. *See also* Nelson,
    Richard R and Winter, Sidney G.
  in Aristotle   69
  in Marx   81–88
  in Weber   89
  inner   21
  national   74
  neoclassical   81, 88
  neuro-economics   67. *See also*
    Fehr, Ernst
  non-market   68
  political   75, 81
  primitive   67, 71–76
  tribal   74
ecosystem   30, 44
ego   4, 50

INDEX   161

Einstein, Albert   1. *See also* theory of relativity
Eldredge, Niles   18
Elsasser, Walter   23
emancipation   5–6, 8, 80, 90
   national   94
emotion   36, 45, 50, 79, 122, 145
endogamy   12–13
enemy   48–49, 98
Engels, Friedrich   17, 79–80, 135
environment   7, 8, 15, 17, 36, 44, 65, 69, 89, 102, 121
   and adaptation   17, 25–26, 28–30, 33, 65, 103
   and behavior   130
   and culture   25–28, 30–31, 41–44, 46–48, 64, 73, 96, 104, 106, 125, 127
   and metabolism   18, 63
   developmental   42
   inorganic   36
   social   27
   superorganic   36–37
enzyme   22
equilibrium   129
   cultural   58, 62–63
   demographic   60
   ecological   60
   eugeny   9
   organism   21
   punctuated. *See* Theory, Punctuated equilibrium
Eurasia   135
Europe   52, 59, 119, 136, 140
   Eastern Europe   90
   European expansionism   97
   European powers   53
   European races   95
eusociality   37, 39
evo-devo. *See* Evolutionary developmental biology
evolution, evolutionism   2–3, 7–9, 14, 17–19, 24, 26–28, 30, 35, 37, 42, 44, 54–56, 63–64, 66, 75, 111, 125, 128, 13, 1, 134–35, 137, 141, 146
   biolinguistic   7
   biological   3, 10–11, 19–22, 25, 29, 39, 45–48, 64–65, 105
   cultural   3, 8, 10–11, 14, 20–22, 25–31, 45–47, 63–65, 126, 147

Darwinian theory of   32, 46. *See also* Darwin, Charles
evolutionary developmental biology   137. *See also* Carroll, Sean; Müller, Gerd
   gene-culture   28, 30
   genetic   20, 25, 27, 30
   human   125
   inorganic   36
   molecular   22
   of language   134–35
   sex   11, 16
   social   56
   Spencerian theory of   34–37. *See also* Spencer, Herbert
evolutionary game theory   15–16. *See also* Trivers, Robert
evolutionary reversibility   8
Extended Evolutionary Synthesis   32, 137

Fanon, Frantz   94
father   9, 38, 98
feedback   21, 29, 44, 63, 88, 123
Fehr, Ernst   67
Feigl, Herbert   23
Feldman, Marcus W.   29–30
Fernald, Anne   45
Feuerbach, Ludwig   5, 50, 76–79, 85, 99
fire   8, 57, 118
Fisher, Ronald   13, 134
Ford, Henry   93
freedom   22, 71, 73, 100
Freud, Sigmund   4, 50–51, 85
friend, friendship   57, 73, 79
function   36, 62
   chemical   21, 22
   language   133
   organism, organ   54, 56
   political   90
   social   56–57, 120
functionalism   62, 83, 129

Galton, Francis   9
Geertz, Clifford   40, 110, 121–26
Gehlen, Arnold   100–6, 123, 125–26, 128
gender   5, 57
   female   13, 16, 38, 104
   male   38

gene 2, 8, 9, 12, 15–20, 24–29, 38–39, 42, 74, 131–32, 134–35
  and meme 10–11
  and the environment 18
  flow 48, 50, 64, 75, 135
  gene pool 9, 16
  phenotypical effects 20
  propagation 10
  recessive 12
  regulation 137
  selfish 10, 16–17, 21. See also Dawkins, Richard
  transmission 19, 27, 41
gene-culture coevolution 26–28, 30
general systems theory 18, 63. See also Bertalanffy, Ludwig von
genetics 4, 11, 14–15, 21, 31, 44, 126, 142, 146
  genetic change, alteration 7, 14, 30, 123
  genetic exchange 39
  genetic introgression 135
  genetic variants 25
genocide 53
genome
  cultural 11, 19
  human 132
genotype 14, 43
Geoffroy, Étienne 7, 136
geography 48–49, 52, 60, 65, 71, 86, 95
germ 11–12
German Historical School 58
gift 73, 75–76
Gil-White, Francisco José 28
Gintis, Herbert 67
God 77–78, 99, 148
Godelier, Maurice 84
Goethe, Johann Wolfgang von 143
Gould, Stephen Jay 18, 131n6
Gouldner, Alvin W. 73
Graeber, David 63, 70–71, 84
grammar 107, 116–18, 136, 140, 147
  generative 1–2, 26, 61, 130–33, 137, 139–41. See also Chomsky, Noam
  language 47, 107–8, 117, 129, 131–32, 140, 144
  philosophical 143
  Port-Royal 140
  social 28
group 13–16, 25, 27–28, 35–37, 42, 60, 90, 143

alienized 4, 74
  and genetics 41
  and gift 75. See also Mauss, Marcel
  competing 60
  cultural 25–28, 41–42, 44, 49–50, 64, 98, 127
  ethnic 28, 60
  gene 131
  human 3–5, 11–13, 26–29, 41, 43, 47–48, 50, 52, 57, 62–63, 73–74, 84, 86, 97–99, 108, 116, 126–27
  isolated 47, 51
  linguistic 95–96, 98, 108
  moral 75
  primitive 68
  social 46, 53, 73, 79
  taxonomic 13
growth 36
  cultural 39
  economic 66, 80, 90
  population 9–10, 80

Habermas, Jürgen 82
Haddad, Ana Estela 1
Haldane, J.B.S. 15, 17, 18, 134–35
Hamilton, William D. 14, 15, 37–38
Hamilton's Rule 14–15. See also Hamilton, William D.
Hare, Hope 38
Harris, Martin 46
Harris, Zellig 136
Hartmann, Nicolai 101, 123
Hayes, Carlton 92
Hegel, Georg Wilhelm Friedrich 50, 76, 77–79, 85, 99, 126, 148
Heidegger, Martin 95, 99
Herder, Johann Gottfried von 96–101, 126, 128, 139
heredity 10, 14, 18, 39–40, 134
heterogeneity 35, 51, 54, 92
Hicks, John R. 86
history 4–6, 41, 45, 47, 51–52, 54, 58, 65, 69–70, 79, 84, 86, 93, 95–96, 99, 121, 126–27, 147
  developmental 49, 127
  economic 66, 89
  historical forms, patterns 68, 73, 79
  historical phenomena 41, 92

history (*cont.*)
   historical processes   53, 65, 77, 120, 126
   historical transitions   5, 58
   in Marx   81–85, 91–92
   natural   140
   of evolution   27
Holocene   27
homeostasis   21–22, 32, 63
Homer   72
Homo (genus)   125, 135
Homo heidelbergensis   135
Homo sapiens   72, 123, 125
homogeneity, homogenization   35, 51–53, 56, 65, 93
horde   54, 58, 70
Humboldt, Wilhelm von   4, 96, 134, 140, 142–45
hunting, hunter   36, 65, 68, 70–71, 74, 104
Huxley, Julian   64*n*2

idealism
   Hegelian   5, 77, 79, 85
identity   3, 5–6, 47, 58, 77, 84, 92, 98, 115
ideology   65, 92
impulse   128–29
   biological   10, 50
   human   103, 123, 128–29
   incest   12, 50–2, 57
   religious   93
   sexual   51
India
   caste system   60
individual   8–9, 10, 16, 24, 36–37, 39, 42, 72, 141–42, 146
   alienizated   50
   altruistical   14
   and culture   11, 25–26, 29, 40–41, 44, 46, 53, 62, 75, 84, 120
   and genes   10, 12, 16–17
   and group selection   13–14
   and language   96, 107, 111, 127, 129–30, 133, 136, 140, 144–45
   and memes   10, 29
   and reproduction   13
   and sex   17
   and society   55–57, 79, 87–88, 90
   and species   9, 13
   cooperative   39
   selfish   14
individuation   29
information   8, 27, 40–41, 43, 122, 130
   cultural   25, 27, 60, 127
   genetic   8, 26, 32
   meme   22. *See also* Dawkins, Richard
   scientific   8
   symbolic   32
   technological   8
Ingold, Tim   2, 46, 47–48, 84, 141
inheritance   32, 43, 56, 91, 125
   cultural   20, 27, 116, 147
   genetic   21, 29, 39, 41, 43, 50, 146
   niche   30
   symbolic   32
insect   14, 24, 35–39, 72
instinct   43, 45, 47, 79, 99, 100, 102–3, 123–24, 126–32
   animal   39, 99–100, 103
   kin   26
   language   45, 101, 127, 129–32, 139, 142. *See also* Pinker, Steve
   religious   45, 74–75, 127, 132
   tribal   28–29, 45, 74–75, 92, 126, 132
institution   28, 49, 54, 65–69, 101, 103, 123–24
   coercive   28
   community   69
   economic   68–69
   family   69
institutionalism   65–66
Integrated Causal Model (ICM)   41–43. *See also* Tooby, John; Cosmides, Leda
integration   35, 64, 68–69, 73–74, 90
intelligence   10, 36, 39, 78, 130
   animal   101
interaction   44, 124, 144, 146
   allosteric   22
   animal   74
   between physiology and psychology   44
   brain   31
   cultural   31
   gene-culture   26
   genes and environment   18
   group   60
   human   79
   interdependence   11, 43, 74
   metabolic   18
   mind-brain   23
   social   44, 146
   with environment   25, 44

isolation   1, 7, 47–48, 51–52, 55, 60, 80, 95, 111, 132
  cultural   52
  geographical   60
  reproductive   49

Jablonka, Eva   30–33
Jacob, François   3, 24, 105, 137, 139, 141–42, 148
Jakobson, Roman   61
James, William   101, 127–29, 131

Kant, Immanuel   97, 99, 104–5, 109, 138–39, 143
Kienpointner, Manfred   116n3
Kluckhohn, Clyde   124
Kohlberg, Lawrence   126
Kroeber, Alfred L.   26, 37–41, 58, 60, 124

labor   68, 70, 76, 86–87, 89, 94, 120
  division of   36, 56, 58, 80
  in Marx   76, 80, 82–83
  slave   53, 86, 90
  spiritual   77
Laland, Kevin N.   29–30, 32
Lamarck, Jean-Baptiste de   7, 34
Lamb, Marion J.   30–33
language   1–2, 5, 17, 19, 24, 26, 32, 34, 45, 47–48, 78, 80–81, 83, 85, 95–103, 107–20, 125–26, 128, 130–40, 142–46
  acquisition   112, 132–34, 145
  animal   99–100
  computer   138
  contact   31
  Creole   133
  language instinct   45, 129, 132
  Romance   94
  sign   8, 36
  symbolic   3–5, 18, 27, 32, 45, 47, 70, 75, 84–85, 95, 100–1, 105, 126–27, 129, 135, 142, 147
  written   93–94
Latin America
  colonization   52, 53
learning   26–27, 41, 104, 119, 121, 124–25, 130–31, 146
  cultural   147
  language   112, 115, 129–30, 133
  social   43

technical   8
Lee, Dorothy D.   110
Lehrman, Daniel S.   127n5
Lenneberg, Eric   110n2, 129, 134
Lerner, Abba P.   17–18
Levinas, Emmanuel   4, 47
Levins, Richard   18, 46
Levinson, Stephen C.   135n7
Lévi-Strauss, Claude   12, 51–54, 59–62, 84, 127
Lewontin, Richard   18, 131n6
linguistics   1–2, 4, 7, 11, 18, 63, 96, 105–10, 112–16, 120, 125–26, 129, 132–34, 146–48
  anthropological   136
  behavioral   112
  Cartesian   139–40
  Chomskyan   138–44
  Humboldtian   142
  structural   61
List, Friedrich   74
logic   20, 21, 31, 46, 64, 75, 77, 85, 113–14, 148
  combinatory   54
  formal   4
  in language   130
  of accumulation   89
Lorenz, Konrad   127, 138
love   56, 77, 79
Lowie. Robert   59
Lucas Jr., Robert E.   66
Luhmann, Niklas   34, 88
Lula, Luiz Inácio da Silva   1

Macy Conferences   63
magic   71–72, 119–120
  magical thought   117–18, 120
  Neolithic   119
Malinowski, Bronislaw   62, 73, 124, 129
Malthus, Thomas   9–10
Margenau, Henry   23
Marx, Karl   5, 50, 67, 74, 76–77, 79–89, 92
Marxism   66–67, 82, 84–92
  classical   66
  Soviet   66
Massachusetts Institute of Technology   1
materialism   81
  anthropological   82
  contemplative   5, 77, 79, 85. *See also* Feuerbach, Ludwig
  historical   2, 4–5, 81–86, 89, 120
  Marxist   76–79

mathematics 61, 113–14
matter 33, 35, 145
  inorganic, inert 2, 22
Maturana, Humberto 89
Mauss, Marcel 72, 75–76, 84, 120
Maxwell, Clerk 63
Mayr, Ernst 7–9, 49, 58
Meillassoux, Claude 84
meme 11, 19–20, 22, 27. *See also* Dawkins, Richard; Blackmore, Susan
  altruistic 10
  and culture 11, 19, 25, 29
  meme pool 10, 19
  memeplex 20, 29
  religious 10
  selfish 10
memetics 20, 24, 28–29, 37
memory 19, 57, 93, 128, 142
Mendel, Gregor 134
Menger, Carl 68n3
metabolism 18, 22, 29, 32
Miller, Geoffrey F. 45
mind 1, 19, 23–24, 31, 40–42, 44, 57, 85, 99, 109, 131
  and culture 40
  and language 96, 145
  architecture 44
  mind-body interaction 101
  mind-brain interaction 23, 40
  mindset 124
modern synthetic theory 7–8, 17–18, 21, 32, 134–35. *See also* Fisher, Ronald; Haldane, J.B.S.; Wright, Sewall
molecule 2, 11, 22, 55, 137
  inorganic 55
monism 41, 71, 101
Monod, Jacques 21–24, 32, 41, 136, 142
morality 8, 10, 13, 28, 47, 54–55, 73, 75–76, 80–81, 119, 126
Morgan, Lewis 47
morphology 49, 102
  language 108, 110
  social 54
mother 36, 38, 45
Müller, Gerd 137
Murdock, George P. 124
mutation 8, 12, 17–18, 31, 64, 137
mutualism 72–73
  coevolution 27

meme 10
myth, mythology 61, 71–72, 74–75, 77, 139

Nairn, Tom 91
nation 5, 7, 20, 29, 35, 45, 74, 87, 89–92, 94, 96–99, 110, 145
  and language 145
  nation-state 89, 92
nationalism 20, 91–96, 98
nature 39, 53, 67, 69, 72, 75, 79–80, 96, 100–1, 119, 128, 144–45
  and culture 4, 31, 59, 70, 71
  and men 76–84, 102, 121
  and nurture 4, 25, 31, 44
  and spirit 85
  and symbolic language 3
  biological 3
  cultural 3, 24. *See also* Jacob, François
  dialectics 18, 135. *See also* Engels, Friedrich; Marx, Karl
  human 20, 25, 41, 43, 59, 77, 124, 145
  objectification 4, 72
Neanderthal man 135
Nelson, Richard R. 67
Neolithic 121
  Revolution 57, 70–71, 74, 76, 86–87, 94, 119–20
neuron 23, 40, 130
neurotransmitter 23, 40
niche 18, 29–30, 32, 60, 64–65, 105, 137, 147
  cultural 53, 65, 147
  social 60
North, Douglass 66–67, 81, 140
Nowak, Martin 37

objectification 4, 72, 88, 120–21
  human 85–86
observation 22–24, 36, 44, 107, 112, 136
  empirical 61
Odling-Smee, John 29–30
ontogenesis 42, 126, 132, 147
ontology 46, 71, 84, 101, 121, 123
organ 21, 56
  fight and flight 102
  mental 43, 123
  reproductive 103
  sense 23, 104
organic 9, 25, 35, 36, 37, 39–40, 61, 101–2, 136–37, 142

organic (*cont.*)
  and culture 40
  being 9, 39
  in language 140
  non-human 24
organism 10, 12, 14, 21–23, 33, 38, 42, 54, 56, 80, 84, 104–6, 137–38, 142, 146
  and culture 58–59
  and cybernetics 21
  and environment 18, 20, 29, 33, 44, 106, 130
  and genes 10, 15–16, 20–21, 29
  and language 110
  and memes 10, 19, 22
  and natural selection 35
  as social species 54, 56
  complex 11, 138
  metabolism 18
  multicellular 55–56
  sociological 93
  superior 13, 33
  unicellular 55
other, otherness 3–5, 48, 51, 66, 72, 74, 79, 81, 112, 126, 143, 146

Pääbo, Svante 135, 142, 146–47
Paleolithic 52, 70, 121
  poverty 67
Parsons, Talcott 34
parthenogenesis 13
Patterson, Orlando 73
Peirce, C.S. 138
people 28–29, 48, 51, 54–55, 57, 60, 69, 74–76, 81, 91, 96–97, 111, 125, 146
  African. *See* African peoples
  Amerindian. *See* Amerindian peoples
  and language 108–9, 112, 114
  history 52
  indigenous 115, 126
  isolated 1, 95, 111, 114–15
personality 19, 29, 78, 144
phenotype 12, 14, 20, 27, 29, 40, 45
  and genotype 14, 43
  behavior 8
philosophy 8, 11, 34, 139
  analytic 20, 110
  Comtian 34–35, 54
  German 76
  Hegelian 77–78

Herderian 76, 101
Kantian 97
language 110–13, 140, 143–44
Marxist 80–81
Spencerian 37
Wittgensteinian 114–17, 121
phylogenesis 42, 64, 126, 147
physics 2–3, 7–8, 10, 11, 19, 21–24, 35, 38–40, 44, 60, 105–6, 115, 141–43
  body 24
  physical nature 3, 24, 145
  physical-chemical processes 3, 19, 35
  quantum 23, 105, 141
physiology 21–22, 33, 54, 106, 142
  human 4, 40, 108, 122, 125
  mind 44
  neurophysiology 23, 40
Piaget, Jean 126
Pinker, Steven 31, 45, 129–32, 134
plant 12, 28, 39, 47, 58, 72, 80, 143
  domesticated 71–72, 86
Pleistocene 26, 31, 84, 125
Polanyi, Karl 67–69, 73–74
politics 5–6, 10, 36, 62, 70, 88, 90–93, 122
  in Brazil 1–2
  Marxist 89
Popper, Karl 23
population 12, 15, 17, 43, 48–49, 55, 134–35
  human 9–10, 25–27, 44, 71, 80, 95, 132
Port-Royal 144
  grammar 148
  logic 148
positivism 3, 37, .60, 113. *See also* Comte, Auguste
potlatch 75
predator 17, 102
primate 8, 12, 24, 36, 125, 134, 147
production 67, 69, 75–76, 80–83, 87–88
  artefact 101
  means of 86, 90
  mode of 82
  relations of 88–89
  symbol 147
progress 10, 34–35, 39, 46, 52–54, 56, 61, 64, 66–67, 99, 124
  moral 47
  technical 87
progressivism 6
property 36, 57, 73, 81, 90, 97

pseudoscience, 3, 148
psyche 40, 128
　relationship with culture 43
psychism 4, 40
psychoanalysis 12, 50–51. *See also* Freud, Sigmund
psychology 25, 28, 31, 45, 56, 108, 122
　and culture 40–45
　animal 45
　cognitive 31
　evolutionary 28, 31, 40–45, 47, 74, 92, 100, 122, 126–29, 131
　functional 129
　innate 25, 28, 41–42
　psychic structure, architecture 1, 42, 44
　psychological mechanisms 31, 42, 44–45, 131
　psychological phenomena 55–56
　psychophysical organization, conditions 106–7
　social 31

Quine, W.V.O. 110–15, 117, 147

Raatikainen, Panu 112
race 5–6, 51, 58, 95–96, 98, 134
racism, racialism 42, 44
Radcliffe-Brown, Alfred 59, 61–62
reciprocity 15, 19, 30, 49, 60, 68–69, 73–74, 130
reductionism 5, 7–8, 11, 21, 46. *See also* Mayr, Ernst
religion 5, 10, 20, 29, 34, 37, 45, 48, 56, 65, 70, 72, 74–78, 81, 90, 92–93, 98–99, 110, 120, 127, 132
　in Feuerbach 77–79, 99
　in Hegel 77
　in Marx 85–88
replicator 2, 10
　gene as 19
　meme as 19–20, 25, 28–29
reproduction 4, 19, 55, 57, 86
　germs 11
　material 119
　sexual 11–13, 14, 16–17, 19
r-evolution 3–4, 17, 21. 24, 45, 49, 58, 63, 74–75, 105, 121, 126, 148
revolution 76, 86, 92
　anti-imperialist 94

biolinguistics 7
bourgeois 90
　Industrial 86–87, 92, 94, 119–21
　Marxist 92
　modern 89
Ribeiro, Sidarta 105
Richerson, Peter J. 25–28, 45
Rig Veda 72
Roman Empire 55
Romer, Paul M. 66
Roscher, Wilhelm 74

sacrifice 13–14, 88
Sahlins, Marshall 63–70, 73–76, 81–83
Said, Edward 91–92
Sapir, Edward 95–96, 107–10, 142, 145
Sartre, Jean-Paul 46
Saussure, Ferdinand de 136
scarcity 4, 67–69
schismogenesis 4, 62–63
Schlegel, Friedrich 139
Schmalhausen, Ivan 18
Schmoller, Gustav von 68n3
Schrödinger, Erwin 23
Schwarz, Roberto 1
science 5, 7, 9–10, 38–40, 42, 53, 57, 72, 87, 107–8, 113–14, 117–21, 123, 132, 137, 138–39, 142, 148
　cognitive 130
　experimental 121
　modern 41
　natural 140
　social 2, 33–34, 36–38, 41–42, 108, 110, 113, 148
Searle, John 143
selection 22, 25–26, 30, 125
　artificial 9, 71
　cultural 29, 75
　group 13–16, 25, 27, 35, 37, 143
　kin 14, 16, 28, 38
　natural 8–9, 12–14, 16–17, 19, 25–27, 31, 35, 43, 71, 131, 134, 136
　semispecies 49, 58, 61
Service, Elman R. 64–66
sex 6, 11, 13, 16–17, 24, 38, 80, 102, 135
　and culture 51
　and domination 58
　and evolution 17
　and genes 17

sex (*cont.*)
   and psychology   45, 56
   and reproduction   12–13, 16–17, 19, 43
sister   38
Skinner, B. F.   130–31
slave, slavery   4, 53, 57, 62, 69–70, 73, 86, 94
Smith, Adam   74
Smith, John Maynard   12–13, 15, 17, 24, 51, 135, 142
Sobera, Grecia de la   1
sociability   73, 129
   animal   101
   insect   39
social science   111
   and science   113–14
socialization   29, 41
society   4, 9, 13, 26, 28, 34, 48, 53–58, 67–68, 70, 79, 81, 108, 117, 120
   agglutination of   57
   class   10, 76–77
   composite   59
   ecological   4, 84
   economic   4
   feudal   68
   history of   5, 58
   human   7, 24, 35–36, 39, 54–56, 58, 72, 105, 148
   hybridization   56
   industrial   69–70
   insects   36–39
   market   68
   modern   25–26, 68, 70, 121
   organization   54
   Paleolithic   121
   poly-segmental   56
   pre-industrial   91
   pre-modern   121
   primate   24
   primitive, archaic   95, 119, 121
sociobiology   13–14, 20, 24, 27–28, 32, 34–35, 37–39, 41, 71
sociology   23–24, 29, 34, 36, 54–55, 64, 93, 96, 122, 126, 143
   Comtian   34
   Durkheimian   55–56
   Luhmannian   88
   Spencerian   34–36
   Weberian   89–90
Socrates   130

soul   39, 47, 100
Souza, Paulo César de   50
species   4, 8–9, 12–13, 16–19, 28, 30, 33, 38, 41, 43, 47–51, 55, 65–66, 99, 104–5, 132
   animal   33, 58, 100
   biological organization   1
   cooperation between   72
   cultural   11, 63–64
   human   2, 5, 8–10, 19, 28–30, 42, 45, 47, 49–51, 57–58, 75, 100–3, 105, 107, 123, 125, 131, 135–36, 142–43, 145, 147–48
   interchange between   72
   plant   58
   social   54
   species-being   81
Spencer, Herbert   34–37, 47, 65
Spinoza, Benedictus de   77
Standard Social Science Model (SSSM)   41–42
state   85, 89, 91
   absolutist   90–91
   modern   90–94, 97
Steward, Julian   63
Strathern, Marilyn   2, 62
structuralism   84, 126, 127, 136, 140. *See also* Lévi-Strauss, Claude; Jakobson, Roman; Trubetzkoy, Nikolai
structure   62, 101
   anthropological   53
   chemical   137
   cultural   46, 59, 61, 81, 84
   economic   66, 81
   linguistic   47, 61, 107, 109, 130, 132, 134, 138, 140, 143, 145
   mental   47, 143
   political   91
   population   43
   psychic, psychological   1, 44
   social   28, 36, 44, 54, 61, 122
subject-object relation   2, 4, 71–72, 80, 82, 84, 86–89, 92, 104, 119–21
subjugation   4, 57–58, 62–63, 73, 75–76, 86, 121
subspecies   58
Sumeria   57
superorganism   14, 36–37, 39, 52, 54. *See also* Spencer, Herbert; Kroeber, Alfred L.
   cultural   19, 26
   social   35, 53

superspecies 49, 58, 61, 75. *See also* Mayr, Ernst
superstructure 51, 81
survival 9, 16–17, 20, 25, 35, 42, 102–3, 118, 122, 130
  gene 16
  meme 10
  species 13
system 22, 35, 63, 68, 83, 88, 101, 114, 116, 119, 124
  behavior 41, 103
  belief 114, 116
  brain 40, 43
  colonial 94
  cultural 31, 61, 63, 65, 125, 127
  cybernetic, computational 22, 33, 133, 138
  economic 70, 73, 87–88
  effector 33, 104, 106
  endocrine 21
  genetic 142
  guidance 42
  immune 11, 136, 142
  impulse 103, 123
  inheritance 32
  kinship 61
  linguistic 61, 107–10, 116, 129, 140, 143
  metabolic-homeostatic 32
  nervous, neural 21, 104, 130
  operational 42
  organic 56
  phonological 61
  physical 23
  receptor 33, 104, 106
  regulatory 34
  semantic-pragmatic 134
  sensory-motor 134
  sign 94
  social 44, 48, 60–61
  symbolic 33, 104, 106–7, 122–23, 139
  teleonomic 22
Szathmáry, Eörs 13, 135, 142

Tarnita, Corina 37
Tattersall, Ian 135
technique 8, 10, 47, 66, 67, 82, 87, 91, 93, 103, 106, 119–21
technology 65, 67, 69–70, 81, 87, 89

theory 5–6, 79–80, 82–83, 113–14, 138
alienation 50, 85
alienization 99
biological 103–5. *See also* Uexküll, Jakob von
Chomskyan 138–39
consciousness 24
Darwinian 30–32, 35, 134. *See also* Darwin, Charles
dependency 66
diffusionism 66. *See also* Sahlins, Marshall; Service, Elman R.
economic 68, 81, 88, 91
evolutionary 4, 8–9, 11, 13–16, 27, 29, 30–32, 34–35, 42, 46–47, 63–64, 134, 147
group selection. *See also* selection
imperialism 66
inclusive fitness 38
instinct 127–28
language acquisition 132
linguistic 83, 113, 117, 137, 142, 147
Marxist 67, 81, 83, 92
niche construction 18, 30, 105, 147. *See also* Lewontin, Richard; Levins, Richard
physics 141
political 91
population 9–10
pre-synthesis 7
punctuated equilibrium 18. *See also* Gould, Stephen Jay; Eldredge, Niles
Spencerian 36
systems 89, 127, 141
theory of relativity 1, 105–6, 114. *See also* Einstein, Albert
Thurnwald, Richard 68
Tomasello, Michael 4, 110n2, 132–33, 142, 146–48
Tooby, John 31, 40–45, 122, 131
tool 8, 47, 86, 98, 124
tradition 68, 96, 116
  Anglo-Saxon 52
  Arab 53
  Cartesian 140
  Chinese 53
  cultural 64
  Germanic 52
  Greek 52

tradition (*cont.*)
  philosophical 76
  Roman 52
  social 125
  sociological 34, 143
  transmission 47
  Western 40
transcendence 2–3, 22–24, 32, 40, 44–45, 142
translation 19, 109–12, 114–16, 128, 130
Tremlett, Paul-François 127
tribe 13–15, 26, 28, 35, 45, 48, 57, 59, 71, 75, 97–98, 109
Trivers, Robert 15, 38
Trubetzkoy, Nikolai 61, 136
Tylor, Edward Burnett 47, 63

Uexküll, Jakob von 33–34, 63, 103–6, 110, 125, 138–39
Umwelt 104, 110, 138
Unheimlich 4, 50, 85. *See also* Freud, Sigmund
United States 46, 95, 136, 140

Varela, Francisco 89
variation 3, 30–31, 64
  by natural selection 35
  climate 26–27
  cultural 25, 41
  environmental 125
  linguistic 136–37
  phenotypical 14

variation-selection 3, 8, 11, 18, 35, 126, 148
Veblen, Thorstein 65, 74n4
vitalism 24, 33, 141
Vrba, Elisabeth 131n6
Vries, Hugo de 7

Waddington, Conrad Hal 18
Wagner, Moritz 7
Wagner, Roy 62
Wallace, Alfred Russel 32, 134
war 10, 75, 89–90, 92, 98
  Second World War 62
Weber, Max 7, 89–90, 92, 99
Weil, Simone 94
Wengrow, David 63, 71
  West 40, 59, 89–90, 143
White, Leslie 63
Whorf, Benjamin Lee 18, 63, 105–10, 114, 116–17, 125–26, 129, 138
Wiener, Norbert 21
Wilson, David S. 13–14
Wilson, Edward O. 13–14, 20, 32, 37–38, 45
Wilson, Margo 45
Winch, Peter 110, 117–19, 121, 125–26
Winter, Sidney G. 67
Wissler, Clark 124
Wittgenstein, Ludwig 110, 114–18, 121, 125–27, 147–48
World-Systems Theory 58
Wrangham, Richard 57
Wright, Sewall 134
writing 37, 57, 94, 129

www.ingramcontent.com/pod-product-compliance
Lightning Source LLC
Chambersburg PA
CBHW070627030426
42337CB00020B/3938